MANAGEMENT, W~
AND ORGANISATI~

Series editors: **Gibson Burrell**, The Mar
Mick Marchington, Man
Paul Thompson, Departr
University of Strathclyde

This series of new textbooks covers the areas of human resource management, employee relations, organisational behaviour and related business and management fields. Each text has been specially commissioned to be written by leading experts in a clear and accessible way. The books contain serious and challenging material, take an analytical rather than prescriptive approach and are particularly suitable for use by students with no prior specialist knowledge.

The series is relevant for many business and management courses, including MBA and post-experience courses, specialist masters and postgraduate diplomas, professional courses and final-year undergraduate courses. These texts have become essential reading at business and management schools worldwide.

Published

Paul Blyton and Peter Turnbull **The Dynamics of Employee Relations** (3rd edn)
Sharon C. Bolton **Emotion Management in the Workplace**
Peter Boxall and John Purcell **Strategy and Human Resource Management**
J. Martin Corbett **Critical Cases in Organisational Behaviour**
Keith Grint **Leadership**
Marek Korczynski **Human Resource Management in Service work**
Karen Legge **Human Resource Management**: anniversary edition
Stephen Procter and Frank Mueller (eds) **Teamworking**
Helen Rainbird (ed.) **Training in the Workplace**
Jill Rubery and Damian Grimshaw **The Organisation of Employment**
Harry Scarbrough (ed.) **The Management of Expertise**
Hugh Scullion and Margaret Linehan **International Human Resource Management**
Adrian Wilkinson, Mick Marchington, Tom Redman and Ed Snape **Managing with Total Quality Management**
Diana Winstanley and Jean Woodall (eds) **Ethical Issues in Contemporary Human Resource Management**

For more information on titles in Series please go to www.palgrave.com/busines/mwo

Invitation to authors

The Series Editors welcome proposals for new books within the Management, Work and Organisation series. These should be sent to Paul Thompson (p.thompson@strath.ac.uk) at the Dept of HRM, Strathclyde Business School, University of Strathclyde, 50 Richmond St Glasgow G1 1XT

Emotion management in the workplace

Sharon C. Bolton

First published in 2005 by
PALGRAVE MACMILLAN
Houndmills, Basingstoke, Hampshire RG21 6XS and
175 Fifth Avenue, New York, N. Y. 10010
Companies and representatives throughout the world.

PALGRAVE MACMILLAN is the global academic imprint of the Palgrave Macmillan division of St. Martin's Press, LLC and of Palgrave Macmillan Ltd. Macmillan® is a registered trademark in the United States, United Kingdom and other countries. Palgrave is a registered trademark in the European Union and other countries.

ISBN 0–333–99017–X

This book is printed on paper suitable for recycling and made from fully managed and sustained forest sources.

A catalogue record for this book is available from the British Library.

Library of Congress Cataloging-in-Publication Data

Bolton, Sharon C., 1960–
  Emotion management in the workplace / Sharon C. Bolton.
     p. cm. — (Management, work and organisations)
  Includes bibliographical references and index.
  ISBN 0–333–99017–X (paper)
     1. Organizational behavior. 2. Emotions. 3. Employee motivation.
  4. Work—Psychological aspects. 5. Organizational sociology.
  6. Industrial management. I. Title. II. Series.

HD58.7.B65 2005
648.3′14—dc22   2004054296

10 9 8 7 6 5 4 3 2 1
14 13 12 11 10 09 08 07 06 05

Printed and bound in China.

To Derek Ditchburn (Dad) with love

Contents

Acknowledgements

There are many that are owned thanks for their contribution to the completion of this book. They have all offered moral support and continued words of encouragement as well as practicalities. For that I would like to thank all of my colleagues in the Department of Organisation, Work and Technology, Lancaster University Management School; especially Jean Yates for sanity saving chats 'over the fence', Prof. Frank Blackler for his continual support and good humour and Dr Steve Fleetwood for important feedback on early drafts of chapters. Particular thanks go to Prof. Stephen Ackroyd who had travelled with me on this intellectual journey and provided priceless guidance and friendship throughout. Dr Maeve Houlihan receives a special mention for her tireless reviews of the book's contents and unstinting support. This book would not have been conceivable without their continued, open-hearted generosity. Similarly, thanks go to Dr Chris Warhurst and Prof. Paul Thompson who inspired me to start the journey and gave me the confidence to finish. And to Ursula Gavin of Palgrave for her endless patience. Finally, I am indebted to my family. Thoughts are with Lynne Marlor, my closest friend who died suddenly September 2000 but whose influence remains. I will never be able to repay my sister, Beverley, for being there and for being human, as she always is. I thank my mother for showing me what a mixed blessing mixed feelings are, my dad for instilling the will to succeed and his eternal faith that I would and, of course, my children, Jack and Geordie, just because they're gorgeous. But most of all I thank my husband, Steve, for the love and generosity of spirit which has made it all possible.

Sharon C. Bolton., 2004.

1

Why emotion, why now?

Emotion on the organisational agenda

This book will talk about emotion in organisations. There are three main themes that will be explored. First, why and how emotion has become such an important topic in organisation and management studies? Second, why is such a dismal, one-dimensional picture of organisational life presented in many recent accounts of the emotional organisation? Third, how can emotion in organisations be thought about differently? Bringing these three themes together, the main body of the book will introduce a typology of workplace emotion that offers a multidimensional portrayal of organisational life – with all of its pains and its pleasures. The core aim is to introduce the idea of people in organisations as skilled social actors and multi-skilled managers of emotion.

Emotion in organisations, of course, is no longer the mystery it once was. Thanks to the rising service sector and resultant growing army of front-line service workers who must create desirable emotional climates and the resource-based view of Human Resource Management that focuses on emotion as a valuable resource to be harnessed in order to gain employee commitment and competitive advantage, emotion has now been firmly placed on the organisational agenda. It is now widely recognised that 'organisations have feelings' (Albrow, 1994, 1997); that they are sites of 'love, hatred and passion' (Fineman, 1993); that the 'commercialisation of feeling' (Hochschild, 1983) is a common occurrence and, of most importance for many writers, emotion is a valuable resource readily available for development by management (Ashforth and Humphrey, 1993, 1995; Ashkanasy *et al.*, 2002; Dulewicz and Higgs, 1999; Goleman, 1998a; Morris and Feldman, 1996, 1997).

So, why this book, why now? Originally the conceptual journey began with a sense of dissatisfaction with the way it is assumed that the emotion management skills of employees have been, or have the potential to be, entirely captured by the organisation. There appears to have been a re-drawing of the boundaries between the public and private worlds of emotion management which represents a certain turn in how social actors are conceived (Hochschild, 1983, 1989b, 2003). It seems that capitalism has appropriated all of our feelings so that there is no longer any room for sentiments, moods or reactions that have not been shaped and commodified via the 'commercialization of intimate life' (Hochschild, 2003). This pessimism concerning the (over) managed heart is shared by both writers on organisation and social commentators (Deetz, 1998; Hopfl, 2002; Meštrović, 1997; Ritzer, 1999; Townley, 1994) to such an extent that it has become a very influential force in the study of workplace emotion.

There are, of course, many other contributions to debates on emotion in organisations. There are studies that celebrate the recognition of emotion as a vital part of organisational life (Fine, 1988; Fineman, 1993, 2000, 2003; Mumby and Putman, 1992) and others who constantly seek creative solutions to organisational problems such as poor customer service or employees' emotional exhaustion (Ashforth and Humphrey, 1995; Kinnie *et al.*, 2000; Morris and Feldman, 1996). Nevertheless, though emotion in organisations has been studied from a variety of perspectives two common themes become apparent. First, there is a neglect of any conflict and contradiction which may occur due to demands made by organisations for employees to manage their emotions in certain ways. Second, and directly related, there is an underlying implication of normative control, that is it is assumed that organisational actors' emotions are being captured and irretrievably damaged in the velvet cage of corporate culturism. In such a narrative, we are left with two very different, though equally one-dimensional, portrayals of organisational life. Accounts of social engineering, objectified social actors and comparisons with Orwell's 1984 are frequently found, but equally vacuous notions of humanity are found in portrayals of eager workers with bright and welcoming smiles.[1] It is suggested here that the implications for the study of organisational emotionality are immense. Even though emotion is a lived interactional experience, when reading recent accounts of organisational life one begins to ask 'where is the laughter, where is the compassion, where is the day-to-day interaction?' This is not to deny the importance of recognising emotional burn-out in front line service work, the everyday stresses and strains of organisational life and the darker sides of working with people; bullying and harassment, for instance. But the important thing to recognise is that not all emotion is controlled by the organisation. Employees are social beings who enter an organisation with life histories and certain ways of being. They may enthusiastically take on organisationally prescribed roles but they also make friends, they experience frustrations, they have to present themselves differently to customers or client – all of these things mean that there are no definitive divides between the public and private worlds of emotion.

Viewed in this way, the originality of this book's contribution lies in its ability to conceptualise the organisational actor as an active, knowledgeable agent. By utilising a sociological approach to workplace emotion the human subject is placed firmly at the centre of organisational analysis. The performances, feeling rules and motivations that make up the emotional life of an organisation are explored in detail via the introduction of a typology of workplace emotionality that offers a multidimensional view of the emotional life of an organisation. But before introducing the contents of the book it is worth considering in more detail what the background to the contents that follow might be. For instance, contemporary debates concerning emotions in both social and organisational life suggest movements in the way feelings are used in society that impact upon how the social actor is thought about. *The public and private worlds of emotion management* attract considerable attention and form a core part of the analysis throughout the book. Closely related to this is how it arises that attempts are made to rigidly prescribe employees' emotions at work which distorts interaction with customers so that it can no longer be likened to social interaction in that it is an *unequal exchange*. The control of the emotional labour process is a central concern in the proposed attempt to introduce new ways of thinking about emotion at work which, in turn, leads to the introduction of just how we might think about the *management of emotion* and who might help us to do this. A theoretical partnership is used in order to support the introduction of the typology of workplace emotion and to bring the multi-skilled emotion manager to life. Unusually in the study of emotion both Labour Process Analysis (LPA) and Goffman offer a detailed, realist account of workplace emotion.

The social view of emotion which will be developed and deployed throughout the book involves the view of the actor as a purposive agent. It also allows an understanding that, in negotiating between the feeling rules that are operative in different situations, actors are usually highly skilled from the point of view of the management of their emotions. These observations offer a range of potential insights into the employee as social actor, in that the individual may select from sources of conflicting feeling rules and often creatively interpret and manipulate them. For example, social groups in and around work – work groups, professions, peer groups are all sources of clues, accepted norms and feeling rules, which are to some extent observed. There is a need to ask how certain feeling rules are regarded as being more important than others. Beyond this, just how they are negotiated and managed should be the subject of extended examination. To date, much of this territory has not been analysed by investigators and it will be the purpose of this book to undertake an extended analysis along these lines. The following sections set the scene by briefly reviewing the major sources of insight that inform the overall character of the book.

The public and the private
worlds of emotion

There are competing accounts concerning developments in how emotion might be viewed. Some (Wouters, 1989a and b) suggest that the boundary between the public and the private spheres are being re-drawn as the result of a general 'informalization of feeling': 'There is enough empirical data to show that during approximately the last hundred years the models of emotion exchange have become more varied, more escapable and more open for idio-syncratic nuances, thus less rigid and coercive' (1989a, p. 105). Wouters takes evidence of the breaking down of social barriers in modern society to show how social actors are all now much more familiar with different cultures than their own. They have developed the ability to switch and swap faces according to the demands of many different situations (Wouters, 1989a and b). Nevertheless, the informalisation of emotion has not led to a breaking down of the order of social interaction. On the contrary, the wider variances available to social actors in the presentation of self has led to the need for a greater awareness of rituals of deference and demeanour and as a result, men and women 'have become more strongly integrated into tighter knit networks of interdependencies in which the level of mutually expected self-restraint has risen' (Wouters, 1989b, p. 449).

For others the focus of their analysis is on the very opposite of informalisa-tion. The pressures of modern life have led to a move toward the routinisation of emotion, leading to claims of a post-emotional society. This does not mean that society is emotionless but that the emotions which are presented are man-ufactured states devoid of human feeling. Within this approach there is a growing body of thought that mourns the death of 'real' feelings. It seems that a neo-Orwellian nightmare of insidious all-embracing controls has materi-alised with the result that we have become alienated from our own feelings and only 'McDonaldized petrified, routinized' emotions remain (Meštrović, 1997, p. 147). This, apparently, is most especially the case for service-sector employees who are now mere simulacrums on the organisationally designed emotional stage: hollow service workers dealing with hollow customers

(Hopfl, 2002). In this 'post-emotional society' the notion of the 'noble savage' is celebrated where real, authentic and natural feelings rule the day (Hochschild, 1983, 2003; Meštrović, 1997). There is growing confusion over the mechanisation of work and the mechanisation of the self; as though they can be classified and analysed as one and the same thing. In effect there has been a dangerous division in the sacred and the profane: both consumers and producers have been moved from the 'fat and the living to the thin and the dead' (Goffman, 1961a, p. 152). This 'vulgar tendency', as Goffman usefully describes it, portrays a lifeless, if not bleak, picture of organisational life, devoid of humanity.

There is little doubt that much of customer service is routinised and predictable but that does not mean it consists of a McDonalidized, off-the-shelf package of artificial humanity (Archer, 2000). Emotion is a lived, interactional experience with traffic rules of interaction framing how it is expressed and shared. Employees draw on professional, organisational and commercial codes of conduct and social feeling rules in their interactions with others. The fragile accomplishment of social interaction is continually maintained through, not only formal exchanges, but also through episodes of compassion and shared laughter. The aim of the book is to counteract this dim portrayal of organisational life and demonstrate that the workplace is far from a lifeless landscape; rather it displays the emotional life of an organisation as a particular social world, with all of its pains and pleasures. It is, therefore, suggested that organisational life would be better understood if it were recognised that emotions are social things and that humanity is expressed, shared and supported in a myriad of ways as part of the 'interaction order'. And, that rather than dividing the emotional life of the workplace into the prescribed and the liberated, that it is recognised that expressions of humanity continually cross organisational boundaries; from the profane to the sacred. In other words, the mechanisation of the labour process should not be confused with a mechanisation of the self.

An unequal exchange

For social commentators such as Wouters (1989a) developments in society mean that social encounters can be likened to a game and he denies the need to theorise emotion management as having any connection with the capitalist labour process. However, as Hochschild (1989b) points out, organisational life is not a game to be played lightly. What Wouters does not recognise is that an analysis of the capitalist labour process is very relevant when analysing the unequal emotional exchanges which occur as part of service encounters. What is also apparently neglected is the fact that management is increasingly taking new initiatives in the control of emotions at work. This sort of development was a key innovation prompting Hochschild's (1983) seminal work, *The Managed Heart*. It is notable when examining encounters which are clearly part of the labour process that the 'rules of conduct', which usually govern general social encounters ensuring that everyone 'acts appropriately and receives his due' (Goffman, 1967, p. 55), do not apply to the interaction which occurs between service-provider and customer. The exchange becomes 'unequal' (Hochschild, 1983) in that the customer does not have to follow the 'traffic rules of interaction' and make the effort to maintain the correct balance. The rules in this particular 'ritual game' (Goffman, 1967) are different to those of the general social encounter.

This can be further understood in the context of the recent emphasis on the 'sovereignty' of the customer that has created raised consumer expectations (du Gay and Salaman, 1992). It is especially relevant to the British public services where the rhetoric of the enterprise culture has re-classified patients, students and housing tenants as customers, thereby putting extra pressure on front-line staff to ensure the consumers of their services go away 'happy with their lot'. Often, in the absence of adequate funding to provide the required service, there can be unpredictable outbursts and, in such instances, the irate, dissatisfied customer demands a skilful performance of emotion management to diffuse the situation. In these instances, as in many service encounters in the for-profit sector, there is no mutual 'self-restraint'. The rules of social encounter change and the emotional exchange clearly becomes unequal – consumers feel within their 'rights' to display dissatisfaction, yet the service provider is expected to meet aggression with pleasantries, sympathy, or at worst, calm indifference. As Hochschild states: 'Where the customer is king, unequal exchanges are normal, and from the beginning customer and client assume different rights to feeling and display. The ledger is supposedly evened by a wage' (1983, p. 86).

It is worth noting, however, that the very same demanding customers are seemingly prepared to accept the obviously feigned sincerity that occurs within many face-to-face encounters between customer and service provider. The provision of familiar rituals and scripts by companies such as McDonald's create predictable interactions between customer and worker where there is little doubt in anyone's mind that the worker is merely acting out a given role. The worker's private feelings have clearly not been 'transmutated', yet lack of genuine sincerity on behalf of employees has not prevented companies such as McDonalds runaway success. Perhaps its success lies in the very predictability of worker's reactions. In an 'informalized' society this can be seen as a haven for the 'anxious customer longing for predictability' (Ritzer, 1996, p. 81) and would help to sustain the necessary 'ontological security' (Giddens, 1984) which human nature appears to require. Goffman stresses how important it is that the right balance be achieved during normal social encounters – that the actors involved in the interaction be treated with 'proper ritual care' (Goffman, 1967). Quite clearly, in such contexts, employees may not be treated with 'proper ritual care' according to general social feeling rules, but even exposed to verbal and physical abuse. In effect, there is no 'audience tact' or 'moral order' when the motive behind service encounters is not social ceremony (Goffman, 1961a) but merely the creation of profit.

Goffman, labour process analysis and the management of emotion

A detailed analysis of social interaction rests upon a particular sociological understanding of emotion and who better to guide us than Goffman, who can be described as 'an observational genius' (Harré, 1990) concerning the 'interaction order' and the detailed study of human activity. It is the processes of interaction that are of interest to an understanding of emotion, the minutiae of everyday life and the norms that inform its conduct (Goffman, 1991). Going 'public' with emotion, what Goffman (1967) would describe as presenting a 'face', shows how it is interwoven with social life. But more than this Goffman offers a comfortable resting place on what can be a complex theoretical journey with his wonderful view of humanity. Goffman presents social actors who are capable of moral commitment, who are involved with society *and* whose activities take place within multiple and layered frameworks of action (Goffman, 1967). He, therefore, forges a link between the 'expressive order', the micro-world of social arrangements where the order of the 'proper' is meticulously observed, to the 'practical order'; 'those social arrangements by which the means of material existence are generated' (Harré, 1990, p. 354). From this place it is possible to see quite clearly how emotions are social things, derived from a 'natural' substrata but mediated by active, reflective agents through the situations (which both constrain and enable) they confront (Archer, 2000). Thus Goffman, unlike the majority of interactionists with whom he is associated, offers layers of reality by taking us through various 'frameworks' of activity at all times conscious of the 'large, sturdy, and durable institutional structures that distribute the resources of interaction' (Berger, 1974). As Goffman states 'social life is dubious enough and ludicrous enough without having to wish it further into unreality' (Goffman, 1974, p. 2). And who better to aid Goffman in his pursuit of a realist analysis of social action than Labour Process Analysis?

Labour Process Analysis allows an understanding that emotion work can be 'hard' and 'productive' as well as just something that people do. This type of analysis focuses on management attempts to control work, physical or other, and shows how organisational actors are sometimes constrained to comply with managerial prescriptions. Applied to manual work this approach suggests that the capitalist labour process aims to extract the maximum surplus value from every employee's labour. Using this perspective it seems clear that some managerial regimes now aim to realise similar advantages through extending control over emotional aspects of labour. Instead of proscribing emotions, as has been the traditional stance, management has devised policies for prescribing them. With reference to organisational feeling, recent portrayals give accounts of the various mechanisms management is employing in order to control an actor's emotionality. It appears that employers want more than mere compliance from their employees, they want emotional commitment to the aims of the enterprise thereby eradicating the possibility of discord. Some recent accounts suggest that attempts at normative control and the introduction of surveillance techniques have succeeded in this objective (Hopfl, 2002; Rose, 1999; Sewell and Wilkinson, 1992; Willmott, 1993).

However, LPA accepts conflict as an inherent part of the employment relationship and recognises that management control regimes are unlikely ever to be completely successful in securing the full compliance of labour. The recognition of the potential of employees to resist managerial demands is also applicable to an understanding of what might be called 'the emotional labour process'. Goffman adds detail to this analysis in his realist analysis of role, his appreciation of how organisational actors are able to stand apart from the dictates of prescribed roles and his wealth of detail concerning the 'underlife' of an organisation. If management in the past have experienced difficulty in fully utilising the physical labour of employees, how much more onerous is their task of controlling emotional labour? The realisation that organisational emotion is not an empty space but already a matter of extensively controlled 'performances' suggests that workers, as active, knowledgeable subjects, have in fact been brought back into an analysis of the labour process. In the terms used here, management may have the ability to prescribe new feeling rules but this is more likely to result in a self-consciously empty or inauthentic performance. At best, newly imposed feeling rules are likely to produce compliance rather than commitment. Leaving management to inexpertly judge if there is any feeling behind the face.

The book

In its examination of *Why emotion, why now?* this chapter has set the terrain upon which the rest of the book will travel. In an attempt to put the subject back into organisational analysis and place the actor as the central focus in an analysis of the emotional organisation, Chapter 2 begins the search for an adequate understanding of workplace emotion. It *brings emotion onto the organisational agenda* in its coverage of over a century of organisational analysis. The chapter reviews the major contributions to management and organisation studies from classical management theory to post-structuralist analysis and onto more recent dream-making management prescription, in order to examine how the subject of emotion in organisations has developed. The review also acts as a means of assessing the ability of various perspectives on organisations to theorise the organisational actor as a skilled emotion manager. The result of this review is that much of existing organisational analysis has little to say about emotion. As such it requires a reworking, a mixing and matching of existing views and an acknowledgement of their strengths and weaknesses in order that a conceptual framework will be produced which allows emotionality to be put onto the organisational agenda.

Chapter 3 is a focused literature review which investigates Hochschild's (1979, 1983) work and that which has followed; in what might be described as an emotional labour bandwagon. Hochschild's concepts of 'emotion work' and 'emotional labour' are presented in some detail displaying how and why her work is so important to the study of emotion in organisations. In its examination of *The (over)managed heart*, this chapter highlights the analytical weakness in using only one blanket term such as 'emotional labour' to describe a complex phenomenon such as emotion management in organisations. The significance of the commercialisation of human feeling to the state welfare sector is a new arena in the field of organisation studies and this chapter explores some of the literature that investigates the emotional elements of public sector caring professionals' work. It goes on to highlight the inadequacy of using one descriptive phrase to understand the complexities inherent in the labour process of caring professionals.

A sociological understanding of emotion is introduced in Chapter 4. Strengths from a variety of viewpoints are gathered in order to discover a suitable way of theorising the interplay between structure and action. As a basis for further theorising, the origins of emotion are discussed. Drawing on constructionist ideas emotion is conceptualised as a social construct. However, so that the overly deterministic nature of constructionism is mediated it is combined with a much weaker version of a constructivist understanding of emotion. Social actors are portrayed as knowledgeable agents who are able to calibrate their performances of emotion management depending upon the feeling rules of particular situations. In this chapter Labour Process Analysis and Goffman are introduced as the foundation for a sociological understanding of emotion in the workplace. The labour process analysts show the political and economic structures which surround the capitalist labour process. They enable an understanding of how, upon entering an organisation and in exchange for a wage, the social actor is compelled to comply with organisational prescription. They give valuable insights into how control of the labour process is never complete. On the contrary, attempts to intensify control only serve to create conflict and contradiction as workers resist and struggle to come to terms with the demands made of them. Contradiction and conflict is not confined to the capitalist labour process but can be identified in the labour process of public service professionals, especially in the recently restructured British public services. For this reason it is suggested that the labour process analysis of capital–labour relations be expanded to an understanding of how the introduction of a market rationality has altered the labour process in the public welfare sector. To supplement this structural analysis, Goffman introduces social actors. He complements an labour process analysis in his examination of an actor's ability to either present a 'sincere' or 'cynical' performance. This adds to the understanding that workers' performances may not always be committed to the aims of the enterprise.

Building upon this theoretical framework, and in answer to the dissatisfaction with existing conceptual devices, Chapter 5 introduces a *Typology of workplace emotion*. It presents four types of emotion management: *pecuniary* (emotion management according to commercial values), *prescriptive* (emotion management according to organisational/ professional rules of conduct), *presentational* and *philanthropic* (emotion management according to general social feeling 'rules'). These concepts allow the interweaving of social and instrumental motivations. In other words they recognise the variety of means an organisation employs in order to achieve its ends whilst also acknowledging the subjective experiences of its members.

The conceptualisation of emotion introduced in Chapter 5 is explored in more detail in Chapters 6 and 7. Chapter 6 utilises the concepts of *prescriptive and pecuniary* emotion management in its exploration of what it means to be a member of an organisation or profession. It shows how organisational feeling rules act as a script so that organisational actors arrive at a certain understanding of 'how to be'. Focusing on organisational, professional and commercial feeling rules it shows how during goal-orientated activity emotions are managed according to a variety of motivations with a wide range of results. The concept of *prescriptive* and *pecuniary* emotion management according to different feeling rules display the variety of motivations that lie behind organisational actors performances of emotion management and how this impacts upon whether performances will be invested with feeling. In this chapter the concept of the customer is explored in some detail showing how commercial feeling rules define how *pecuniary* emotion management will be enacted and that motivations to comply with commercial feelings rules are really very different to those linked with professional feeling rules. In this way the concept of contradiction is introduced into the analysis, with special attention paid to public sector professionals and the imposition of commercial feeling rules into their work.

In its examination of the spaces within, between and around organisational, professional and commercial feeling rules, Chapter 7 shows how *presentational and philanthropic* emotion management according to social feeling rules continually crosses organisational boundaries and contributes to all aspects of organisational life. Within organisations there are spaces for misbehaviour, spaces for a bit of a laugh, spaces for occupational communities, spaces for organisational violations, spaces for a gift exchange and spaces for the creation and maintenance of identity. *Philanthropic* emotion management is presented as a special case in that it represents a gift of an extra effort in the management of emotion. However it is stressed, as with *presentational* emotion management, that the concept of a gift is not confined to particular spaces in organisations but can be offered as an added dimension to *prescriptive* or *pecuniary* emotion management. The combination of Chapters 5, 6 and 7 present a thorough examination of different facets of people's working lives: formal professional training and rules of conduct (*prescriptive* emotion management), the dimension of providing a customer service (*pecuniary* emotion management) and the 'spaces' workers are able to create where they offer kindness and support to each others and colleagues or let off steam through instances of misbehaviour, or act out wider social divisions and engage in bullying or sexual harassment (*philanthropic* and *presentational* emotion management). In this way organisational actors are portrayed as multi-skilled emotion managers who both comply with and resist the organisational constraints which exist around them.

Finally, Chapter 8, *Mixed feelings*, reviews the core arguments that are presented throughout the book. It does not, however, arrive at any conclusions but valuably brings to light numerous contradictions. For instance, front-line service workers are asked to generate the profitable product of customer service but are not empowered to do so. Instead imposed scripts and impossible targets create a distorted form of social encounter that results in a dissatisfying and alienating experience for all involved. Turning to the public sector, the book, in highlighting the complexities inherent in the emotional labour process of caring professionals, raises many questions concerning the nature of care work and its value, not just in the labour market but to society as a whole. In a similar vein the concentration on social actors as multi-skilled emotion managers emphasises the irony that in a national skills hierarchy emotion work is barely recognised at all. In turn, this is inextricably linked with the notion that emotion is a very social thing and, as such, emotion work represents and reproduces wider social divisions. All in all, the book presents organisations as being full of mixed feelings and that, even allowing for all of the pleasures and pains involved in being a member of an organisation, endorses the view that we would not wish it any other way.

Note

1. That is, once the problems of emotional burn-out have been effectively solved via the latest management prescription.

2

Bringing emotion onto the organisational agenda: a century of organisational analysis

Searching for the emotive subject

Over the past 20 years various accounts of the worker as an emotive subject have brought attention to the way in which organisations have been traditionally viewed. In place of the orthodox account of the organisation as a formal structure populated by rational office holders, it is being claimed that organisations have feelings and that organisational actors utilise emotions in the course of their work. A good deal about organisations has changed, including the way they are supposed to work and, to some extent, this simply reflects social change. The decline in manufacturing, the rise in service industries and the restructuring of the working population this has entailed are important factors, as are changing emphases in skill requirements. Less demand for the formally skilled male, manual worker and increasing demand for people dealing with customers – typically women – using more obvious interpersonal skills, are key developments. In addition to these structural changes employers are now faced with ever greater demands from workers who wish to be more 'fulfilled' in their work.

Clearly work has changed significantly creating new areas for study and a growing need for a conceptual framework for the study of emotion in the workplace. This is not to deny that, in classical theory (Fayol, 1949; Maslow, 1954; Mayo, 1946), organisation men and women were recognised as having 'sentiments' and that their various 'needs' would have to be satisfied in order to maintain organisational efficiency. Emotions have always been present in organisations but, for much of the last century, they were assigned to an 'unanalysed motivational reservoir' (Albrow, 1997). However, in more recent accounts employees' 'sentiments' have become the central focus of analysis. Though the focus and intent of such studies varies a great deal, there can be little doubt that emotions are now acknowledged not only as an unimportant by-product of organisational life which can be safely excluded from consideration, but as a vital and necessary part of an organisation and something which ought to be studied.

The rapid transformation of the passionless bureaucracy into the emotional organisation raises the question of how the emotional elements of working life are best to be understood. What conceptual developments have to be made to understand more adequately why writers now refer to organisational actors as 'emotional labourers' (Hochschild, 1983), 'sentimental workers' (Strauss *et al.*, 1982) or the 'emotionally intelligent' (Goleman, 1998a)? Why are leaders instructed to become 'social architects' (Senge, 1996), organisational designers enjoined to ensure that 'giants learn to dance' (Gerstner, 2002; Kanter, 1990) and what is so important about the mysterious motivational 'factor X' (Blanchard and Bowles, 1998; Peters, 1987)? In various ways, recent accounts highlight subtle and not so subtle changes in the way that the organisational actor is conceived. Whether it be management prescriptive literature which calls for employees to commit themselves with zeal to organisational values, or critical writers who decry such demands as an encroachment on an employee's own subjectivity, there is little doubt that the image of organisational actors has changed dramatically over the last century. Since it is now recognised that sexuality, violence, love and humour make important contributions to organisational life it would seem that some adjustments in our ways of understanding organisations are needed.

To develop an understanding of the emotional organisation a typology of workplace emotion is proposed and will be introduced in detail in Chapter 5. The complexity of organisational emotionality is indicated by the fact that the typology designates four distinct kinds of emotion management in contemporary organisations. These are *presentational* and *philanthropic* emotion management (according to social feeling rules), *pecuniary* emotion management (according to commercial feeling rules) and *prescriptive* emotion management (performed according to professional feeling rules). However, before this new way of conceptualising emotion and the processes by which it is regulated in organisations can be fully explored it needs to be situated within current debates concerning the use and control of emotion in organisations and the various conceptual approaches to an understanding of workers as emotive subjects. The purpose of this chapter and the one following is to create such a context.

This chapter begins the search for an understanding of how various 'paradigms' in organisation and management studies approach the topic of emotion in organisations and how, or if, they view the organisational actor as social actor and emotion manager. In an attempt to arrive at an adequate understanding of the organisational participant as a competent emotion worker, a review of different theoretical perspectives is undertaken. The approach adopted is to appraise broadly different perspectives drawn from almost a century of writing on organisations in order to assess what they say or do not say about emotions and emotionality. It soon becomes clear that some ways of looking at organisations say very little about the subject in hand, and are unhelpful as even initial sources of insight.

The little cogs

In Weber's description of the 'ideal' bureaucracy we find the origins of the idea of the organisation acting as an instrument. Much like a machine, the bureaucratic organisation is seen to be the 'most rational system of harnessing energies to the fulfilment of specialised tasks' (Giddens, 1972, p. 47). Based on his 'fundamental categories of rational legal authority' Weber's rational bureaucracy is expected to consist of a systematic division of labour; to have a formal hierarchy in place; to regulate conduct by the imposition of rules; to have administrative staff who are separated from ownership of the means of production; to make decisions and formulate rules; to select candidates for office on the basis of technical qualifications and remunerate office holders with fixed salaries (Weber, 1947). As such, the organisation is expected to function in a routine, efficient and reliable way; it is a means to an end, the centre of goal-oriented activity and, therefore, the bureaucratic type of 'administrative organization ... is, from a purely technical point of view, capable of attaining the highest degree of efficiency ... . It is superior to any other form in precision, in stability, in the stringency of its discipline and in its reliability' (Weber, 1947, p. 337).

Although Weber was one of the first to lay down explicit principles of the 'ideal' type of bureaucracy, the first American and European writers on management and organisation theory did not rely on this account as Weber's work was not translated from German until much later, in the 1940s. Nevertheless, Weber's work did go through a process of 'Americanization' where the formal and methodological characteristics were selectively reproduced. As a result, there are some obvious points in common between Weber's ideal type of bureaucracy and managerialist writings also formulated in the early part of this century. The early classical management writers look for methods which will first set up and then fine-tune the organisational machine to reach greater efficiency. Whereas Weber defines his 'ideal' type of bureaucracy as just that, an ideal that may rarely if ever be realised, classical management writers actually set out in the belief that organisations can run just as efficiently as machines, following a set of explicitly formulated principles which any manager could apply. For the first time, a body of work dedicated to the design of organisations was produced.

One of the celebrated examples of the mechanistic view of organisations is that of scientific management. Frederick Taylor (1911) utilises the idea of the specialised and extreme division of manual labour in his approach to work. Using a formal analysis of work, later to be developed into time and motion study, Taylor examines the work of a manual labourer and arrives at several conclusions: workers should be specifically chosen for their suitability to carry out precise tasks, the process of work should be broken down into easily achieved tasks that would require the minimum of training, workers should not be required to think about what they are doing and finally they would be progressively rewarded for their efforts in monetary terms. Taylor continually strives to find the 'one best way' to achieve maximum output by his application of an analytical approach to the design of work. For Taylor, the worker is an individual unit of production and he thinks that the way to satisfy both individual and organisational needs is through the application of such methods: the individual could rationally pursue their personal ambitions of creating more economic wealth and the organisation would achieve greater production output.

Taylor's work is part of what Weber suggests is the progressive rationalisation of economy and society, which includes developments in industry such as Henry Ford's assembly line. The kind of society which developed, involving the continuous rationalisation of work through increasingly specialised divisions of labour combined with bureaucratic controls, has come to be associated with Fordism. There is indeed considerable debate as to whether this era has come to its end; but, even if we have entered a phase of post-Fordism or neo-Fordism, there is little doubt of the importance and impact of the original ideas which are introduced by the likes of Fayol (1949), Ford (1924) and Taylor (1911).

Coming within the category of the orthodox school of thought are classic management theorists such as Barnard (1938) and Fayol (1949). Much like Taylor, but aimed at administrative methods rather than shop floor methods, these management writers propose principles which need to be followed if executives of the organisation are to fulfil their functions efficiently: 'The soundness and good working order of the body corporate depend on a certain number of conditions termed indiscriminately principles; laws, rules'

(Fayol, 1949, p. 19). Not surprisingly, the principles bear a very close resemblance to those of scientific management: division of labour, discipline, unity of command, centralisation of authority, remuneration and the 'subordination of individual interests to the general interest'(Fayol, 1949, p. 19). It is notable how this portrayal of the efficient organisation is based very much on Weber's 'ideal type' in that it insists on functional departments, precisely defined job descriptions and clear patterns of authority running through hierarchical structures, with the emphasis being very much on 'top-down' control. The classic view of organisations never doubts their status as completely rational systems, designed to operate in a smooth and efficient manner.

Orthodox writers of this period frequently compare the organisation to a human body: note Fayol's (1949) use of the term 'body corporate' or Barnard's (1938, p. 216) description of an executive's role: 'The functions with which we are concerned are like those of the nervous system, including the brain, in relation to the rest of the body.' In this way, each department clearly relies on one another for survival. Despite their emphasis on functional departments and specialisation of tasks, writers such as Barnard and Fayol clearly feel that the design of a formal structure will be enough to ensure that the organisation achieves equilibrium: 'there must be a place appointed for each thing and each thing must be in its appointed place' (Fayol, 1949, p. 36).

In this mechanistic view, organisational actors are not seen as thinking, feeling beings who have an element of choice in how they conduct their daily lives. Taylor's workers are not 'paid to think', they are expected to be reliable, efficient and, most of all, predictable. Fayol's managers are meant to remain impartial and carry out orders from their superiors unquestioningly; personal opinions should be 'put aside': 'ignorance, ambition, selfishness, laziness, weakness, and all human passions tend to cause the general interest to be lost sight of in favour of individual interest and a perpetual struggle must be waged against them' (Fayol, 1949, p. 26). Both of these views represent the worker as the little 'cog', personal feelings are subordinated to the 'organization personality' (Barnard, 1938) and work becomes a 'sentence of bondage' (Clegg, 1990) within the vast mechanism of bureaucracy – the iron cage. Once again, it is easy to see a comparison with Weber's description of the 'ideal' bureaucrat: 'The dominance of the spirit of formalistic impersonality, sine ira et studio, without hatred or passion, and hence without affection or enthusiasm. The dominant norms are concepts of straight-forward duty without regard to personal considerations' (Weber, 1947, p. 340).

However, unlike Weber, writers such as Taylor and Fayol do not show concern about the issues of the place of organisations in wider society or share Weber's pessimism concerning the increasing bureaucratisation of organisational life. Despite his 'metaphysical pathos' (Gouldner, 1955), Weber recognises that it is possible for the irrational to prove to be a powerful counter-force to the rationalisation process and his work is full of references to feelings. His descriptions of different types of social action, coupled with his understanding of formal and substantive rationality, clearly differentiate Weber from the classicist organisation writers who only recognise one type of actor – 'organisation man'[1] – whose behaviour is formally rational and goal orientated.

For these early management writers the bureaucratic personality is the only permissible kind and if maximum efficiency is to be achieved then emotion definitely cannot be written into an organisational actor's script. This is not to say that emotion is not recognised as occupying a place in organisational life, but it cannot be seen to interfere with goal-oriented systems of activity (Parson, 1956). Through the creation of rationally defined ways of organising, expressed in the form of formal structures, hierarchies and rules, it was thought that the method had been found whereby all subjective interferences could be managed 'out' of working life. This, in turn, led to the refinement of further practices such as sophisticated accounting and time and motion techniques which, as Reed points out, would allow 'recalcitrant and wasteful human beings (to) be transformed into governable and efficient organizational members' (Reed, 1992, p. 41).In this way, the classic management theorists think they have found the 'one best way' to organise and that they have solved organisational problems forever.

However, the portrayal of a social actor as a formally rational 'organisation man', what Weber refers to as a 'little cog', does little to further an understanding concerning the realities of organisational life. To writers within the classicist frame of reference, the organisational actor, whether he or she be a shop floor labourer or a company executive, is only ever portrayed as an unfeeling automaton who blindly behaves according to corporate regulations within the formal organisation. Taylor's concern with actors as individual factors of production and Fayol's obsession with executive 'functions' mean that the organisational actor is only ever seen within a managerial frame of reference, which dare not acknowledge emotion of any sort lest it interfere with the efficient completion of tasks. The only acknowledgement of any human passion is when writers such as Barnard (1938) and Fayol (1949) speak of the 'esprit de corps' and they advise executives to 'build strength' through 'union' and thus avoid any deviance from prescribed forms of action. It is notable how, when mentioned at all, emotion is described as something to be 'excluded', 'controlled', 'subordinated' and, at all costs, 'avoided'. Hence the portrait of the emotionally 'crippled' actor (Mouzelis, 1975). Such a narrow view, which believes so devoutly in its ability to control all aspects of organisational life, makes it impossible to understand anything but the formal aspects of organisation. It is, therefore, clearly unhelpful when trying to theorise organisational actors as having multiple interpretations of reality and as being competent emotion workers.

The human side of enterprise

Increasingly, the deficiencies of the mechanistic structure loomed large in management thinking. It was seen to be rigid and unable to adapt to environmental change. There was concern over the dehumanising effects of scientific management and the mindless and unquestioning face of bureaucracy which neglected the basic fact that the worker does not always behave according to the rules of the formal organisation. With the idea that organisational actors are not mere 'automatons', but complex human beings with their own variety of motivations, needs and desires, an organisational theory which concentrates on the informal aspects of the organisation begins to be developed. The work of the 'Human Relations' school of management originated with devising ways of managing 'the human side of enterprise' in order that the often unintended consequences of a rigid bureaucratic structure may be avoided.

Research conducted during the 1920s at the Hawthorne Plant, by Roethlisberger and Dickson (1939), discovers what they call the 'logic of sentiment' and that the perceived irrational logic possessed by workers often differs from the organisational 'logic of efficiency'. Elton Mayo (1946), who directed the infamous Hawthorne studies, arrives at the conclusion that values and beliefs which emerge from the social interaction of individuals create an informal social system which develops its own rules and norms. Despite the inconclusive results and questionable research methods used in the Hawthorne studies (Carey, 1967), a new branch of organisation theory is developed and the Mayoites continue to attempt to explore group behaviour, morale, motivation and the effects of these variables on the level of production.

This new management theory differs greatly from classical management theory in one major respect: that is it recognises that the design of work is influenced on a day-to-day basis by the social interaction of individuals and that the individual can find ingenious ways to circumvent the formal structure of an organisation. The development of the new theory is built on the idea that individuals and groups in an organisation are a part of the organism as a whole and will only function efficiently when, like a living organism, their needs have been satisfied. These 'needs', however, are perceived by the human relations theorists as pathological problems suffered by individual workers which can be remedied via careful counselling from managers who know what is best for the worker. It is Mayo's (1946) belief that he has discovered how a 'harmonious and efficient' organisation can be achieved through the control and management of workers' unreasonable 'urges' and 'desires'. Through the satisfaction of workers' social needs and by creating a new society within the plant, the informal and formal organisations will work together toward the same ends.

Following Mayo, many theories of human motivation are put forward endeavouring to find the answer of how to secure employee commitment to organisational goals. They all tend to follow the same theme through their criticism of the classicist's 'rabble hypothesis' (where workers act purely out of rational self-interest) and base their theories very much on Mayo's (1946) discovery of the social needs of the working man and woman. Writers such as Hertzberg (1966), Maslow (1954) and McGregor (1960) stress 'organisation man' as 'social man'. They advocate job enrichment where employees are given more autonomy and recognition in their work, emphasising the fact that monetary incentives are not enough to secure the commitment of employees. Maslow (1954), for instance, suggests that human beings operate according to a hierarchy of needs; when basic survival needs have been satisfied then the human being moves to the next level and seeks to satisfy social needs and from there they move up to the satisfaction of psychological needs. In the 1960s and 1970s the ideas of increasing production through the creation of the 'satisfied' worker grow in momentum.

Just as Taylorism firmly sets the foundations for many work processes in operation today, the ideas put forward by the early human relations theorists still dominate management literature. The 'must do' of recent prescriptive and human resource management literature relies entirely on the human relations view of the organisational actor, a review of which will be conducted later in the chapter. Other highly respected and influential academic accounts of workplace emotion, that rest within this framework, offer well-meaning investigations into the consequences of management prescription and organisation structure combined with the emotional elements of organisational life. A general view is that organisational effectiveness could be improved if emotion is recognised as a vital element of motivation, leadership and group dynamics. Unsurprisingly, much of contemporary research within this body of thought is concerned with the efficacy of emotion work in the context of customer service. As a result, various studies seek to ascertain the variable, that is 'highly expressive', 'self-monitoring', that will enable management to predict which 'type' of employee can be guaranteed to express 'positive' emotion all of the time (Morris and Feldman, 1996, 1997; Rafaeli and Sutton, 1990). Analysis also tends to focus on the consequences of emotion work where disaffected workers, exhausted managers and, perhaps most prominently, dissatisfied customers, are a matter worthy of extended investigation with the result that ever more inventive management prescriptions are offered as a means to satisfy the needs of all involved (Ashforth and Humphrey, 1993, 1995; Morris and Feldman, 1996, 1997).

Despite this perspective stressing, throughout its long history, the 'human' element of organisational life, the organisational actor still never really comes to life as a distinct entity separate from the organisation. Admittedly, workers are no longer treated as individual units of production, as they are in classic management writings. The social interactions of workers are recognised as an important element of organisational life and attempts are made to shape the sentiments of workers. However, just as the Mayoites believed that any signs of worker discontent were signs of maladjustment on behalf of the individual personality more recent accounts continue with this assumption and we are led to believe that important workplace issues such as stress, burnout and emotional exhaustion are individual crises that arise due to an individual's lack of capacity to cope. Despite huge developments in this band of thinking there continues a serious neglect of the political, social and economic factors that provide the social framework in which interpersonal relations at work are embedded. Though many of these studies are well-meaning in intent their blinkered approach means that conflict in the workplace is never acknowledged and 'human sentiment' is only ever seen in terms of worker motivation and job satisfaction.

For this stream of thinking, cooperation is the key to an organisation's survival and the continual invention of new management theories are aimed specifically at this achievement. Despite the human relations school's claims of improving on the mechanistic ideas of organisation, their recognition of the organisational actor barely differs at all. Of course, they do recognise the organisational actor as 'social man' (more recently including an acknowledgement of 'social woman'), but still overemphasise the power of management techniques to 'manage' subjective interferences. Through their research and analysis of human sentiment in the workplace, they display a generally patronising air towards organisational actors, as if they know what is best for the workers. It appears to be their belief that they are able, through management prescription, to make the organisational actor a whole and contented person.

The body of work produced by writers belonging to the early human relations school (Maslow, 1954; McGregor, 1960; Hertzberg, 1966) forms an enduring interest in the 'human side of enterprise'. However, the original naivety of this view tends to remain and contemporary accounts of organisational life still reproduce a 'top down' view and narrow perspective of the organisational world meaning that their view of 'social man/ woman' is in fact not too far removed from the mechanistic 'organisation man'. Such a perspective leaves no room for the analysis of any action other than that which is orientated to achieving an organisation's ends. Where sentiment is acknowledged, it is only in order that a new management method may be invented to prevent it causing interference.

The human relations school, and associated behavioural approaches, find a place for emotions in organisations but emotions had better know their place (Archer, 2000, p. 81). The simple equation is that 'happy' workers equal 'productive' workers and to that end they seek to merge the individual's needs with the organisation's needs. Early human relations writers show little recognition of or interest in the inherent emotion management skills that social actors possess or the possible value of such skills to an organisation's success. Quite the opposite is true of their new millennium contemporaries where many interesting studies emphasise the important role of emotion in organisational life. However, despite these changes in the direction of research, there remains a general lack of attention to the subject of emotion as anything other than an irrational force that is to be developed and channelled into certain forms by management. It is unlikely, therefore, that a frame of reference which relies so much on a behavioural approach to emotion, and thus only partially recognises the important social aspects of human emotion, can contribute to furthering a genuine understanding of the organisational actor as an emotive subject.

Organisations as 'Open Systems'

The 'systems-approach' to organisations, much like the classicists and human relations school of thinking, treats the organisation as a system of interdependent parts. However, unlike the earlier theorists who concentrate solely on the internal workings of an organisation, the systems theorists recognise that organisations do not operate as closed systems, but interact and are dependent upon the environment for survival. The 'open-systems' approach, based on Bertalanffy's principles of 'General Systems Theory', treats the organisation as a living organism that must achieve equilibrium with its internal sub-systems and external environment.

Emphasising the study of contextual factors in the environment that may affect the survival of organisations, contingency theory remains within the systems thinking framework but concentrates on how different 'species' of organisation are required, depending on the kind of environment in which they have to exist. One of the most convincing studies is Burns and Stalker's (1961) which examines the differences between 'mechanistic' and 'organic' organisations and how this affects their survival in different environments. They find that stable environments can be handled by 'mechanistic systems', for example bureaucracies, whereas an environment which is constantly changing requires an 'organismic system' that is flexible in its responses to changing circumstances. These examples are used to represent the two extremes of a continuum, along which most organisations can be placed.

Burns and Stalker's (1961) research has proved to be influential in linking organisation structure with the external environment. It has been widely supported by other studies: Joan Woodward (1965), for instance, links the effect of technology with the type of structure adopted by an organisation and the Aston Studies (Pugh and Hickson, 1976) find that it is organisation size that determines the type of structure. Similarly, relying heavily on the analogy of the organisation as a living organism, Lawrence and Lorsch's (1967) research reveals that organisations cannot be viewed as homogeneous entities. The various sub-systems of an organisation may develop in a variety of ways in order to adapt to the different demands made of them from their 'sub-environments'. Additionally, they state that it is as equally important that an adequate structure is in place to ensure the organisation is not only 'differentiated' but also 'integrated'.

As can be seen by the wealth of research which has been produced, the contingency view of organisations has been very influential in the field of organisation and management studies and remains so today in the form of a systems approach to organisational design and change (Attwood *et al.*, 2003; Checkland, 1999; Gharajedaghi, 1999). Give its emphasis on equilibrium it is hardly surprising that much of today's prescriptive management literature can be found to refer to this theoretical base. Mintzberg's (1983) 'adhocracy' is very similar to the idea of an organic structure. Tom Peters (1987, 1995, 2003), as well as referring to internal strategies to create a company culture, also frequently refers to the need to be flexible and able to adapt and change in order to keep pace with a turbulent environment. Blanchard and Bowles' (1998) 'Gung Ho' principle bears a close resemblance to Barnard's biological view of the organisation when they advise that observations of the natural world can be used to motivate employees. And Pedlar *et al.* (1997) and Senge (1990, 1996, 1999), in their concept of the learning organisation and leadership, explicitly refer to systems theory as a conceptual framework. A more detailed review of recent management prescription will be conducted later in this chapter but, for now, Senge summarises the position very well:

> Systems thinking is a discipline for seeing wholes. It is a framework for
> seeing interrelationships rather than things, for seeing patterns of change rather

than static 'snapsots'. ... And systems thinking is sensibility – for the subtle interconnectedness that gives living systems their unique character. ... Systems thinking is a discipline for seeing the 'structures' that underlie complex situations, and for discerning high from low leverage change (Senge, 1990, p. 68–9).

Though clearly this approach has proved itself useful when studying the formal relationship between organisations, structure and environment it does suffer from some very severe limitations, mainly its ignorance of the organisational actor. This is hardly surprising when coming from a perspective that views organisations as having a distinct life of their own, wholly independent of the actions of its members. A view such as this leaves little or no room to acknowledge the ability of actors to actively construct the world around them. It does recognise the presence of the human element and there has been a general shift towards a 'softer' version of systems theory in an attempt to overcome the general neglect of the social actor and account for the variability of human conduct (Checkland, 1999). Nevertheless, despite these good intentions, the over dependence on systems theory as a 'problem solving methodology' and the view of organisations as organic systems underplays the possibility of conflict. It is always assumed that the subsystems, with a little help from the soft systems approach, will act together, automatically achieving equilibrium and, thus, an organisational actor's personal needs and wishes will be fulfilled through involvement in the organisation.

This confirms the view that theoretical perspectives can be a way of seeing but can also act as a means of not seeing and, quite clearly, systems theory chooses not to truly 'see' organisational actors lest they should disrupt their consensual approach to organisational life. Whilst systems theorists do acknowledge emotion they, like their first cousins the human relations school, dismiss it as the 'irrationality' of workers. Therefore, for all its volume and variety, research conducted within the systems theory framework has done little to alter the classicist perceptions of organisation design. Even when the informal activity involved in organisational life is recognised, this is merely seen as something to be controlled and directed by management prescription within the formal structure. In effect, the classicists' and systems' view of the formal structure hardly differs at all.

Enter the active actor: the action frame of reference

In response to the domination of organisation theory by perspectives that neglect the organisational actor, a new generation of theory begins to develop. One of the earliest contributors to this approach to theory is Silverman (1970), who portrays organisations as social constructs which are created through the actions of their members: 'If the reality of the social world is socially sustained, then it follows that reality is also socially changed' (Silverman, 1970, p. 135). This view is directly opposed to the orthodox view, which sees an organisation as a concrete, independent structure that affects the actions of its members but remains unaffected by them. In highlighting the 'action frame of reference', Silverman enables the understandings of how organisational rules are quite fluid due to their re-negotiation through the actions of individuals. In turn, this stresses the ability of actors to influence their environment and represents a major challenge to the overdeterministic view of both classicists and systems thinkers. Silverman points out 'both roles and structure merely provide a framework for action; they do not determine it' (Silverman, 1970, p. 134).

This frame of reference has been used for social analysis for some time (Blumer, 1962, 1969; Berger and Luckman, 1966; Goffman 1959, 1961a, 1967; Schutz, 1967). Writers use the basic notion of a distinctive micro-social world where 'reality is socially constructed' (Berger and Luckman, 1966) and is continually sustained through the interaction of its members, according to its own peculiar rules and processes. A whole school of thought has grown around the central premises that (1) people act towards things, and each other, based on the meanings they have for them; (2) meanings are derived through social interaction and (3) meanings are managed and transformed through an interpretive process used to make sense of what constitutes their social world (Blumer, 1969; Denzin, 1984; Hughes, 1958; Snow, 2001; Strauss, 1970). Symbolic interactionism encompasses a broad range of thought concerning human action, interpretation, social constraints and 'the interaction order', with some recent accounts even giving interactionism a postmodern slant (Denzin 1993; Fine, 1993). Nevertheless, there is a common thread that binds this heterogeneity together; they focus their analysis at the level of the local. As Goffman points out, efforts continue 'to promote acceptance of this face-to-face domain as an analytically viable one – a domain which might be titled, for want of any happy name, the interaction order – a domain whose preferred method of study is microanalysis' (Goffman, 1991, p. 4).

It is not, however, until the late 1960s and early 1970s that symbolic interactionist and social action theories begin to be developed as a theory of organisations that advocate a way of understanding the 'micro' elements of organisational life. In this way, the interactionists are able to move the emphasis away from studies of organisations as purely technical means of achieving predetermined goals. They attempt to show how the organisation is not a concrete entity in its own right but derives its meaning from the 'attitudes of everyday life and in socially sanctioned common-sense typifications' (Bittner, 1973, p. 269).

Many empirical studies have been carried out using this approach. Where system theorists look for causal and law-like explanation based on generalisable knowledge, the social action theorists tend to use qualitative methods as a way of accounting for the processes through which members constitute their meanings of everyday life.Classic studies such as Bittner's (1967) 'Police on Skid Row' and Zimmerman's (1971) 'The Practicalities of Rule Use' show how an organisation's formal rules are constantly re-negotiated by organisational actors and that control, through the imposition of a formal network of rules, can never be complete. In fact, Zimmerman's (1971) study of how receptionists enact the rules of a bureaucratic public sector organisation shows how, in many cases, the violation of set rules and procedures actually leads to a more efficient use of an organisation's resources. Similarly, in the case of Bittner's (1967) policemen, it is shown how the actor creates his or her own rules to deal with the situation as it is encountered on 'skid row'; an area of urban life which is seen to 'live apart from normalcy'. As Bittner (1967) points out, it is not necessarily 'specific legal formula' that dictates how law is enforced, rather it depends on how policemen interpret the situation with respect to the actual state of particular social situations on skid-row.

Cases such as Zimmerman's (1971) and Bittner's (1967) highlight how the symbolic interactionist goes farther than seeing the actor as merely reinterpreting the existing rules. Each scenario displays how understanding is created through the negotiated action of individuals and without the continual 'negotiation' between social actors organisations would have no meaning or life. There can be little doubt that both the action frame of reference and the symbolic interactionists, which together are known as the interpretative paradigm,take account of the important part actors play in organisational life. Unlike the classicist or systems view, the interactionists concentrate on the subjective meanings which actors bring to an organisation and allow for the influence of emotion on both the formal and the informal aspects of organisational life.

Using this approach, valuable contributions have been made to organisational analysis which further an understanding of the 'emotional life' of an organisation. For example, Strauss *et al.* (1982) attempt to theorise organisational emotionality with their concept of 'sentimental work'. Whilst studying the work of a nurse, Strauss and his colleagues recognise that there is more to nursing work than the completion of technical tasks. Much of a nurse's time and energy is consumed by working on both their own and the patient's emotions in order to create the correct climate and 'get the job done' (Strauss *et al.*, 1982). Fine's (1988) study of humour in a busy restaurant kitchen, Pilnick and Hindmarsh's (1999) detailed examination of professional/ patient interaction in an anaesthetic room and Goffman's (1961b) revelations in *Asylums* concerning 'hospital underlife' clearly shows how the interactionist paradigm can prove to be useful when attempting to understand the organisational actor as a skilled emotion 'worker'. Their 'micro' studies of interaction, between both workers and clients and workers and co-workers, enable an understanding of how work is not purely a matter of following procedural rules. They also, unlike the human relations school's recognition of 'sentiment', insightfully display that human sentiment is not something that is confined only to the realm of the 'informal' organisation, but plays a vital part in all walks of organisational life.

However, despite the detailed descriptions of the minutiae of everyday organisational life, the portrayal of organisational actors as having the ability to construct their own meaningful world neglects the existence of official mandates that attempt to structure and direct action in organisations. Where formal rules are recognised it is to signify how they are constantly re-interpreted by organisational actors and any power these rules may be able to exert over the organisational actor tends to remain a vague concept in the interactionist's analysis of organisational life. The emphasis placed on the con-stant reworking and modification and, in some cases, the actual construction of rules tends to overplay the ability of organisational actors to freely construct their own 'organisational arrangements' with very little constraint or interfer-ence from 'outside' forces. It can be clearly seen how the interpretative per-spective differs so dramatically to the systems theorists and how they are both seen as being on completely opposite ends of the macro/micro continuum. This leaves both theoretical perspectives open to the same type of criticism – their particular way of 'seeing' tends to restrict the reader's view of organisa-tional life. Whereas the systems theorists tend to over-concentrate on the 'macro' aspects of organisation, such as formal structure and environment, the interactionists overestimate the 'micro' side of organisational life by portray-ing the organisational actor as creating their own realities within a very limited framework.

The interpretative way of seeing organisational life allows a clearer picture of actors as emotive subjects than the orthodox perspective would allow. However, whilst this recognition of the individual is to be applauded, the over-concentration on the power of the organisational actor to construct a mean-ingful world does little to further an understanding of the structural factors which provide the context in which this 'minutiae of everyday life' will be con-structed. As Reed (1992, p. 92) points out: 'there is too much attention to "structures in process" and not enough to the "structuring of process" '. In effect, there is an overemphasis on the day-to-day, here and now, elements of organisational life and we are given a snapshot of action where only half a picture can be gained. For instance, when the actions of Bittner's (1967) police are described, they are set firmly within the micro-world of skid row. There are no clues as to the social background of the policemen and no concern for the social, economic and political forces which both create and sustain this particular aspect of urban life, neither are there questions concerning who would wish for this 'primordial jungle' to be so neatly contained. Bittner (1967) continually speaks of the 'ad hoc' decision-making processes of the police on skid row and yet never reveals what influences, apart from the actors who live and work within this closed world, may bear upon how they arrive at their judgements. Equally, there is no acknowledgement of a formal authority structure within the city police department or what effect this may have on the day-to-day policing of skid row.

Without full consideration of the 'outside' influences that guide action in certain frameworks, the meaning of the action cannot be fully understood. The interactionists often leave us with what Hochschild (1983) would describe as 'fractured islands of reality', with no 'structural bridge' to link the islands of action together. However, to summarily dismiss all interactionist accounts as solipsistic is to miss their variety and value. There is little doubt that the interactionists can be relied upon to give vivid portrayals of particular situations and, as in Goffman's work, the 'rules' of that micro-world are acknowledged as having a powerful influence over the way the scene is enacted. In fact, as argued throughout this book, Goffman can be relied upon to expand the interaction order into different and larger frameworks of analysis. There is an implicit recognition of layers of reality throughout his work, made explicit in *Frame Analysis* (1974) and *Asylums* (1961b), and he often carries his analysis out of the micro-worlds of the 'closed institution' and the face-to-face encounter into the wider social realm. It is also becoming increasingly recognised within the symbolic interactionist paradigm that a concentration on interaction at the micro-level only allows the situation to be placed into very limited frameworks where meaning and motive can only be partially understood. More and more accounts place their analysis of social interaction on a material stage though, with few exceptions (Goffman, 1974; Schwabe, 1993), there remains an attachment to the notion that individual and society only exist in relation to each other.

Elements of symbolic interactionism, in all its forms, are invaluable in understanding an emergent and interactive process such as emotion. With recent developments in the field and Goffman's 'loose-coupling' of enduring structures and seemingly fleeting interactions, it becomes possible to draw on this paradigm to begin to understand how the organisational actor comes to be such an efficient 'emotion worker'. Nevertheless, its political naiveté compromises any account it may have concerning how 'emotional labour' can be compared with physical labour in that it has become a valuable commodity in the 1990s workplace.

The labour process: a radical view

Labour process analysis sets out to develop an understanding of the organisation of work, and employee responses to it, by placing it in the context of institutionalised structures of domination and control. This is a critical response to the lack of structural analysis in the interpretative framework and the way the systems theorists reify organisation structure. Rather than taking for granted that there is a consensus amongst the participants in organisations, LPA assumes that conflict arises from the unequal distribution of resources available to different groups in society. Unlike the systems perspective, it is argued that conflict cannot be treated as a minor aberration that can be eradicated from society or its constituent organisations. To LPA conflict is an integral part of capitalist organisation and society and differences between groups can only ever be reconciled to a limited degree. Organisations are a key location in which contradictions between the interests of groups are acted out with a resultant 'gap' in the employment relationship. It is the indeterminacy of labour that is at the heart of LPA – that is the gap between the effort organisations demand and the effort labour actually offers, often referred to as the effort bargain. In theory, and this is highlighted within the prescriptive texts reviewed above, the gap is bridged through management intervention and various control mechanisms. LPA is interested in what actually happens in practice.

As its name suggests, LPA examines the changing nature of the labour process believing it to represent identifiable features of the nature of work in contemporary organisations. The division of labour, the deskilling tendencies in increasingly technologised production techniques, the separation of conception and execution and the control imperative and resultant 'struggle' are all central concerns of LPA. Adopting a structuralist viewpoint, labour process writers analyse which institutional structures impact upon an organisation. They believe organisations cannot be understood without looking at their place and role within the capitalist society in which they are both spatially and temporally embedded. By analysing the relationship between the macro-level of economy and political system with the micro-level of the organisation and its operations, the analysis of structure is carried down to the organisational actor via the labour process and the politics of production. LPA asks to what extent it is possible, through patterns of control and conflict, for groups to re-make the world in small ways. This acknowledgement of the relevance of both macro- and micro-levels of analysis allows the identification of particular strategies of control that are used in organisations and the way these generate both consent and resistance.

Described as a 'seminal contribution' (Thompson, 1989), Braverman's (1974) work, 'Labour and Monopoly Capital', influenced a generation of writers in the United States and Britain. Arguing that the capitalist mode of production requires efficient means of extracting work from workers and controlling the workforce, Braverman shows that, for much of the recent history of the industrial United States, effective control of labour has been achieved through the use of Taylorism. Braverman concentrates on the way that Taylorism has entailed the 'degradation of work'. Through the separation of 'conception and execution' management is seen to be exercising tight and ever tighter controls over the labour process. By such means they ensure that power remains firmly in the hands of those at the top of the organisation's hierarchy. Alienation in work is seen as a result of the predominance of the mechanistic design of work:

> Thus, if the first principle is the gathering together and development of knowledge of the labour process, and the second is the concentration of this knowledge as the exclusive preserve of management – together with its converse, the absence of such knowledge among workers – then the third step is the use of this monopoly of knowledge to control each step of the labour process and its mode of execution. (Braverman, 1974, p. 119)

Building on Braverman's 'de-skilling' thesis, other writers have tried to identify ways in which management exerts 'direct control' through the imposition of scientific management type principles (division of labour, separation of 'knowing and doing'). Various methods of controlling the labour process have continued to be developed that acknowledge the organisational actor as an active agent. Edwards (1979) notes that forms of management control have evolved in conjunction with the historical development of the capitalist labour process. 'Simple' control, as advocated by Taylorism, may be still found in small, owner-controlled workplaces, but has generally been supplanted by forms of structural control, such as 'technical' control. This has been achieved through the implementation of mechanised forms of work and 'bureaucratic' controls that rely on formal hierarchies and clearly defined administrative structures. However, it is also noted that structural forms of control are complemented by other kinds of efforts to mobilise workers' consent. For example, Richard Edwards (1979) cites 'welfare capitalism' whereby social and other benefits can be provided by employers. Andrew Freidman (1977) identifies 'responsible autonomy' as a means of producing a level of participation from the workforce. Here managerial authority is maintained by workers' identification with the overall aims of the enterprise, thereby requiring the minimum amount of supervision. Burawoy's (1979) account of everyday life on the shop floor is pivotal in involving labour as an active subject in the labour process. He shows how interactions between workers and managerial regimes can 'manufacture consent'. In the factory he studied, Burawoy found that workers defined their lived experience of the labour process through their daily game-playing activity at work.

By the 1980s a whole body of work had developed which used this sort of framework for analysis. By examining the labour process, and management strategies of control and worker resistance, research from the labour process perspective serves to highlight how control over workplace relations is a 'contested terrain' (Edwards, 1979). Studies such as Beynon's 'Working for Ford' (1973); Nichols and Armstrong's 'Workers Divided' (1976); Nichols and Beynon's 'Living with Capitalism' (1977) and Thompson and Bannon's 'Working the System' (1985) use qualitative research methods in an attempt to 'make sense' of organisational practices. Work in this vein continues, offering valuable insight into the changing nature of work, the move from external to internalised modes of control, and workers' reactions to these changes (Callaghan and Thompson, 2001; Delbridge, 1998; Garrahan and Stewart, 1992; Taylor and Bain, 1999). Accounts such as these bring the organisational actor to life. This makes it possible to understand the importance of shop floor joking practices (Burawoy 1979; Collinson 1992; Delbridge, 1998), workers' own perceptions of subjects such as redundancy (Nichols and Beynon 1977) and the existence of both collective and individualised resistance 'on the line' (Beynon 1973; Callaghan and Thompson, 2001; Garrahan and Stewart, 1992). However, unlike the interpretative accounts of organisational life, the radical writers ensure that the actor's subjective views are firmly 'situated within cultural and historical contexts, embroiled in organized structures and relations of the wider society' (Collinson, 1992, p. 237).

Within this framework, we also find some of the first research concerning 'organisation women'. Feminists argue that previous accounts of organisational life reflect a 'deep rooted male bias'. In response to this, studies such as: Cavendish's (1982) 'Women on the Line', Pollert's (1981), 'Girls, Wives, Factory Lives', Westwood's (1984), 'All Day, Every Day', Cockburn's (1983) 'Brothers' and Wajcman's (1998) 'Managing Like a Man' have used a Marxist analysis of class and a socialist-feminist analysis of gender to reveal the reality of working life for women working in a patriarchal system that has capitalism as a close partner (Cockburn, 1991).

Though their recognition of micro-influences is limited, the LPA of organisations comes close to portraying the organisational actor as capable of being an efficient emotion manager in the workplace. Research carried out by Ackroyd and Thompson (1999), Burawoy (1979) and Collinson (1992) shows how game playing and humour are not only a hidden part of the informal organisation but have both beneficial and non-beneficial effects on the labour process. Furthermore, feminist accounts such as Westwood's (1984) highlight how the social construction of gender affects workplace relations. Interestingly, along with a general trend in organisation studies and management writing, recent labour process accounts have also come to recognise management's attempts to control organisational emotionality and the peculiarities of the 'emotional effort bargain' (Bolton and Boyd, 2003; Callaghan and Thompson, 2002; Sharma and Black, 2001; Taylor 1996, 1998). Callaghan and Thompson's empirical study of call centre work highlights how customer interaction is not entirely divorced from social interaction when the customer service agents re-interpret the company script in order to 'help' elderly customers. This serves to further emphasise the indeterminacy of labour, especially where the control of emotion work is involved. Often, during social encounters in the workplace, a 'gift' exchange takes place that has little or nothing to do with the production of a profitable product. The 'gift' may inadvertently reinforce the quality of a consumable product, such as in a face-to-face service encounter, but it is not something which is directly controlled as part of the capitalist labour process and the freedom to offer or withdraw the gift remains with the organisational actor.

There is little doubt that recent LPA accounts show an extended conception of agency. This, however, is seen as inadequate by one particular branch of LPA which, during the 1990s, has moved away from a materialist stance and changed the existing structural framework by analysing subjectivity and identity formation at work. Using a post-structuralist approach it is shown how an actor searches for a secure identity through work thus enabling organisations to capture and control their subjectivity through various cultural management programmes. In these accounts 'identity rather than labour is the site of indeterminacy' (Thompson and Smith, 2001). The precarious nature of *postmodern* identities means that actors become subjugated to the disciplining demands of the organisation (Knights, 1990; Knights and Vurdubakis, 1994; Knights and Willmott, 1989; O'Doherty and Willmott, 2001; Willmott, 1993). This very different concept of control and agency has caused a rift within LPA with little hope of any form of consensus ever being reached due to fundamental ontological differences. The post-structuralist turn in organisational analysis will be analysed in more depth later in this chapter. Suffice to say, there is a general view from the orthodox branch of labour process theory that this new dimension adds nothing, and in many cases detracts, from the mainstream LPA framework. Apart from the fact that post-structuralist analyses engage with disturbing 'discourses of despair' (Thompson and Smith, 2001, p. 56) the case for a 'Foucauldian labour process' (Bahnisch, 2000) within an LPA framework is difficult to sustain. LPA deals in 'concrete' relations of production, post-structuralism deals in discursive constructions. LPA examines the tension inherent in the capitalist labour process and views agency as a creative force, post-structuralism views agency as something of a gaping black hole. For LPA, indeterminacy of labour is at the heart of their analysis, for post-structuralism there is no indeterminacy, labour is already determined as it is both a 'medium and outcome of power relations' (Knights and Willmott, 1989, p. 538).

This, however, is not to say that LPA alone is able to offer necessary insights for the study of emotion in organisations. Although various labour process accounts do acknowledge the micro aspects of organisational life, they tend to over-concentrate on the collective attitudes of workers, giving their day-to-day activities political meaning and placing them in a perpetual power struggle with management.[2] In addition, their description of labour (both physical and emotional) as a commodity limits an understanding of certain aspects of the non-capitalist labour process, such as work in the public sector and amongst professionals. There are complexities involved in applying LPA to the public sector, even though, as Cousins (1987) notes, public sector managers are often 'constrained to act as capitalists'. Perhaps most importantly LPA, by its own admission (Thompson, 1989; Thompson and Smith, 2001), shows limited ability in examining the intricacies involved in the individual's management of emotion, making it difficult to create an understanding of the skilled emotion worker and how he or she is capable of behaving in social encounters. Despite labour process accounts enabling an understanding of the patterns of conflict and accommodation that characterise workplace relations, they analyse the resulting contradictions mainly in terms of attempts at management control and workers' ability to resist within the confines of the capitalist workplace. In effect, they are unable to conceptualise fully non-political or non-commercial aspects of organisational emotionality, leaving areas of organisational life only partially explained.

To be fair, LPA is very aware of its limitations and recognises that 'all theoretical frameworks have natural limits to their scope' (Thompson, 1989, 1990; Thompson and Smith, 2001). This admission is a major strength of this paradigm and means that they are willing to engage with new ideas and borrow from other conceptual frameworks that can help to compliment their own analysis. Contrary to commentators believing LPA has been 'defeated' by recent innovations in management (Spencer, 2000) and that contemporary LPA accounts are 'confined to the rehearsal of a familiar labour process meta-narrative' (O'Doherty and Willmott, 2001, p. 469) there are recent insightful studies concerning subjectivity and the emotional labour process (Callaghan and Thompson, 2002; Ezzy, 1997; Sharma and Black, 2001; Sosteric, 1996) offering optimism for further research in this area.

Management prescription and the human resource

The late 1970s and early 1980s saw a growing disenchantment with the all-out 'macho' management approach, methods which were deemed to be no longer applicable to a world 'turned upside down' (Attwood *et al.*, 2003; Hirschborn and Gilmore, 1992; Peters, 1987, 1994, 2003). The classicist portrayal of the passionless bureaucracy where emotion is a by-product, an interference to be locked outside, rapidly altered. Where the orthodox view portrayed modern organisations as being rigid, functional, standardised and de-skilled, it is claimed we now have the postmodern organisation that reverses these trends (Clegg, 1990). Today's organisation operates through corporate culture and a committed workforce, rather than hierarchical bureaucratic control structures (Drucker, 1981; Handy, 1989; Kanter, 1990; Peters, 1987, 2003; Senge, 1999). Employees are now human resources and caring, sharing managers attempt to create an image of the company as an 'anti-authoritarian, no-boss set-up' (Thompson and McHugh, 1990, p. 34) where, in an atmosphere of 'love and empathy' (Albrow, 1992), everyone subscribes to corporate core values. Through involvement with the 'tripod of success' (flexibility, quality and teamwork) (Wickens, 1993) it is now said employees are empowered and, instead of direct control, the postmodern employee has gained responsible autonomy. Apparently, the corporation in the new millennium is intent on capturing the hearts of its employees and relies heavily upon an 'emotional' culture.

It is worth noting how obviously reminiscent the recent management guru literature is of the human relations school. For instance, Mayo's (1946) ideas concerning worker motivation following the Hawthorne experiments; Maslow's (1954) hierarchy of needs as an account of human motivation; McGregor's (1960) Theory X and Theory Y (with Theory Y recommending a 'softer' approach to management) and Hertzberg's (1966) 'hygiene' and moti-vation factors along with the concept of 'job-enrichment'. Much of the current prescriptive management literature appears to be merely 'repeating and embellishing prescriptions advocated by post-Taylorist management theory' (Willmott, 1993, p. 523). The 'new' human resource management writers advocate many of the same 'must-dos' as the human relations school (Cornelius, 2000; Dale *et al.*, 1997; Guest, 1987; Schuler and Jackson, 1999) and are open to the same criticisms.

Although contemporary prescriptive literature embraces emotion as a valuable resource, it still tends (as classic management writers have before them) to overestimate its abilities in harnessing workers' emotions in order to achieve a company's ends. It is notable how these writers assume that the organisation is able to easily achieve equilibrium through the patronising ministrations of management who 'know best'. For writers like Senge it is much more than simply restructuring the organisation. He describes leaders as 'social architects' and is clear in his view that a new 'moral order' can be achieved: 'the first task of organisation design concerns designing the governing ideas of purpose, vision, and core values by which people will live' (Senge, 1996, p. 293). Similarly, Kotter (1996) exhorts management to instil a sense of 'urgency' in his Herculean approach to major change, Pedlar *et al.* (1997) recommend methods to assess the 'energy flow' of an organisation and Peters offers a magic formula that will generate the 'wow' and 'x' factors reinvigorating demotivated employees (1987, 1995).

A relatively recent addition to management dream-making literature is the hugely popular concept of emotional intelligence (EI). Originally introduced by a group of academic psychologists, EI is defined as the ability to monitor and regulate one's own and other's feelings and to use feelings to guide thought and action (Mayer and Salovey, 1993). The concept has been quickly appropriated by the guru faction in management literature and exaggerated claims are made about the relationship between a person's emotional quotient (EQ) and organisational performance. Daniel Goleman (1998a) popularised EI as a managerial tool in his 1998 book *Working with Emotional Intelligence* which presents it as a relatively simple solution to age old management problems. Grand claims are made concerning various empirical studies, many subsequently revealed to be of doubtful pedigree (Fineman, 2000, 2003; Mayer, 1999), that show how EI is a 'must' for effective leadership, dealing with difficult co-workers, motivation and, perhaps most importantly, improving sales performance (Goleman, 1998a, 1998b). In what has been described as every 'spin doctor's dream' (Woodruffe, 2001), the good news, as Goleman tells it, is that 'emotional competencies' can be learned. EI's greatest appeal, however, lies in its package as a science. Relational qualities that are deemed to be valuable work based attributes, frequently referred to as 'people skills', have been given a scientific credibility with the claim that they can be reliably measured

(Caruso, 2001; Dulewicz and Higgs, 1999; Mayer, 1999). As a quantifiable competence, it strips the irrationality and unpredictability from emotion management and enables it to be contained and sold as a tangible fix for organisational problems. There are no shortage of advocates of this approach and a general consensus has emerged within the field of management prescription that 'well tapped, it will enable organizations to realize strategic stretch' (Huy, 1999).

Literature such as this continues the myth that all a worker has to do to achieve a happy and fulfilled existence is to follow the prescriptions of these newer versions of systems and human relations theory. As Senge states: 'Much of the leverage leaders can actually exert lies in helping people achieve more accurate, more insightful, and more empowering views of reality' (Senge, 1996, p. 295). This is achieved by offering a vision of the promised land and creating 'cult-like cultures' (Collins and Porras, 2002; Peters, 2003). Goleman (1998a) claims he can guarantee that management will be less of an art and more of a science and even the less embroidered claims concerning EI's beneficial qualities seriously propose that EI is a valid and accurate predictor of organisational success (Caruso, 2001; Dulewicz and Higgs, 1998, 1999). And what about obstacles that potentially upset the status-quo or those employees who don't achieve the required sense of reality and don't fit within the company's emotional competency framework? The simple answer is to 'get rid of structural, cultural and system obstacles' (Kotter, 1996, p. 111) and ensure that all barriers are 'ejected like a virus' (Collins and Porras, 2002). In turn, the science of EI will help support these exclusionary mechanisms via tests that confirm particular employees are emotionally unintelligent thus requiring extensive training in how to become emotionally competent according to the organisation's remit, or are beyond redemption and are labelled as having certain disorders and, therefore, of no use to the company.

Prescriptive management literature is often aptly referred to as 'pop management' due to the continuously changing, though persistently positive and buoyant, portrayal of organisational life (Thompson and O'Connell Davidson, 1996). In the interests of organisational efficiency the past is deracinated, realities re-shaped and the new model worker repeatedly reproduced. There is actually little of the 'human' in much of the recent human resource and associated management literature. Talk of the 'wow' and 'x' factors and desirable emotional competencies bears little resemblance to everyday organisational life. Emotion is talked of in very narrow managerially defined terms, what is or is not an emotional competence is identified by those who have the power to do so and a consideration of emotion is contained within the parameters of organisational performance. These approaches include emotion in their analysis but at the same time, in their arrogance, neatly exclude any notion of employees as skilled social actors who offer a wide variety of emotion management performances depending on context and motivation – and certainly not always according to management's desires. As a result, we are left with much the same portrait of an emotionally inadequate actor that the orthodox management literature presents. It becomes clear that this particular brand of management writing can serve little or no purpose when looking to develop a suitable theory of organisational emotionality other than to highlight the way that emotion has become top of the prescriptive management writer's agenda – but strictly on their terms.

The captured subjectivity in the velvet cage

Despite much of the recent management literature having the same flavour as that of the human relations school, there does appear to be a much more complicated agenda and management prescription today seems to have higher aspirations where the workforce is concerned. 'Soft' human resource management techniques are said to be aimed at winning the hearts and minds of the workforce although there is also the definite impression that it wishes to capture their very souls. In other words, management has been given the job of seducing employees into 'loving' the company, its product and its customers. In order to do this it is deemed necessary to reconstruct 'the conduct and self-image of employees' (du Gay, 1994, p. 136). There is an emphasis that 'control by the old standards is out of control by the new standards' (Peters, 1987, p. 395, 2003) and in the 'romantic' (Kanter, 1990, p. 281) entrepreneurial corporation the new psychological, emotionally charged contract ensures a more binding kind of control: 'self-control born of involvement' (Peters, 2003, p. 363). The implications of this are that post-bureaucratic organisations need to be managed through values rather than rules. It is believed control is brought about by managers being portrayed as spiritual leaders, creating a shared and inspiring vision in which an employee dedicates all their mental, physical and emotional energies to the company, resulting in salvation for all those concerned.

To many writers this attempted seduction of the employee's soul is equal to an involvement in an Orwellian nightmare of invasive management practices where employees have lost control of their own identities and have become 'manipulable bodies'. Views such as these clearly draw upon a Foucauldian philosophy concerning surveillance and power: 'the body is directly involved in a political field, power relations have an immediate hold upon it; they invest it, mark it, train it, torture it, force it to carry out tasks, to perform ceremonies to emit signs' (Foucault, 1991, p. 173).

Much like his own theory of power, Foucault appears to be a creeping, ever growing force within organisation studies. His views concerning discursively produced subjectivities appear now to be readily accepted as unarguable facts. We find writers increasingly relying upon a Foucauldian analysis to theorise the contemporary organisation. Burrell (1988, p. 232) states that as individuals we are 'incarcerated within an organizational world' and suggests there is 'no escape' from their discipline. Rose (1990, p. 1) writes it is quite clear that 'thoughts, feelings and actions ... are socially organized and managed in minute particulars'. In the same vein, Townley (1994) believes that human resource practice renders human 'subjects as objects' and the very soul becomes open to management interrogation. Grey (1994, p. 483) argues that the accounting labour process is better understood through Foucault's emphasis on the 'panoptic gaze' that produces 'self-disciplined forms of subjectivity'. Deetz (1998) believes that powerful management discourse is so successful in its constitution of our subjectivities that we actually 'strategise our own subordination'. Total Quality Management (TQM) is regarded as nothing less than 'Total Management Control' (Delbridge et al., 1992), where the worker's subjectivity is captured in the prison of quality discourse (Knights and McCabe, 1999). An additional array of writers (Delbridge et al., 1992; Fernie and Metcalfe, 1998; Willmott, 1993; Sewell and Wilkinson, 1992) give convincing accounts of various management regimes as an 'Orwellian nightmare', where 'Big Brother' watches our every move whilst the 'iron fist in the velvet glove' manipulates our very soul (Willmott, 1993). So convincing are these accounts of organisational life that there seems little room for further debate: 'a pattern has taken shape in whose web we all, modern men and women, have become entangled' (Rose 1990, p. 9). Furthermore, though resistance is recognised as central to a post-structuralist analysis of work, it seems there can be no escape from the network of power and, therefore, opposition is futile as it merely alerts management to weaknesses in their control regimes (Burrell, 1988; Deetz, 1998; Townley, 1994) or actually serves the interests of the organisation (Knights and McCabe, 1999). Foucault's (1991, p. 182) prediction that 'discipline produces subjected practised bodies, "docile bodies" ' has, according to much of current opinion, been realised.

Literature concerning the emotional organisation can be seen to be particularly prone to adopting a post-structuralist perspective when it is suggested that 'in the realm of feeling, Orwell's 1984 came in disguise several years ago, leaving behind a laugh and perhaps the idea of a private way out' (Hochschild, 1983, p. 23). Clearly it can be seen how Foucault's focus on a 'network of power', which is 'everywhere and nowhere' (Thompson, 1993, p. 199) working in invisible ways to render the 'soul as effect and instrument' (Foucault, 1991, p. 177), can be compared to Hochschild's (1983, p. 218) description concerning the 'transmutation' of private feelings. In effect, employees' feelings are used as a means of achieving corporate goals and, in order for this to be successful, the employees must subjugate their private selves to corporate wishes. Through what Hochschild describes as 'deep acting', it is shown how the employee comes to identify with corporate values often losing a sense of self in the process. In Thompson and Findlay's (1996) words, the 'subject has gone missing'.

Through the popular discourse of the 'excellence' pop-management literature and the acceptance of a Foucauldian view within organisation studies, we are presented with the picture of an 'emotional organisation' where the 'subjectification of work, involving the saturation of the working body with feelings, emotions and wishes' (Rose 1990, p. 244) has finally taken place. This portrayal of the organisation, however, does not claim it has been derationalised. It infers the iron cage is now made of velvet (du Gay and Salaman, 1992) indicating that the 'final frontier of control' has at last been crossed. From this picture it is easy to assume the contemporary organisation has gained the full co-operation of its employees; that they are prepared to 'give of themselves' for the sake of corporate goals. In effect, we are being told that corporate wishes and personal wishes have become one and the same thing through the 'transmutation' of feeling. This appears to amount to a blurring of the boundaries between the public and the private. What was once thought of as non-rational and belonging strictly in the private domain has now been welcomed into the public world of work. Not only has the irrational made itself available for open public viewing but is being used as a valuable management tool. Acts of private emotion management have fallen 'under the sway of large organizations, social engineering, and the profit motive' (Hochschild, 1983, p. 19).

Such a negative view is typical of the post-structuralist stance toward the individual who, despite claims that agency lies at the heart of their analysis, they only ever recognise in a limited way. Whilst many accounts of organisational life using this perspective give some valuable insights into emotion in organisations, this particular way of seeing reduces the wide diversity of human experience to the force of 'coercions' that shape the social actor (Foucault, 1991). Their view of the 'subject' restricts the possibility of individuals ever being active agents, who through negotiation are able to break the 'chain' of power and 'make their own histories' (Giddens, 1987, p. 97). Clearly, the neglect of the potential power of actors hinders any use this theory may have for the analysis of organisations. As Thompson (1993) states 'the flaws vastly outweigh any benefits', most especially in the investigation of a 'lived, interactional experience' (Denzin, 1984) such as emotion in the workplace.

Institutional structures and all that

The institutional perspective in organisational analysis comes in a variety of guises. As pointed out by instutionalists themselves 'there is little consensus on the definition of key concepts, ... and nor is it associated with a standard research methodology' (Tolbert and Zucker, 1996, p. 175). Hence, institutionalism has been defined in a wide variety of ways and has many 'faces'. As Scott (1987, p. 493) notes 'the beginning of wisdom in approaching institutional theory is to recognize at the outset that there is not one but several variants'.

A broad description of institutionalism would emphasise how such an approach recognises the value-laden nature of an organisation's environment. Traditionally, where open-systems theory recognises organisations as production systems affected by environmental conditions such as technology and markets, the institutional view directs attention to the symbolic aspects of organisations and their environments (Aldrich, 1992; Scott, 1987). As already mentioned, within this broad definition there are several variants. This is not surprising considering institutionalism's 50 year history, dating from Selznick's (1957) recognition of the 'natural' dimension of organisations, through to Meyer and Rowan's (1977) elaboration of 'formal structure as myth and ceremony'; DiMaggio and Powell's (1983) theory of 'isomorphism' and Tolbert and Zucker's (1996) work on the process of institutionalisation. Basically institutional theory can be understood as being an adaptive response in reaction to pressures from internal groups and clearly linked with the values of the external society:

> as an organization is 'institutionalized' it tends to take on a special character and to achieve a distinctive competence or, perhaps, a trained or built-in capacity . . . institutional theory traces the emergence of distinctive forms, processes, strategies, outlooks, and competences as they emerge from patterns of organizational interaction and adaption. (Selznick, 1996, p. 271)

It is interesting to note how the 'new' institutionalists (Selznick, 1996) have claimed Berger and Luckman (1966) as their own in their attempts to move toward a more phenomenological approach to organisational analysis (Tolbert and Zucker, 1996). To the 'new' institutionalist (Di Maggio and Powell, 1983; Tolbert and Zucker, 1996), institutionalisation is achieved when actions become so familiar that they become habitual. It takes little effort or thought on behalf of the actor involved to invoke the required action. Therefore institutionalisation can be seen as a process of creating 'reality' (Aldrich, 1992) and writers such as DiMaggio and Powell (1983) suggest that, as a consequence, individuals fail to reflect on the meaning of situations as they accept the taken-for-granted, shared (institutionalised) meaning as their own view of the world.

Many third parties label the defining characteristics of institutional theory as falling firmly within the structuralist functionalist mode (Burrell and Morgan, 1979; Mouzelis, 1975). Admittedly, these writers refer to the early work of Selznick (1957) and his prescriptive writing on how to retain equilibrium through the instilling of company values. Although the 'new institutionalists' attempt to distance themselves from the 'old institutionalism' (Scott, 1987; DiMaggio and Powell, 1983; Selznick, 1996), with some going so far as to label themselves as phenomenologists (Tolbert and Zucker, 1996), there is a basic commonality in all of their writings. They pursue different avenues of enquiry but their analyses rest upon the same assumptions: organisations are open-systems, the system must achieve equilibrium with both internal and external environments if it is to survive, management have the ability to design formal structure and, according to Meyer and Rowan (1977), manipulate informal aspects of the organisation to meet the system's needs and, finally, organisational actors are always assumed to be at the top of the hierarchy. When institutionalists speak of organisational values, what they mean is the values of those at the top that are imposed upon those at the bottom of the organisation's hierarchy. These commonalities can only lead to the conclusion that institutional theory is explicitly related to the family of system theory.

Despite their claims to the contrary, the institutional theorists present us with a picture of 'oversocialised' individuals who unquestioningly follow social norms and are only capable of routinised, hence institutionalised, action. Apart, that is, from those decision-makers who make a conscious decision to change the organisation structure (Tolbert and Zucker, 1996; DiMaggio and Powell, 1983; Selznick, 1996; Scott, 1987). Many criticisms of institutional theory can be traced to its relationship with systems theory and the belief that institutionalised structures are symbolic universes which have their own empirical reality. It can, therefore, be concluded that such a limited theory, which clearly chooses to ignore the influence of organisational actors upon the organisation and its environment, can make no contribution to an understanding of the complex role emotion management plays in organisational life.

Conclusion and implications for an understanding of emotion in organisations

The previous review of various perspectives on organisations emphasises how there are indeed different ways of 'seeing'. Depending on which stance is taken a completely different picture of organisational life may emerge. This is particularly true of portrayals of organisation men and women over the years. For classicists such as Fayol (1949) and Barnard (1938) emotion is something to be excluded from organisations; Taylor does not even recognise the 'human' side of work and the Mayoites, whilst recognising the 'informal', see any expression of feeling as a pathological hiccough to be smoothed over. In more recent accounts, emotion, as a vital contribution to all aspects of organisational life, has clearly been recognised but in vastly differing ways. Contemporary behavioural approaches, firmly rooted in human relations and systems theory, either seek to capture and control the emotional energies of employees, or offer well-intentioned prescriptions to help individuals cope with their inability to manage emotion on the job. If a post-structuralist view were to be taken this would suggest that the corporation has captured the employees' hearts and minds and that there is no room in the organisation for the 'private' self to operate. In these accounts, all emotional activity is controlled and directed by management as a means to achieving an organisation's aims. On the other hand, the interactionists portray organisational actors as recreating the meaning of formal 'rules' through the power of human interaction. Actors operate in very limited frameworks with no acknowledgement of any 'outside' forces that may impinge upon their negotiated order. In contrast, attempts at controlling emotion as a vital part of the capitalist labour process are recognised in labour process accounts. However, many of these management attempts at control are seen as precursors to new forms of employee resistance and 'misbehaviour' and the actor comes to life in only a very limited way. All of these perspectives portray completely different versions of the organisational actor as a skilled emotion worker, that is when such an actor is acknowledged at all.

Whichever of the more recent perspectives on organisations is taken, it becomes clear that the contemporary organisation has recognised the value of 'emotion work'. The 'iron cage' is clearly still very much in existence; only it has now unlocked its doors and invited emotion in. Therefore, in so far as it is accepted that the public world of work encroaches more and more into the private realm of emotion management, the reasons for the blurring of these boundaries should be questioned. It surely cannot be claimed that the rhetoric of the 'velvet cage' is created by corporations simply as a powerful means of capturing the worker's subjectivity. The question must remain how it serves a corporation to engage in the seemingly sinister game of creating an Orwellian nightmare of insidious control mechanisms. There is little doubt that changes have taken place but, if the cause is to be laid at management's door, it should be asked why they would want to go to such incredible lengths in order to capture the hearts and souls of their employees.

If questions such as these are to be answered, an adequate conceptual framework needs to be found which acknowledges the power of human interaction as well as being able to appreciate that actors have often to contend with forces much more powerful than themselves. Already, from the review in this chapter, the multifaceted nature of organisational life begins to be revealed. The next chapter will examine recent accounts that engage with the concept of 'emotional labour' as one particular way of 'seeing' emotion in organisations. Together this and the next chapter help to highlight the inadequacy of existing approaches, their assumptions concerning the emotive subject and the terms they use to describe organisational emotionality, emphasising the need for a new method of conceptualising the complex nature of emotion management in organisations.

Notes

1. Organisation 'woman' is notably absent in early accounts of organisational life.
2. An exception being Ackroyd and Thompson (1999) who include more individualised forms of recalcitrance and resistance in their account of organisational 'misbehaviour'.

3

The (over) managed heart

Organisations do have feelings

Recently the subjects of love, intimacy and emotion have entered centre stage of general sociological debate. Research concerning the ideologies of 'love and intimacy' (Duncombe and Marsden, 1993), attempts to theorise being 'in love' (Jackson, 1993), and a feminist analysis of gender and the social meaning of emotion (Crawford *et al.*, 1992; Shields, 2002) have all helped to fill a gap left by British sociology's previous neglect of the issue of emotion. Declarations that 'even sociologists fall in love' (Jackson, 1993) cannot fail to capture attention. Furthermore, the continuing lively debate concerning an adequate theoretical background for the sociological study of emotion guarantees that the 'sociology of emotions' remains an engaging subject.

As the last chapter shows, the writing in of emotion has been a welcome development in organisational analysis, leading to the publication of a wide range of literature on the subject. It is due to the recognition, for example, of the importance of research concerning 'emotional labour' (Hochschild, 1983), organisation sexuality (Hearn and Parkin, 1987, 2001), 'the social regulation of feelings' (Fineman, 1993, 2000; James, 1989); 'sexuality and the labour market' (Adkins, 1995) and 'emotion and power at work' (Newton *et al.*, 1995) that it has become accepted that human emotions are an important factor within organisations. Studies such as these acknowledge that organisations recognise the potential power of emotion and attempt to suppress, hide or manage feelings. This is never more apparent than in the array of management 'guru' literature continually reproduced which encourages managers to use 'instinct' and generate the mysterious 'X-factor' throughout the organisation or various 'how to' texts extolling employees to 'become emotionally intelligent'. All of which are quick fix solutions to complex problems that are intuitively attractive to desperate managers. Best selling titles such as: 'Working with Emotional

Intelligence' (Goleman, 1998a); 'The Emotional Energy Factor' (Kirshenbaum, 2003); 'The Pursuit of Wow' (Peters, 1995, 2003); 'A Passion for Excellence' (Peters and Austin, 1985); 'The Heart of Change' (Kotter and Cohen, 2002) and 'Gung Ho: turn on the people in any organisation' (Blanchard and Bowles, 1998) highlight how feelings are no longer excluded from prescriptive management literature, but are increasingly recognised, if not accepted as an established management 'truth', as a valuable management tool. There is little doubt that the study of emotion adds a new dimension to how organisations are understood. Ideas that organisations are constructed by the ebb and flow of feelings and that emotion management adds a valuable commercial element to the labour process have enabled doors to be opened and feelings are being allowed to enter the study of organisations.

This chapter will focus on contemporary literature concerning the emotional aspects of organisational life, most especially the use of the term 'emotional labour', including that which is relevant to a study of emotion management in the public services. This, of course, in no way covers all of the literature that could come under the 'emotion in organisation' umbrella. For instance, it does not give more than a second glance to management 'guru' material which calls on companies to create a culture which acts as the 'glue' of an organisation and encourages managers to foster the feelings of employees (Peters, 1987, 1995, 2003). The continued popularity of behavioural approaches to emotion management receives but a cursory summary, including that of the topic of emotional intelligence. Neither does it dwell on the critical management literature which recognises and examines how various corporate culture programmes aim to control employees' identities (Casey, 1995; Deetz, 1998; Delbridge *et al.*, 1992; du Gay, 1996; Grey, 1994; Willmott, 1993). All of these are covered in more depth in the review in the second chapter 'Bringing Emotion on to the Organisational Agenda.'

The focus of this chapter will be on selected contributions to the debate concerning the conceptualisation and control of emotion management in organisations, highlighting the ways in which organisational emotionality is portrayed by various writers. For example, emotion in organisations has been explored in its many forms. Investigations reveal what emotion 'does' to an organisation and, conversely, what an organisation 'does' to emotion. Descriptive terms such as 'emotion work', 'sentimental work', 'bounded rationality' and, most commonly, 'emotional labour' are used to define the type of emotion being discussed. An in depth review of much of the existing literature reveals that the term 'emotional labour' is now common parlance. This is particularly unfortunate in some cases as the phrase carries with it many connotations, as will be shown by the review of Hochschild's (1979, 1983) major works on the subject where the term originates. These connotations become significant when continual use of 'emotional labour' to describe so many different forms of emotionality (not always in the workplace) results in the presentation of a confusing picture of organisational life. This analysis will review a variety of existing literature concerning emotion in organisations but in particular it will question the frequent use of the phrase 'emotional labour' in a variety of settings, and will attempt to define whether or not it serves as an adequate descriptive device and gives enough conceptual clarity in certain situations.

Working on emotion in the contemporary organisation

Emotion has long been recognised as making important contributions to organisational life. For example, the enactment of 'display rules' in service industries has never ceased to be a popular subject (Fine, 1988; Goffman, 1967; Parkinson, 1991; Rafaeli and Sutton, 1990; Sutton, 1991; Whyte, 1948) and methods for managing the social side of organisational life (Hertzberg, 1966; Maslow, 1954; Mayo, 1946; McGregor, 1960) continue to reappear in a variety of guises within a broad spectrum of management literature (Ashforth and Humphry, 1995; Drucker, 1981; Morris and Feldman, 1996, 1997; Peters, 1987, 1995, 2003; Van de Vliet, 1994).

However, recent accounts attest to qualitative changes in the type of emotion management performances demanded of employees. These demands 'represent a significant scaling-up of institutional and executive privilege over the ownership of emotion' (Fineman and Sturdy, 1997, p. 2) and indicate that emotion is no longer seen as something to be managed 'out' but as a resource to be harnessed as a means of achieving an organisation's ends. This development is said to be due to the movement toward a post-industrial era where global markets have become volatile and organisations must be able to adapt through the deployment of a more flexible workforce. Companies are supposedly post-bureaucratic and are bound, not by rules and structure, but by the bond of a strong corporate culture where employees love the company, the product and the customer. Employers are now engaging with hearts and minds and, some would say, souls as a means of harnessing employee commitment and gaining competitive advantage.

Though many sectors of British industry are reportedly experimenting with a variety of 'soft' human resource management techniques, encouraging employee involvement and autonomy through quality initiatives and team work, the rising service sector is particularly reliant on its employees' ability to display the correct demeanour. For example, workers in the entertainment industry must produce 'laughter and well-being', in other service industries the sale of a product depends upon employees' interaction with potential customers and the survival of a company in a competitive market relies on employees' ability to deliver quality service to customers. Whereas examples such as Walt Disney were once seen as the extreme, they have now become the normative model which service sector organisations wish to achieve. The 'smile factories' (Van Maanen, 1991) have their rules and employees often have to work hard on their emotions in order to abide by the company's feeling rules and present the 'correct' face.

Amongst contemporary literature perhaps the greatest contribution to advance an understanding of emotion in organisations is Hochschild's (1983) work concerning the 'Managed Heart'. Her empirical study of air-stewardesses highlights how actors' emotion management skills have become a saleable commodity commonly referred to as 'emotional labour' (Hochschild, 1983). Hochschild successfully links the ideas of work and emotion, thereby recognising that social actors are able to carry out emotion work which can be used as a vital part of the capitalist labour process (Hochschild, 1979, 1983). Hochschild's work has proved to be enduringly popular and there is little that has been written concerning the subject of emotions and organisations in the last 20 years that does not refer to the 'Managed Heart'. Many recent accounts use the term 'emotional labour' to highlight emotion as a new area of study in organizations and to emphasise how organisations seek to regulate an employee's emotion management as part of the labour process. However, the term is not benign and the implications of its continued use for the study of organisational emotionality are immense. This cautious approach to the use of the term 'emotional labour' is mainly due to Hochschild's overemphasis on the divide between the public and private performances of emotion management and the way she tends to use the terms 'public' and 'commercial' interchangeably. In Hochschild's account of organisational life there is little room for emotion management performances within the organisation which are not appropriated for commercial use; when an employee may offer their emotion management as a 'gift' to a colleague or client for instance. Hochschild's concern with management attempts to seduce employees into 'loving' the company, its product and its customers, creates an illustration of emotionally crippled actors. Despite her recognition of both 'surface' and 'deep' acting, her concept of emotional labour is ultimately 'absolutist' in its implementation and consequences (Korczynski, 2002; Tolich, 1993; Wouters, 1989a and b). For Hochschild, offering cynical performances in the form of 'surface acting' results in ultimate alienation from one's 'true self' and deep acting, that is efforts to conjure up sincere performances, results in 'altering' one's self (Hochschild, 1983, pp. 186–8). Either way, feelings become 'transmutated' by the organisation and the 'smile', 'mood', 'feeling', or 'relationship', 'comes to belong more to the organization and less to the self' (Hochschild, 1983, p. 198). The prominence given to captured feelings in Hochschild's account of organisational emotionality arguably disqualifies the possibility that employees may exert an 'active and controlling force' in relationships with both management and customers (Callaghan and Thompson, 2002; Paules, 1996, p. 265).

In addition, Hochschild openly admits that the concept of emotional labour is little suited to the study of workers outside of the commercial service sector. However, she stresses that this is due to the autonomy held by public sector professional groups over how, when, and for whom they perform emotion work. She neglects to note how much more emotionally complex the work of, say, a caring professional in the state welfare sector is compared to that of a commercial service worker such as an air-stewardess. For these reasons, Hochschild's 'emotional labour' would appear conceptually inadequate for the understanding of work in the public sector services. Nevertheless, this has not prevented the term being used widely in this context.

Nonetheless, despite these apparent weaknesses in Hochschild's conceptualisation of emotion work in organisations, as already indicated, the value of much of the recent contribution to the debate concerning emotion in organisations rests upon Hochschild's (1979, 1983) pioneering work in identifying social actors' skilled emotion management performances and their potential value to the capitalist labour process. Her observations concerning the 'public' face of emotion management, and the possible consequences of its commercialisation, has been described as the 'watershed' in the sociology of emotions (Kemper, 1990). Due to Hochschild's important place in the literature, the concept of emotion as productive labour will be further explored with a consideration of her views on the subject.

Hochschild's 'Managed Heart'

Hochschild (1979, 1983) gives deep insight into the social actor's ability to work on emotion in order to present a socially desirable performance and capitalism's appropriation of that skill. The greatest contribution is her emphasis on how the management of emotion can entail hard work and that, in the same way as workers becomes alienated from their physical labour, they can also become alienated from their 'emotional labour'.

When looking for a clearer understanding of two of the most popular terms used to describe emotion in organisations: 'emotion work' and 'emotional labour', there is little doubt that Hochschild is the place to begin. In her earlier work, Hochschild attempts to put the subject of emotions firmly on to the sociological map by linking 'emotion work, feeling rules and social structure' (1979, p. 276). Her concern to show that emotion is not 'a periodic abdication to biology' (1983, p. 27), but something which is subject to acts of personal management, according to implicit 'feeling rules', has allowed Hochschild to wrest the study of emotion away from 'its traditional guardians', the psychologists (Fineman, 1993).

To carry out emotion work is the act of attempting to change an emotion or feeling so that it is appropriate for any given situation. In order to be able to asses the situation correctly, and produce the expected feeling, social guidelines are used: 'a set of shared, albeit often latent, rules' (Hochschild, 1983, p. 268) which help fit together the emotion and the situation, for instance feeling sad at funerals but happy at weddings. The use of the word 'work' to describe the management of emotion stresses that it is something which is actively done to feelings. It is an effort directed toward the production of 'suitable' emotions: 'I tried not to laugh', 'I forced myself not to cry', 'I was determined not to show my anger'. As Hochschild points out, 'work' differs from the usual concept of controlling or suppressing emotion: "Emotion work" refers more broadly to the act of evoking or shaping, as well as suppressing, feeling in oneself' (1979, p. 266).

The ability to manage emotion according to the 'rules' of the situation emphasises the need to acknowledge the power of the 'social': as socialised beings actors 'try to pay tribute to official definitions of situations, with no less than (their) feelings' (Hochschild, 1979, p. 257). Emotion work is a gesture in everyday social exchange; the 'rules' exist to ensure social stability and the well being of those involved. Nevertheless, the giving and receiving of emotion work is not always a smooth transaction. The gesture may be carried out half-heartedly, it may not be carried out at all; either in ignorance, dislike or complete disregard for the 'rules' of the situation. On the other hand, a person may 'work' harder at emotion management than would normally be expected: if they care for the people involved or feel the situation is special then a generous 'tribute' is offered. As Hochschild suggests, depending on actors' perspectives of the situation (their reading of the rules), some expression of emotion work may seem more generous than others:

> Any gesture – a cool greeting, an appreciative laugh, the apology for an outburst –
> is measured against a prior sense of what is reasonably owed another, given the sort

of bond involved. Against this background measure, some gestures will seem more than ample, others less. (Hochschild, 1979, p. 273)

The acceptance of the view that, within the social framework, actors can 'do' varying degrees of emotion work, that there is choice in what, when, how much and to whom they give, allows the introduction of the concept of the 'gift exchange' (Hochschild, 1983, p. 76). As social beings, emotion management is a way of 'paying respect with feeling'; it is a personal gift given freely, sometimes unconsciously, without the counting of costs:

> We put emotion to private use. Through deep acting we share it and offer it in exchange. … Rules as to the type, intensity, timing, and placing of feelings are society's guidelines, the promptings of an unseen director. The stage, the props, and the fellow members of the cast help us internally assemble the gifts that we freely exchange. (Hochschild, 1983, p. 85)

With the idea of personal management of emotion as a 'gift', Hochschild questions what happens 'when deep gestures of exchange enter the market sector' (Hochschild, 1983, p. 86). When people are no longer free to negotiate their own rate of 'exchange', when emotion management becomes another aspect of saleable labour power, then feelings become 'commoditized': 'Just as gestures of emotion work can be exchanged in private, so they can be exchanged in the marketplace' (Hochschild, 1979, p. 277). In the 'Managed Heart' Hochschild introduces the term 'emotional labour' to describe emotion management with a 'profit motive slipped under it' (Hochschild, 1983, p. 119). Her study of air-stewardesses highlights how emotion management is being increasingly appropriated by organisations in a 'service-producing society': 'commercial love' is now becoming an essential part of much routine face-to-face service jobs (Hochschild, 1983, p. 10).

Hochschild states quite clearly that jobs that require emotional labour have three distinct characteristics in common:

> First, they require face-to-face or voice-to-voice contact with the public. Second, they require the worker to produce an emotional state in another person – gratitude or fear for example. Third, they allow the employer, through training and supervision, to exercise a degree of control over the emotional activities of employees. (Hochschild, 1983, p. 147)

Moreover, in the case of Hochschild's airline stewardesses and debt collectors ('The toe and heel' (1983) of emotional labour), there is a fourth criterion which needs to be fulfilled before the term emotional labour can be applied: the creation of a profitable product with the use of emotional labour as a major factor in its production. Using the stewardess as an example we see how they induce or suppress feelings so that they match the airline's advertised image, thus giving the company a competitive edge and selling to customers on the strength of the quality of service delivered by the stewardess. It could be said that the profitable product manufactured by the airline stewardess is 'passenger contentment'. Hochschild neatly summarises this in her description of the 'emotional labour' airline stewardesses are expected to perform:

> The company lays claim not simply to her physical motions – how she handles food trays – but to her emotional actions and the way they show in the ease of a smile. ... For the flight attendant, the smiles are a part of her work, a part that requires her to co-ordinate self and feeling so that work seems to be effortless. To show that enjoyment takes effort is to do the job poorly. Similarly, part of the job is to disguise fatigue and irritation, for otherwise the labor would show in an unseemly way, and the product – passenger contentment – would be damaged. (Hochschild, 1983, p. 7/8)

Whilst Hochschild does not speak of the creation of surplus value as being one of the essential characteristics of jobs calling for emotional labour, her emphasis throughout the 'Managed Heart' is on the important contribution it makes to a 'profitable product'. Even without this distinguishing feature, Hochschild does warn that many jobs that appear to employ emotional labour do, in fact, not demonstrate all of the defining characteristics. The feature most frequently missing is the third: 'the employer, ... exercise(s) a degree of control over the emotional activities of employees' (Hochschild, 1983, p. 147). There are several professions, many of them belonging to the public sector 'caring' services, doctors, nurses, social workers, that require skilled emotion management as an essential 'tool of their trade'. The need to manage potentially difficult situations by working on their own and clients' feelings has long been recognised by the caring professions. However, they are basically different to the majority of workers who produce a service in that they are not closely supervised in their 'emotion work'; their skilled status allows them to retain autonomy, within the confines of professional norms and client expectations, over how they carry out the emotional part of their job (Hochschild, 1983). And, of course, until recently they have not been involved in the direct production of a profitable product, such as 'customer contentment'.

The originality of Hochschild's work has meant that 'The Managed Heart' is continually used as a reference point and has taken centre stage in the debate concerning emotion in organisations. From the above discussion, it can be seen why the use of the terms 'emotional labour' and 'emotion work' have become so popular; such simple descriptive phrases to describe such a complicated phenomena as organisational emotionality prove to be irresistible.

The emotional labour bandwagon

Such is the popularity of the term 'emotional labour' it could be said that research following Hochschild's pioneering study formed something of a 'Bandwagon', with the term being used in a myriad of ways. Not unexpectedly, this has involved a move away from Hochschild's original definition. For example, its application to the professions[1] who Hochschild believes perform a particular form of emotion work that does not correspond to the emotional labour performed in front-line service work, or applying the term to the interaction between colleagues within an organisation, rather than remaining with Hochschild's focus on customer interaction On the other hand, many accounts build on Hochschild's valuable work concerning the gendered nature of emotional labour (Sharma and Black, 2001; Tyler and Taylor, 1998, 2001; Wellington and Bryson, 2001) broaden its empirical focus and highlight its exploitative potential (Taylor, 1998) and there are also those who repeat and embellish her divide of the public and private faces of emotion work (Harriss, 2002).

Some of the earliest contributions to research concerning emotional labour originates in the North American management literature. Frequently, attention is directed to an employee's inability to match feeling with face and the resultant emotional burn-out, dissonance and low job satisfaction (Morris and Feldman, 1996; Rafaeli and Sutton, 1990). The origins of this are attributed to a variety of destructive factors: role ambiguity, role conflict, poorly defined control systems, constraining work arrangement and, most importantly, poor employee-job fit (Ashforth and Humphrey, 1993, 1995; Mann, 1999; Morris and Feldman, 1996, 1997; Pitt *et al.*, 1995; Rafaeli and Sutton, 1987; Weatherley and Tansik, 1992). Whilst many of these elucidations are rooted in a general dissatisfaction with the limitations of the term 'emotional labour', and its conceptual inadequacies in the understanding of the complexities of emotion in organisations (Ashforth and Humphrey, 1993, 1995; Morris and Feldman, 1996), they all, with few exceptions (Ashforth and Humphrey, 1995; Fine, 1988), share Hochschild's pessimistic concerns about the negative consequences of organisations' attempts to shape and control employees' feelings. In effect, something of a one-dimensional portrayal of organisational life is presented with frustrated managers, emotionally exhausted workers and dissatisfied customers becoming the central focus of analysis.

In Britain and Europe the scope, popularity and accessibility of research concerning emotion in organisation has been considerably broadened by Fineman's (1993) edited collection of papers titled 'Emotion in Organizations'. Fineman explicitly states that by offering an 'unfolding picture of some of the passions and perturbations of men and women at work' it can be shown how 'organizations are emotional arenas' where 'emotions form, de-form and direct organizational processes', whilst a largely invisible world of 'anxieties, fears and yearnings' contribute toward the daily routine of work organisations (Fineman, 1993, pp. 8, 31, 2, 3). When revealing an organisation's emotional 'underlife' many other issues come to the fore and several accounts concerning organisational emotionality can be found in Fineman's collection that investigate the public/ private divide, the 'myth' of rationality, the undervaluation of what is often seen as 'women's work' and the division of emotional labour (James, 1993; Parkin, 1993; Putman and Mumby, 1993) and adding another dimension to the study of organisations as emotional arenas, Hearn (1993) interestingly re-constructs organisation man as an 'emotive subject'.

Nonetheless, despite Fineman's (1993) emphasis on an organisation's different 'emotional zones', there is little evidence of any conceptual clarity with terms such as 'emotional labour' being used to describe any event 'when an employee is in effect paid to smile, laugh, be polite, or "be caring" ' (Fineman, 1993, p. 3). This neglect of occupational complexity in the use of emotion is repeated in later works (Fineman, 2000, 2003; Harriss, 2002) and the policeman, teacher, social worker and nurse are treated no differently than the flight attendant in that they all perform emotional labour, albeit in various settings, with the aim of achieving different goals. The term is used by different writers in different ways: to 'typify the way roles and tasks exert overt and covert control over emotional displays' (Putman and Mumby, 1993, p. 37) and to 'highlight similarities and differences between emotional and physical labour' (James, 1993, p. 95). With Hearn apparently going further than this when he sentences us all to a life of hard emotional labour by using the term as a catchall phrase to describe any and every type of emotion in organisations: 'In one sense all organizational work, membership and presence is emotion labour. ... Indeed the quality of being in an organization – organization-ness – is itself a form of emotion and emotion labour' (Hearn, 1993, p. 161). Indeed, within Fineman's (1993) volume of works, 'emotional labour' is found in a wide variety of possible forms, in many cases moving well away from Hochschild's (1983) original emphasis on the 'commercialisation of feeling'. This is in contrast to Fineman's later work where, though he originally declares that rationality has been 'stripped' away from organisations revealing a 'veritable explosion of emotional tones' (Fineman, 1993, p. 1), he goes on to focus on the 'emotions of control' and gives insightful analyses of the dynamics of control of emotion in organisations (Fineman and Sturdy, 1999; Sturdy and Fineman, 2001).

A recent influential empirical study by Taylor (1996, 1998) builds upon Hochschild's work and highlights emotion management as a highly regulated element of the labour process. His vivid portrayal of the work entailed in being a successful tele-sales agent (TSA) for an airline company known as 'Flightpath' concentrates on the interaction between customers and TSAs. In this way it is shown how management believe the agents sell airline tickets to the customers on the strength of their telephone manner. As the head of the telephone sales states: 'the smile that you send down the phone can be vital' and management's aim is to create an atmosphere of 'customer intimacy' with potential Flightpath clientele (Taylor, 1996, p. 13). In the case of Taylor's (1998) TSAs, their interaction with the external customer shows an explicit example of the performance of emotional labour for direct commercial purposes.

Nevertheless, not all occupations or situations within an organisation can be so easily categorised. Taylor tends to use the term emotional labour to describe a variety of emotion management performances within the organisation, even those enacted between team members themselves. The introduction of TQM, as Taylor states, 'clearly has implications for the emotional labour demanded of the workers concerned' (Taylor, 1996, p. 8). However, if all facets of the working lives of the telephone sales agents are to be understood under the TQM regime, then the different skills required to deal with 'external' and 'internal' customers need to be recognised. As Fineman (1993) mentions, within an organisation there are many different 'emotional zones' where a wide variety of activities take place. Not all of this emotional activity is secured for the company or its customers' benefit. In fact, Taylor himself confirms this by giving explicit examples where TSAs do not always conform to the company's 'feeling rules' and offer tokens of resistance (when they feel they are not being 'watched'). He notes that 'managerial attempts to control such a private, personal realm – while claiming that they wish to "unleash it" – appear to provoke strong resistance from employees' (Taylor, 1998, p. 99). Examples of employees' attempts to resist demands for the performance of emotional labour show that they have not internalised the feeling rules of the organisation, therefore ensuring that management's control of their emotional labour remains incomplete (Taylor, 1998; Tyler and Taylor, 1997).

What the above brief reviews of some of the most noteworthy contributions to the emotional labour debate show is how the term is used (and equally often misused) in a myriad of ways. This is never more apparent than in the way it has been applied to the work of caring professionals, most especially nursing work, with its volume and variety accounting for a significant part of that which may be included in the emotional labour bandwagon.

Introducing complexity: emotion management in the medical setting

Some organisations, such as medical establishments, have long been recognised as 'emotional zones' and Strauss *et al.* (1982, p. 254) were one of the first to coin a phrase ('sentimental work') as recognition that 'there was more to medical nursing work than its physiological core'. Interestingly, they point out that there is nothing particularly new about the idea of 'sentimental work', giving the example of 'tender loving care' in recognition of this. However it is stressed that 'sentimental work' is not only carried out because of humanistic considerations, but as a means of getting the 'work done effectively'. The combination of both subjective and objective considerations in the performance of 'sentimental work' means that it can be equated with both emotion work and emotion *in* labour.[2] In some situations emotion management may be performed out of 'humanistic' considerations; a 'gift' to the patient as a person in a potentially awkward social situation. Whilst in another setting emotion management according to professional rules (emotion *in* labour) may be performed in order to 'get the job done'.

'Sentimental work' is an ideal term to describe the emotion management performed by nurses, it takes into account their subjective experience of dealing with patients as people whilst also recognising the need to complete tasks according to objective criteria laid down by the organisation. Despite this, it is not a term that has caught on and in no way matches Hochschild's 'emotional labour' in popularity. Dent *et al.* (1991) attribute this lack of popularity to its interactionist origins and state that 'emotional labour' 'draws attention, in the way the interactionists are unable, to the labour process implications of the managing of emotions and feelings' (Dent *et al.*, 1991, p. 2). It certainly seems the case that 'sentimental work' gives no weight to the part managed emotion plays in the labour process. Nonetheless 'emotional labour', with its emphasis on the organisation and the commercial, often goes too far in the exclusion of the social self.

Given the nature of nursing work it is not surprising that many writers borrow the term 'emotional labour' in order to stress the important, though undervalued, aspects of a nurse's 'caring' role. Smith (1992) describes the caring aspects of a nurse's work as 'emotional labour' and uses data collected from student nurses in order to stress that it 'does make a difference'. She notes that though it is a vital part of the nursing labour process it tends to be marginalised as a skill female recruits 'naturally' possess and they are therefore offered neither training nor support. In a similar vein, commentators on 'new nursing' and the 'nursing process' note that nursing practice now emphasises a 'close, holistic relationship between nurse and patient' (Aldridge, 1994, p. 722) and 'raises the profile of emotional care' (Smith, 1991, p. 74). However, the difficulty in placing an accepted value on the caring aspects of a professional–patient relationship is not acknowledged, thus leaving the emotion management skills necessary to fulfil the carer's role unrecognised. Commentators such as Smith (1988, 1992) use Hochschild's term in an inexact way and tend to confuse the caring element of the nursing labour process with the 'emotional labour' which Hochschild (1983) describes as a growing part of the capitalist labour process. Even where a 'business model' of health care is recognised (Staden, 1998), and emotional labour's use as a resource to manipulate the image of health care and achieve 'socio-cultural and wider political ends' is acknowledged (O'Brien, 1994, p. 393), care as a 'commodity' in the commercial service sector is never differentiated from care as a 'gift'.

Perhaps one of the most frequently cited examples of 'emotional labour' in nursing is James' (1989, 1992, 1993) work on nursing the terminally ill. Borrowing from Hochschild (1983), she uses the term 'emotional labour' to stress the relationship between emotional and physical labour, 'with both being hard, skilled work requiring experience, affected by immediate conditions, external controls and subject to divisions of labour' (1993, p. 95). The formula produced by James (1992): 'Care = organisation + physical labour + emotional labour' summarises what she sees as the essential components of 'carework'. Organisation meaning both the organisational setting and the management of the provision of 'care'; physical labour focuses on tasks which satisfy daily lived requirements for food, hygiene and medical treatments and emotional labour is said to be 'about action and reaction ... The labourer is expected to respond to another person in a way which is both personal to both of them, but like other aspects of care it develops from the social relations of carer and cared-for and is shaped by the labour process' (James, 1992, p. 500). From her studies of caring for the dying, James concludes that 'emotional labour' can be described as 'productive work', 'hard work', 'difficult' and even 'sorrowful', but that this vital part of the nurse's work remains 'undefined, unexplained and usually unrecorded' due to its link with women's domestic caring role (James, 1989, p. 16/20). She defines 'emotional labour' as the 'labour involved in dealing with other people's feelings, a core component of which is the regulation of emotions' (James, 1989, p. 15). Emphasising the gender division of emotional labour, James applies the term equally to public service care workers, such as nurses, and unpaid female domestic workers, such as 'housewives'. In doing this, James claims that she is 'using the concept in a broader sense than Russell Hochschild' (James, 1989, p. 30) and appears to be trying to blur the boundaries between the public and private, showing how emotion management skills are carried from the private domestic sphere into the public world of work.

It is highlighted by James, when describing the caring relationship between patient and nurse, that 'the expression of emotions is a negotiated process involving a mutual sounding out of what is acceptable' (James, 1989, p. 21). This surely equates with the idea of 'equal emotional exchange' and allows for emotion management to be performed according to social 'rules' rather than organisational prescription. Nevertheless, there will be instances when nurses are not free to negotiate their own rate of 'exchange'. Their position in the hierarchy of the division of emotional labour dictates how nurses perform emotion management (James, 1993) or schedules may be set allowing no time for the negotiation of the caring relationship (James, 1992). At these times emotion management stops being a 'gift' and becomes part of the process of work; that is emotion management carried out according to organisational and professional 'rules'. Despite there being little doubt that the emotion 'work' carried out by nurses who care for the terminally ill is 'demanding and exhausting, and subject to different forms of organisation' (James, 1989, p. 20), it is giving little credit to nurses who, through their skilled performance of emotion management, obviously derive satisfaction from their ability to make a difference to patients' well-being. Clearly the nurses in the study retain a certain amount of autonomy in the delivery of patient care and personal discretion in their negotiation of the 'gift exchange': 'even within this dominant hospital-type system, the nurses had some power in organising details of patient care' (James, 1992, p. 495).

It is difficult to see where the nurses who care for the dying in the hospice perform 'emotional labour' according to Hochschild's (1983) definition. James gives no suggestion that caring for the dying has come to have any commercial value and gives every indication that her nurses retain a great deal of autonomy in their emotion work (James, 1992; Smith, 1988). Smith (1988) states that direct control over nurses' emotion management 'is difficult to apply to British nursing'. Even though some students perceive the Ward Sister as attempting to control their 'emotional activities' and traditional nurse training advises 'detachment' as a means of emotional control, trained nurses once on the ward normally exercise a great deal of autonomy in their emotion 'work'. James' nurses bear no resemblance to Hochschild's (1983) flight attendants, yet the same descriptive term is being used to describe their emotion management at work. However, as a result of developments in public sector management, the potential for elements of nurses' emotion management to be commodified is beginning to be recognised (Phillips, 1996; Smith, 1992). Because of recent changes, it is a very real possibility that nurses will perform emotional labour in a similar vein to those who work in the commercial service sector. Smith (1992) recognises this and compares the nurse with the supermarket assistant, noting that 'the nurse is more vulnerable to the demands of the public' (Smith, 1992, p. 17).

Emotion as a mode of organising?

Emerging from many critical accounts concerning the controlling aspects of emotional organisations is a more egalitarian view of the de-bureaucratised, emotional organisation which states that the 'facade of (organisational) rationality' has finally been stripped away (Fineman, 1993). Management 'guru' literature is just as explicit in flogging rationality as a dead horse, though with far more questionable motives. And yet another view that dismisses rationality as a 'myth' (Putman and Mumby, 1993) offers a very different portrayal of organisational life than those put forward by orthodox organisation writers. Apparently organisations are now postmodern; the employment relationship is based on a psychological contract and employees must display emotional intelligence. Even critical feminist writers suggest a radical transformation of organisation structure where 'bounded emotionality' replaces 'bounded rationality' and emotion management is carried out as part of the process of work 'through substituting nurturance and supportiveness in place of the dualism between mind and body, the use of bounded emotionality merges the conception and execution of work, thus avoiding fragmented and alienated labor' (Mumby and Putman, 1992, p. 476).

Examples of small craft based companies are given to highlight the success of 'bounded emotionality' in achieving flexible, adaptive organisations where in 'an environment of caring' the 'demands of differing values and goals' are comfortably accommodated within a fluid structure (Mumby and Putman, 1992, p. 475). However, more recent empirical research, assessing the success of attempts to implement 'bounded emotionality' in a globally competitive, for-profit company (The Body Shop) (Martin *et al.*, 1998), finds that the caring, sharing organisation may not be quite so desirable in practice. Many employees do not subscribe to the shared corporate culture and feel uncomfortable with the demands for emotional expressiveness. 'Bounded emotionality' in fact becomes 'emotional labour' and appears to be aiming at a 'more intimate and powerful form of organizational control' than corporate culture merchants would ever dream possible (Martin *et al.*, 1998, p. 429).

This example serves to suggest that, however attractive the portrayal of emotional organisations may be, great care needs to be taken when speaking of 'stripping' (Fineman, 1993) away rationality. Organisations are not only sites of 'love, hatred and passion' but also sites of purposeful activity orientated to achieving specific goals. This is something that Weber (1947) clearly recognises in his description of both formal and substantive rationality. Rationality is not a 'facade' to be easily discarded but rather the core of an organisation's being; it is the 'logic of organization' (Clegg, 1990). The contemporary organisation has come to recognise the value of 'emotion work'; it has now become a commonplace resource. Emotion in organisations is no longer seen as an unwelcome interference; once perceived as a dysfunction, the subject of emotion is now being used to invigorate management topics. Emotion management, in all its forms, is proving to be invaluable in an era of shrinking financial funding: picture the bank clerk, the housing officer and the nurse, all fulfilling their role of keeping the customer satisfied. The way organisations have come to feed from their members' feelings clearly indicates that organisational rationality remains firmly in place. In effect, an employee's emotion management is being used as a means to an end.

Revisiting 'The Managed Heart'

As this review has indicated, the originality of Hochschild's work has meant that there is little that has been written concerning the subject of emotions and organisations in the last 20 years that does not take 'The Managed Heart' as a reference point. Key to the popularity of Hochschild's contribution to the debate concerning emotion in organisations is the way she identifies the incursion of management into the area of emotion (emotional labour) and the pre-existing ability of employees to control themselves (emotion work). Hochschild, therefore, contributes a fundamental insight into the conflict of commercial and social feeling rules that explains much of the tension concerning the expression of emotion in the contemporary workplace. However, there are two central weaknesses in Hochschild's (1983, 1989a, 1990) accounts of organisational emotionality that are all but neglected in the literature which has leapt aboard the emotional labour bandwagon.

First, Hochschild overemphasises the divide between the public and private performances of emotion management and tends to use the terms 'public' and 'commercial' interchangeably, creating an oversimplified dichotomy. For Hochschild there is no distinction between emotion work as part of the capitalist labour process, emotion work due to professional norms of conduct, or emotion work during normal social interaction in the workplace. She goes on to reinforce this view in her later work: 'by "emotion work" I refer to the emotion management we do in private life; by "emotional labour" I refer to the emotion management we do for a wage' (Hochschild, 1990, p. 118). Hochschild operates with the underlying assumption that there is no room for the 'private' in organisational life; when operating within organisational boundaries our feelings are 'transmutated' and are, therefore, no longer our own, 'The more the company offers the worker's true self for sale, the more the self risks seeming false to the individual worker, and the more difficult it becomes for him or her to know which territory of self to claim' (Hochschild, 1983, p. 196).

Second, Hochschild mistakenly equates a physical labour process with an emotional labour process. This, again, is based on 'transmutated feelings' becoming a commodified object which exists apart from the worker (Korczynski, 2002). As Hochschild states of the air-stewardesses in her study: 'her have-a-nice-day smile is not really her smile but is an indirect extension of the company smile' (Hochschild, 1989a, p. 440). Just as the factory worker produces tangible goods (Hochschild uses the example of wallpaper) from which she/he feels estranged, then the flight attendant creates the product of customer contentment from which she/he feels equally estranged. On this basis she suggests that just as workers may become alienated from their physical labour then they may also become alienated from their emotional labour (Hochschild, 1983, 1989a). For Hochschild, however, emotional labour carries the greatest personal costs to the worker, as the factory worker who draws upon her/his physical labour does not have to 'love the wallpaper' whereas the air-stewardess has to invest the product of passenger satisfaction with feeling (Hochschild, 1983, 1990). Not to do so would not only damage the product but also the worker's sense of self. As Hochschild frequently alludes, 'neither the passenger nor the worker is really having "a good time" ' (Hochschild, 1983, pp. 135, 187).

There is, of course, some merit in comparing the emotional labour process with a physical labour process, both often require 'patience, tolerance and stamina' (Callaghan and Thompson, 2002) and have exploitative potential. It is in the latter, however, that the differences emerge. It is now well recorded how various normative control devices are implemented in order to create the 'committed employee'. The success of these strategies remains a contested area of debate – just how committed is the committed employee? For instance, an alternative view to Hochschild's would be that flight attendants do not have to 'love' the product, the passengers or the airline. They do not have to feel estranged from the emotional labour process. Unlike the factory worker, they own the means of production and, therefore, the capacity to present a 'sincere' or 'cynical' performance lies within the emotional labourer (Goffman, 1959). Whilst the organisation creates parameters of control defining what constitutes 'good service', via mechanisms such as scripts and customer-care programmes, it is the worker who calibrates how much feeling is invested into the performance. Arguably, the deterministic feel that the term 'emotional labour' carries with it undervalues the vitality and independence of outlook that participants bring to organisations and neglects their ability to carve out 'spaces for resistance and misbehaviour' (Thompson and Ackroyd, 1995) and to produce the 'unmanaged organization' (Gabriel, 1995). Crucially, what Hochschild fails to recognise is that the indeterminacy of labour is further exacerbated within the contested terrain of the emotional labour process.

This is not to deny the importance of Hochschild's seminal contribution. 'Emotional labour' does offer valuable insights into the contemporary workplace and capital's awareness of the value of employees' emotion management skills. There can be little doubt that emotion work in organisations can be demanding, boring, exhausting, tedious, arduous and stressful. It is often exploited as an 'invisible' skill and poorly rewarded (James, 1989; Korczynski, 2002; Tancred, 1995). The 'culture of the customer' bestows a superior status to the consumer and the interaction between service provider and customer is an unequal exchange (du Gay and Salaman, 1992; Goffman, 1967; Hochschild, 1989a). And management prescription invents ever more imaginative ways to extract the maximum, and most sincere, performances from emotion workers (Barley and Kunda, 1992). The term 'emotional labour' captures all of these insights and opens the emotional labour process up to critical scrutiny.

Nevertheless, Hochschild mistakes aspiration for outcome in assuming that capital's attempts to appropriate 'emotion work' will be so successful that our feelings are 'transmutated'. Hochschild offers a view of organisations as flat, lifeless landscapes. Where is any sense of the satisfaction, enjoyment and reward that can be gained from various forms of emotion work? Where is the bullying and harassment from colleagues; the organisational violations that occur outside of the labour process? Where is the innuendo, humour and imperfect customer service? Where *are* the social actors?

Conclusion and implications for an understanding of emotion in organisations

The discussions in this and the preceding chapter concerning emotion in organisations has allowed a review of the diversity of occupations, organisations and the wide variety of people who are employed within them, with emphasis being laid on the major role emotion management plays in organisational life. According to many accounts it is now safe to assume that organisations can be described as 'emotional cauldrons' (Albrow, 1992), with organisation members becoming increasingly skilled 'emotion workers'. Organisational actors manage their feelings according to invisible social guidelines, they control their emotions according to the organisation's rules and regulations and, depending on who they are, emotion management may be carried out according to professional norms. If working in the service sector with its increasing emphasis upon 'consumerism', in exchange for a wage, 'commercial love' is provided as a vital contribution to the profitable product of customer satisfaction. Increasingly, in the absence of adequate financial resources, the human element is being used by management to paper over the cracks: the bank clerk pacifies an irate customer who complains of excessive bank charges, a local housing office deals with eruptions of violence from discontented tenants and a trust hospital's survival relies upon nurses' ability to keep the 'customer' satisfied.

Hochschild's air-stewardesses (1983), James' nurses (1989, 1992, 1993), Taylor's TSAs (1996, 1998), Hearn's 'new' organisation man (1993) and Fineman's 'emotional zones' (1993) have all helped to reveal organisations as emotional arenas and confirm that organisations do 'have feelings' (Albrow, 1997). However, as this review of several studies has discovered, despite differences in the forms of emotion management being enacted they are all described as 'emotional labour'. Following in Hochschild's conceptual footsteps, there is no distinction between emotion management as part of the capitalist labour process, emotion management due to professional norms of conduct or emotion management during normal social interaction in the workplace. In effect, there is no attempt to identify the public and private faces of emotion management: emotional labour appropriated by organisations for commercial gain, emotion *in* labour performed by professionals as a means of carrying out difficult tasks and emotion work used in interaction with colleagues or the extra emotion work which may be offered as a 'gift' to customers, clients or colleagues.

The emphasis by Hochschild (1983, p. 19) on the 'transmutation of an emotion system' when acts of private emotion management 'fall under the sway of large organizations, social engineering and the profit motive', and the lack of detail concerning the possibility of 'equal emotional exchange' within organisations, risks portraying organisational actors as 'perfect company robots' (Wouters, 1989a). In short, organisational actors, through the performance of 'deep acting', internalise company values and become 'playthings' of forces much larger than themselves. Unfortunately, the continual labelling of the 'public-face' of emotion management as 'emotional labour' reduces the view of a person's emotion management skills as a 'newly discovered renewable resource' (Albrow, 1992) and enforces the image of employees as being nothing more than 'cultural dopes' (Giddens, 1992). In other words, the rational organisation has recognised the value of the irrational and the 'iron cage' has taken another prisoner.

Nevertheless, the surface appearance of rationality appears to have been eroded and we are presented with a picture of emotions here, emotions there, organisational emotionality everywhere. There is, of course, an element of truth in this derationalised view of organisational life. Organisational actors do suffer from 'organization-ness' (Hearn, 1993) and control their emotions according to the implicit rules of the organisations as a social setting, not just formally defined rules of emotion management in order to 'get the job done'. The divide between the public and the private is never clear-cut and friend-ships are formed and different 'emotional zones' are created within the work-place. It is well documented that work can be both a source of sadness and alienation, as well as engagement and humour. Taking the view of the 'de-rationalised organisation' allows the recognition that although the 'experience and construction of emotions has to be placed in the context of the experi-ences of organizations' (Hearn, 1993, p. 161) this does not automatically label every emotion experienced within an organisation as 'emotional labour'. Actors may 'work' on their emotions when present in an organisation, but not always in order to achieve company goals. To display pleasure when receiving a gift (Hearn, 1993), to practice constraint in a departmental meeting and to work closely with team members in a 'community' (Taylor, 1996) may be events that constitute parts of any one working day. The success of these 'events' rely on organisational actors' skills in weaving in and out of the different 'emotional zones', just as they do in a social setting outside of the organisation.

In the rush to re-emotionalise organisations little care has been taken to conceptualise the presence of emotions: we have emotional organisations, emotion in organisations, emotion work and emotional labour. What, if any, is the difference? The deconstructed version of organisations (Hearn, 1993) shows that they are emotional arenas; sites of love, hatred, sexuality and pas-sion (Fineman, 1993, 2000, 2003). If, as claimed, 'organizations have feelings' then surely questions should be asked as to how the orthodox picture of organisations has come to be suddenly derationalised on the one hand and then re-created as a menacing Orwellian nightmare of surveillance and 'trans-mutation' on the other.

Developments in the literature suggest there is a need for new ways of con-ceptualising emotionality in organisations and, in particular, for ideas that will help us to understand the ways in which emotions are governed and regulated. In this book the focus will be on what is called 'emotion management'.

Recognising that, although emotions are given more expression within contemporary organisations and indeed are more often central to the ways in which organisations work, their expression is far from being out of control or unregulated. The organisation does not give itself over to passion; on the contrary, the expression of emotion is controlled and directed by employees and their managers in a number of distinctive ways. It is these distinctions which the book wishes to explore, developing a sociological understanding of the management of emotion in organisations with the introduction of a typology of organisational emotionality.

Notes

1. See Harris, 2002; Lively, 2002 for a discussion of emotional labour and the legal profession and the section in this chapter on emotion work and the medical profession.
2. Thanks to Chris Warhurst for the suggested use of this term as a means of highlighting the difference in emotion management which is carried out according to organisational rules in order 'to get the job done' and that which is appropriated for direct commercial gain, i.e. 'emotional labour'.

4

A sociological understanding of workplace emotion

Introducing agency

From the review of literature in Chapter 3 it is clear that, following the successful contribution of Hochschild's (1983) work, attention to the expression of emotion in organisations has grown in recent years. However, as can be seen from the review of organisational analysis undertaken in Chapter 2, the search for effective theoretical accounts of this phenomenon has been largely unrewarded. It seems that established approaches to organisational analysis differ greatly in their approach to, and recognition of, emotion in organisations. It might be expected that early orthodox writers on organisations seek to suppress, exclude or sideline forms of emotionality. Firmly wedded, as they are, to the bureaucratic form of organisation it is hardly surprising that the seemingly irrational will have no place in their portrayals of the typical 'organisation man'. Even contemporary prescriptive writers only have a one-dimensional view of emotionality – that which can be captured and controlled for organisational ends. Researchers who take a more critical view of organisations have, at last, recognised the vital part emotions play in organisational life but with a range of consequences. Shades of agency appear, disappear and just as quickly reappear with every account: employees may be dominated by networks of power, they might be partially in view but generally overshadowed by a focus on capitalism, or agency appears in all its luminosity completely unhindered by any hint of a shadow of any overriding structures. The numerous conceptual approaches reviewed in Chapter 2 clearly rest on diverse views of organisational life and ontological assumptions concerning the nature of the people who work within them. This, in turn, has a major effect upon how the role of emotions in organisations is to be understood.

67

In its contribution to the debates concerning emotion in organisation this book offers its own view of employees in organisations and their emotion management skills. It offers an active agent but one who is necessarily both enabled and constrained by enduring social structures – neither in full shadow or complete light. In order to be clear about the conceptual framework used throughout this analysis first, at a basic level, there is a need to set a sociological/social approach to emotion. Second there is a need to develop an account of the processes by which the expression of emotion in organisations may be thought about more adequately. Beginning with a discussion concerning the social view of emotion, a particular kind of realist account of emotion and an understanding of the management of emotion will be developed. Unusually, and perhaps somewhat controversially, Goffman's analyses of the 'interaction order' will be utilised to display that, although clearly there are social forces shaping and channelling both emotions and expressions of emotionality, there are important limiting factors on these forces. It is argued here that, through an understanding of the independent relationships of agency and structure, it is possible to locate the management of emotion within the biological, social and cultural spheres and that to a large degree, the individual actor retains a sense of him or herself as being in control of emotions. In effect, there are key limits to the extent by which emotions are either biological impulses, psychological intuitions or purely the product of external forces, whether they are social constructions or management prescriptions.

From an over to under socialised conception of emotion

When seeking an understanding of 'what is emotion' clear polarities can be identified: a focus on the internal versus a focus on the external, a concentration on the individual versus a concentration on the social; leading to a focus on the natural versus a focus on the manufactured. Of course, these do not represent simple dichotomies but rather continuums, or fierce 'border skirmishes' (Williams and Bendelow, 1996a), where we can find various combinations of the inner and outer, spontaneous and rule-bound, and instinct and performance. At one end of this spectrum the organismic model posits emotion as an essentially biological process. At the extreme, Darwin states that emotion is based on instinct and he focuses on 'expression of emotion' rather than any meanings which might be associated with them, thus offering emotion as a culturally universal phenomenon (Darwin, 1965). At the opposite end of the spectrum, the social constructionists will tell us that there is no such thing as an 'emotion', only collectively manufactured 'states' (Harré, 1986).

Travelling along this continuum, various approaches to emotion can be found: the many writers, classic and contemporary, who consider emotion to be 'ready-made, as if by intuition' (Sandelands, 1988, p. 443) with a universal, biological basis; Freud with his emphasis on impulses and the unconscious; James (1950) who, in his 'Principle of Psychology', equates emotion directly with bodily states that may be manipulated by drugs or physical intervention but barely by social factors, and the social psychologists, where the importance attributed to the 'social' varies greatly (Greenwood, 1994). Nevertheless, the very nature of its title tells us that social psychology is entering a different realm of understanding emotion in that it seeks to 'go beyond the organism and the physical environment to account for human emotions' (Gerth and Mills, 1954, p. 53). At this position on the continuum the importance of biology and psychology begin to fade and the impact of social structure magnifies, to the point where it dominates. This is the territory of social constructionism and it is within this sphere of understanding that this chapter will begin the search for an effective sociology of emotion. Beginning with the recognition that there is a physiological basis for emotionality – after all if there are no 'basic' emotions what is there to 'manage'? (Murphy, 1995) – it will be argued that the sociology of emotion must concentrate on the public face of emotion. But in positing this, a balance ought to be found between emotion as an agential experience and emotion as a cultural artefact, or in broader terms, a view that neither reduces structure to agency or agency to structure. Social constructionism is continually engaged in just such a balancing act resulting in its very own continuum where at one end social actors are free and unfettered and at the other they are social puppets, whose strings are firmly tied to (and pulled by) social structures. These views need to be explored and understood if a workable sociological understanding of workplace emotion is to be arrived at.

Social constructionism

Social constructionism takes many, often confusing, forms. Strands within this realm can be identified as interpretivism, symbolic interactionism, constructivism or structuralism. There is, however, a common dominator amongst all of these 'isms': that is the primacy which is given to the social. A central premise is that the actual status of a thing – its reality – is determined in the process of nteraction with others in particular social situations or at the level of practice and discourse. Analysis takes place outside of individual psychology, though it varies as to how much 'internal states' are involved in the production of agency and related emotions and where the power of the social lies; the system or the individual. Within the world of social constructionism can be found very different emphases on individualism or structuralism, micro- or macro-sociology: from the symbolic interactionists' rather naïve proposition that society consists of only individuals and their social relations, to the post-structuralists' stance that 'it is not man himself who thinks' (Foucault, 1972), the agent wanders from being fully present and engaged with society, indeed completely involved in its creation and re-creation, to the agent becoming de-centred and almost invisible within the various networks of power. The subject of emotion and the search for an adequate conceptual framework has attracted considerable attention from various quarters within social constructionism, with a plethora of resultant positions on the subject.

At one extreme of the social constructionist viewpoint the independent existence of emotions are denied or made extremely problematic. Some constructionists envisage a 'concrete world' and there is scant, if any, recognition of the psychological and physiological content of emotion. They direct attention to the 'local social world' where cultural factors create 'rules' and ensure a 'local moral order' (Doyle McCarthy, 1989; Harré, 1986; Lutz, 1988). One of the most prominent writers in this field is Harré:

> There has been a tendency ... to abstract an entity – call it 'anger', 'love', 'grief' or 'anxiety' – and to try to study it. But what there is are angry people, upsetting scenes, sentimental episodes, grieving families and funerals, anxious parents pacing at midnight, and so on. There is a concrete world of contexts and activities. We reify and abstract from that concreteness at our peril. (Harré, 1986, p. 4).

In this frame of reference even emotional outbursts are seen as social performances. The physical reactions of emotion, such as crying and rapid heartbeat, are therefore seen as somehow a by-product of and completely incidental to the socially produced 'emotional quality of encounters'. As Harré (1986, p. 13) states: 'Emotions do not just happen, they are part of the unfolding of quite standard dramatic scenarios.' There is some strength in Harré's argument and, to be fair, his work does seem to oscillate in just how much significance is given to an actor's 'involvement' with society. Indeed, Harré represents the eclectic nature of social constructivism very well. At different points he states that 'minds are social products' (Harré, 1990, p. 341) or that emotions are essentially speech acts (Harré and Gillett, 1994) but then goes on to distance himself from more recent constructivist accounts. 'Some of those who have taken up post-modernism have thought that if ontology is grammar then reality is whatever we say it is. A vulgar misunderstanding, I fear' (Harré, 1997, p. 174).

Despite some of its conceptual confusions social constructionism, in its various guises, does offer an explanation of how the circumstances in which it is reasonable to deviate from accepted standards, as well as the patterns of behaviour that might be expected when such standards are not observed, are socially prescribed. It would be seldom if ever appropriate to describe people who behave emotionally as being '*completely* out of control' (Averill, 1994). As Solomon notes: 'there is good reason to suppose that we have never met a raw, unembellished, basic emotion, one not "covered over" with the trappings of culture and experience and constrained and complicated by the "display rules" of society' (Solomon, 2002, p. 118).

From this combination of the 'inside' and the 'outside' it can be seen that sociologists considering emotion in organisations tend to draw on constructionist ideas in a more limited way. They see themselves as analysing the way social processes construct raw emotion and therefore social processes channel, direct or otherwise overlay the biological sources of emotionality. Kemper argues: 'virtually every sociologist of emotions acknowledges a physiological substrate to emotions. The debate turns on how important it is' (Kemper, 1990, p. 20). The sense of being 'gripped', 'seized' or 'overcome' with emotion directly acknowledges the view that 'pure', 'natural', unprocessed emotion does exist (Averill, 1994; Sabini and Silver, 1998). Indeed, many writers insist on this acknowledgement as they are concerned that an over-concentration on the social misses the 'natural', the impulsive and the passionate elements of humanity (Archer, 2000; Barbalet, 2001; Craib, 1995, 1997; Solomon, 2002). Whilst most commentators recognise the biological or physiological basis of feelings, it is also thought to be rare for emotion to be expressed in a natural or even a direct and spontaneous manner (Flam, 1990b; Lyon, 1998; Scheff, 1990; Wentworth and Ryan, 1994). Flam, for example, argues that ' "pure" emotional "man" lurks even behind socialised and constrained emotional "man" ' (Flam, 1990a, p. 45). She differentiates between 'pure' and 'constrained' emotion 'man' by arguing that 'A constrained emotional action model exemplifies a synthetic mix, wherein rational and/or normative action rules interact with 'pure' feelings and shape emotional expression' (Flam, 1990b, p. 232). And Sabini and Silver (1998, p. 231) use the example of the cultural diversity which surrounds events such as funerals and argue that 'real life grief seems to be a blend of the spontaneous and the arranged, of the socially constructed and the not quite socially constructed'.

The conclusion must be that whatever physiological roots human emotions have they are heavily overlaid with social conditioning. In this sense, unusually in the study of emotion, a sociological analysis refutes the authority given to other sciences (Doyle McCarthy, 1989). Nevertheless, the boundary between Kemper's (1990) 'physiological substrate' of emotion and the patterning imposed by socialisation is impossible to identify in many cases. Going back to the example of the funeral cited by Sabini and Silver (1998), even in the most constrained of emotional cultures an outpouring of grief, say in the form of sobbing, would be deemed acceptable, if not expected. It is debatable how much the sobbing is spontaneous or 'not quite socially constructed' (Durkheim, 1971). Moreover, as Archer points out, the aim should be less of an attempt to define or impose boundaries but to 'reunite pathos with human logos' and acknowledge that our 'inner conversation' intertwines with social and cultural properties but cannot be reduced to them (Archer, 2000, p. 194).

The emotional self

Social constructionism varies in how it sees the social actor acquiring an 'emotional self' with many accounts appearing overly deterministic. In the Durkheimian version of social determinism, 'social facts' are the features of social life which act as a constraint upon an individual's scope of action (Durkheim, 1938). The socially constructed actor does not write the script, rather the stage is set and roles assigned and these factors shape the 'self' and prescribe the framework of meanings to be socially transmitted. To many social constructionists these 'facts' are external to the actor and act upon him or her in a way that compels the actor to behave in socially prescribed ways. Increasingly, the determinant influence upon the human subject is stated to be discourse and it is at the level of the local that analysis seems to have come to rest, claiming to have escaped Durkheim's functionalism and resultant determinism but not actually achieving either. Harré is far from alone in his view that 'ontologically the conversation is the primary human reality' (Abu-Lughod and Lutz, 1990; Butler, 1993; Deetz, 1998; Derrida, 1981; du Gay, 1996; Foucault, 1970, 1977; Harré, 1990, p. 352; Harré and Gillett, 1994) resulting in a far more determinist stance than Durkheim could ever have envisaged, or wished for.

Little wonder that this is often referred to as a 'flat ontology' as, at the level of discourse, material realities have an ethereal quality, being simultaneously everywhere and nowhere, leaving social constructionism 'whirling in a maelstrom of total relativity' (Shotter, 1990, p. 213; Thompson, 1993; Willmott, 1997). As a result, an overly 'constructionist' account tends to produce an image of emotionally anorexic social actors and, in some versions, it leads to a complete 'asphyxiation by society' (Archer, 2000, p. 18). Craib ponders on the 'linguistic turn':

> I ask myself what I would feel if somebody walked into my office and said 'I am a social construct'. It would, I think, belong to the same class of reactions that I would have to someone who said 'I am a machine'. It would be a combination of fear and puzzlement at such depersonalisation. By depersonalisation I mean that such a person would be denying that they are a subject – since machines are constructed objects, as are, presumably, social constructs. (Craib, 1997, p. 5).

Social order may well consist of a pattern of 'social facts' and discourse may have a certain transformative power but to mediate an overly determinist view there is a need to acknowledge that social norms 'in no way implement themselves' (Albrow, 1990). At the level of practice they become normative ideals, but there remains 'a world of locatable, powerful particulars' (Shotter, 1990), a real world that anchors a local moral order in a larger context. Within this world social facts, norms and practices are open to change and individuals have the capacity to recognise and work with alternative interpretations of the world around them; as Pearce points out in his discussion of Durkheim's description of 'social facts', '... whilst he (Durkheim) developed an operational definition of social facts as observable, external etc., he conceded that their affectivity was mediated by "representation", which individuals recognized subjectively and dealt with internally' (Pearce, 1989, p. 15).

In stark contrast to the extreme constructionist viewpoint, interactionists such as David Silverman acknowledge the power of the social but would argue that social 'rules' are constantly changing and being re-negotiated through the interaction of individuals. His stance is that society has no existence 'beyond and above' the one created by the interaction of its members (Silverman, 1970). Alternatively, there are interactionists who are less idealistic in that they recognise a 'frame' in which action takes place whilst still emphasising that an individual does not passively accept constructed 'meanings' of himself and 'actively participates in sustaining a definition of the situation' (Goffman, 1961a). In describing the social actor as a 'peg', Goffman draws from a Durkheimian analysis and usefully summarises how actors are 'products' of processes which exist around them but at the same time, through interaction with the 'audience', can be seen to be involved in their own 'self-production':

> In analysing the self, then, we are drawn from its possessor, from the person who will profit or lose most by it, for he and his body merely provide a peg on which something of collaborative manufacture will be hung for a time. And the means for producing and maintaining selves do not reside inside the peg; in fact these means

are often bolted down in social establishments. There will be a back region with its tools for shaping the body, and a front region with its fixed props. There will be a team of persons whose activity on stage and in conjunction with available props will constitute the scene from which the performed character's self will emerge, and another team, the audience, whose interpretative activity will be necessary for this emergence. The self is a product of all of these arrangements, and in all of its parts bears the marks of this genesis. (Goffman, 1959, p. 245)

The attractiveness of this point of view lies in its acknowledgement of 'our all-too-human selves and our socialized selves' (Goffman, 1959, p. 36). When emotion is viewed from this stance it allows recognition of the 'raw' emotion, variable moods and unexpected reactions that are managed according to the perception of what an audience expects.

Building on this perspective emotion can be defined as a lived, interactional experience which must be treated as the 'study of selves and others, joined and separated in episodes of co-present interaction' (Denzin, 1984, p. 61). It is through the process of interaction that meaning is brought into people's lives, how they make sense of the world: 'the stuff ordinary people are made of' (Denzin, 1984, pp. 261, 274). Certain aspects of this view may seem limited, and not a little solipsistic, but it does have a certain appeal when studying a subjective experience such as emotion where an explanation cannot be sought purely from sources external to the individual.

Social structure and social divisions

Whilst resisting the view that emotions are totally socially constructed, we must be aware of the dangers of overestimating the powers of the individual and recognise that social norms act as boundaries around action. In most situations there are feeling rules in operation, what Goffman (1967) refers to as 'traffic rules of interaction', and circumstances which constrain individuals with different degrees of social pressure to observe them. It is the inherent weakness of many interactive accounts of social action that, although 'strong on action', they do not have the ability to deal with issues such as power and conflict. This often leads to a lack of recognition of how actors' skilled performances may be constrained by forces outside their control.

Despite some extreme views, social constructionism does have a valuable contribution to make. Its critics may claim our sense of 'self' 'owes nothing to society' (Archer, 2000, p. 78) but we need to be careful not to overplay the agency hand. Archer offers us an 'active agent who currently weighs his or her circumstances against which the attainment of his or her goals and who alone determines whether he or she can afford the price'. However, *who* determines *what* is often not open for negotiation. Being a member of society involves conforming to prescribed patterns of behaviour and the concept of interactional rules is a barely adequate means of accounting for the differential distribution of life-chances and resources in society. Often expectations, norms and rules are endowed with the power of coercion and control and may indeed be backed by sanctions, so the element of choice the actor has is limited. Weber recognises this in his discussion of legitimacy as a major factor in enhancing the stability of social order: individuals accept the 'rules' as 'social facts' not only for fear of the consequences if they departed from them, but from the perceived advantages if they conform (Albrow, 1990, p. 163). As Durkheim (1938) states, the 'moral conscience' wields a strong influence. Weber helps to illuminate this point with his concept of 'traditional authority' (Weber, 1947); although people act with a certain amount of freedom and choice, pressures to conform can be enormous and the existing primordial beliefs are legitimated by their reproduction. Whilst examining the micro-politics of human interaction, and the important role the management of emotion plays, it needs to be recognised that the interaction order does not exist in a symbolic realm but requires a social stage for its production. It is often the powerful who set the agenda and, therefore, the 'realm of human agency is bounded' (Giddens, 1992, p. 168).

As Goffman frequently points out, 'human nature is not a very human thing' and this is never more clearly explicated than when examining the impact of social divisions upon how emotion work is both given and received. The status of participants in the interaction order will be a defining feature of how emotion work is to be distributed, with considerations of gender, class, race, occupation and, increasingly, vast material inequalities altering the 'rules of the game'. The terms class and gender may be useful analytical social categories that allow stark differences and inequalities to be recognised but they also tend to act as static, objectifying mechanisms, especially in the study of a lived experience such as emotion. Divisions of emotion work have both symbolic and material dimensions and are continually reproduced because being a woman, being black or/and being working class are dynamic and continuing processes, a distinct social accomplishment that is achieved through lived experiences in particular cultural mileuix (Bourdieu, 1990; Charlesworth, 2000; Hochschild, 1983, 2003; New, 1998; West and Zimmerman, 1987). From early childhood we are offered symbolic clues and very particular feeling rules, in what Bourdieu describes as a 'system of structured, structuring dispositions, the habitus' (Bourdieu, 1990, p. 52) that is historically and socially embedded. The habitus tends to exclude divergences from what is seen as the norm and thus there is a certain regularity in the presentation of self that often leads to the misconception of certain embodied capacities as 'natural, individual, moral' ways of being (Charlesworth, 2000, p.158). There is little doubt that assumptions about emotion work are coded according to distinctive social categories, for instance middle-class women are gentle and caring, working-class men are impulsive and aggressive (Charlesworth, 2000; Hochschild, 1983, 1989b; Shields, 2002). However, though categorised in this way, it is often neglected that these modes of 'comportment' are socially mediated and relate directly to material conditions that are a result of social, economic and political relations of domination and exclusion and are, therefore, very much dependent upon social position.

The actor as emotion manager

As noted in the previous sections of this chapter, a weakness of extreme constructionist accounts is that they tend to treat actors as if they are almost infinitely malleable. In fact, through various forms of 'linguistic terrorism' any sense of active human agency has been almost completely dissolved (Archer, 2000, p. 25). To counter this deficiency this chapter has sought to bring agency back into the analysis and the role of the actor in shaping and managing their emotions is extensively analysed. In order to do this it is necessary to set out an argument concerning the way that people respond to, handle and accommodate their emotional experiences. The argument will rest upon the assumption that social actors define their identity as individuals in terms of their capacity to manage their emotions in particular ways, depending upon the levels of commitment to various 'moral orders'. Indeed many, if not most, commentators use the idea of actors actively managing their emotions in particular ways.

For example, Giddens is dismissive of any theoretical understanding of human conduct that relies on the 'content of the unconscious' as a source of the explanation of behaviour. He believes such conduct to be on the level of 'practical consciousness', where the actor has a 'theoretical understanding' of what they are doing and why. Even though much of the action is routinised this does not mean that it is habitually enacted unconsciously:

> a reductive theory of consciousness which, wanting to show how much of social life is governed by ... currents outside the scope of the actor's awareness, cannot adequately grasp the level of control which agents are characteristically able to sustain reflexively over their conduct. (Giddens, 1984, p. 4)

Hochschild (1983), in a characteristically sophisticated formulation, suggests that once public a person's emotionality no longer belongs to themselves. She proposes that an acknowledgement of what 'is emotionally due to another person' results in the exchange of properly managed emotions (Hochschild, 1983, p. 18). What are often referred to in discussions as 'implicit feeling rules' frame the choice of whether 'to be or not to be emotional; to lend a bit of self feeling to one's actions or to withhold feeling, to be overcome by emotion or to hold it in check' (Denzin, 1984, p. 277). Even Harré's particular version of social constructionism supports a certain amount of interpretivism:

> rules are not potent entities driving behaviour but expression of those normative systems by means of which: a) whatever happens is interpreted by those involved (and sometimes by the bystanders too); and b) character is sustained or undermined. Not rules using people to become instantiated, but people using rules to make sense. (Harré, 1990, p. 342)

Goffman's analogy of social action as 'performance' is a useful way of describing how we manage ourselves in social encounters and brings to light the realisation that these performances become extremely polished:

> The whole machinery of self-production is cumbersome, of course, and sometimes breaks down, exposing its separate components: back region control; team collusion; audience tact; and so forth. But, well oiled, impressions will flow from it fast enough to put us in the grip of one of our types of reality – the performances will come off and ... each performed character will appear to emanate intrinsically from its performer. (Goffman, 1959, p. 245)

Giddens (1984) suggests that such performances are necessary if a sense of trust or 'ontological security' is to be maintained. There are mutual responsibilities of communication where actors, not only constantly monitor their own conduct but also monitor the conduct of others, thus sustaining the predictability of much of day-to-day social life. Many routines are tactfully carried out as a means of saving the actor's own 'face' or that of another and agents reflexively adjust their performances accordingly. Without this social actors would appear to exist in a cynical world of self-concerned agents, when in fact 'face', and the corresponding sense of self, is a sacred thing and much of social interaction is centred around not only saving actors' own faces but also those around them. This continuous monitoring and treatment of fellow interactants with 'ritual care' produces and reproduces a moral order: the aim may be to save face but the effect is to save the situation and the 'ritual structure of the self'. (Goffman, 1967, p. 39)

And this is the case even in a complex mass society where there appears to be no commitment to any particular 'rule-book' and the self must be fragmented in order to meet the challenge of diverse audiences. There can be little doubt that the frameworks of social interaction are being re-drawn as the result of a general 'informalization of feeling' (Wouters, 1989a, p. 105). Evidence of the breaking down of social barriers in modern society indicates how social actors are now much more familiar with different cultures than their own. They have developed the ability to switch and swap faces according to the demands of many different situations (Goffman, 1974; Wouters, 1989a and b). However, rather than fragmentation and incoherence, men and women 'have become more strongly integrated into tighter knit networks of interdependencies in which the level of mutually expected self-restraint has risen' (Wouters, 1989b, p. 449). Conditions of late capitalism may have damaged the relations of trust upon which the continued existence of the interaction order depend; nevertheless, we do not see it destroyed but reordered and people ever more sensitive to the process and outcome.

Despite, or because of, the shifting social boundaries social interaction can be viewed as 'a little social system with its own boundary maintaining tendencies; it is a little patch of commitment and loyalty with its own heroes and its own villains' (Goffman, 1967, p. 114). The heroes are those who consistently engage in face-saving activity, what of the villains? In all arenas of social life there will be those who aggressively manipulate the rules of social exchange for personal gain or may not invest in the required level of mutual face-work. In either case the encounter becomes 'less a scene of mutual considerateness than an arena in which a contest or match is held' (Goffman, 1967, p. 24). Interaction becomes strategic and interactants do not fulfil the reciprocal obligations of the interaction order and can be viewed as performers who appear to present 'themselves to others in a false or manipulative fashion' (Giddens, 1987, p. 112). Actors may manipulate a situation but this does not necessarily make them deceptive or unworthy interactants; it may be 'less a choice to be deceptive than it is a choice to survive' (Schwabe, 1993, p. 342).

In summary, the approach to emotions developed here assumes that emotions are actively 'managed' by people according to the 'rules' of a particular situation, set within a wider structure of cultural beliefs and values. In the literature the self-regulation of an agent's responses to a potentially emotional situation is known as 'emotion work' (Hochschild, 1979, 1983) or 'face-work' (Goffman, 1967). The use of the term 'work' indicates that actors are dynamic, knowledgeable agents who fully participate in the creation of various emotion management performances. Though Giddens' and Hochschild's accounts may be described as 'depthless' in their neglect of the independent existence of social structures that are irreducible to the actions of social actors (Willmott, 1997), they do offer a useful account of how it is necessary for social beings to have acquired a form of knowledge that allows them to operate in the social realm. It also shows how emotion not only has an effect on 'social order and disorder, working structures, conflict, influence, conformity, posturing, gender, sexuality and politics' (Fineman, 1993, p. 1), but is in turn affected by it. This understanding of social actors as accomplished managers of emotion rests on a realist understanding of social life. It is alternative to constructionism in that, unlike extreme constructionist accounts such as Harré's (1986), the sociology of emotion introduced here does not rely on accounts which entail the 'surgical removal' of structure from the 'flesh and blood of life' (Rochberg-Halton, 1982). It links the parts and the people, the inside and the outside, the self and society, it talks about our relations with the world but without assuming that they are inseparable.

Conditions for empty performances

As the review of various approaches to an understanding of emotion and social action show, writers vary in terms of the extent to which they see the actor having and being able to maintain autonomy from external control. In the organisational context, it is common for writers to envisage both variations in the ways that employees are committed to the policies of their employers and the extent to which they can evade control. Hochschild (1979, 1983, 1990) refers to the levels of involvement of the individual self in terms of the difference between 'surface acting' and 'deep acting'. But she couples this with a distinctive idea about the inability of individuals to evade what might be described as the colonisation of their mind by managerially designed feeling rules. Hochschild argues that she is drawing directly on Goffman to support parts of her argument:

> As it is for the people observed by Erving Goffman, the action is in the body language, the put-on-sneer, the posed shrug, the controlled sigh. This is surface acting. The other way is deep acting. Here display is a natural result of working on feeling; the actor does not try to seem happy or sad but rather expresses spontaneously a real feeling that has been self-induced. (Hochschild, 1983, p. 35)

Hochschild goes on to describe how 'surface acting' is a device whereby actors can deliberately deceive others about how they really feel, and retain an authentic sense of self. When they become involved in 'deep acting', however, sustaining an independent self is no longer possible. Deep acting is, in effect, a method whereby actors deceive themselves through their own convincing performances: 'by pretending deeply, she alters herself' (Hochschild, 1983, p. 33). However, Hochschild wants to argue that both 'surface' and 'deep' acting are also deliberate manifestations of control by the actor, the latter often being resorted to because the strain of maintaining a 'surface' performance becomes too difficult. In Hochschild's terms, actors are carrying out 'emotion work' as they actively change what they inwardly feel to match their expressive performances (Hochschild, 1983, p. 90). For her there is a reality of external control because, beyond a certain point, the individual cannot sustain psychological distance from feeling rules.

An alternative view is that of Kahn (1992). He gives more emphasis to actors' abilities to choose whether to be 'psychologically present' in that he believes to 'surface act', or to be 'psychologically absent' on some occasions is actually less stressful. It is safer than being fully immersed into a situation that may prove to be threatening. People, therefore, go through cycles of 'psychological presence' and 'absence' as they 'calibrate how fully present they are in response to internal and external factors' (Kahn, 1992, p. 341).

This understanding of the ability of actors to withdraw emotionally from situations takes a much less determinist stance than Hochschild's image of actors being manipulated into moulding their inner feelings according to management prescription. Indeed Goffman's concepts, contrary to Hochschild's attempt to co-opt his ideas to support her views, actually allow an understanding of how actors are continually interpreting the feeling rules of particular situations and adjusting their performances accordingly. Goffman introduces the idea of a 'situated activity system' and illustrates his ideas with an analogy of a merry-go-round:

> As with any face-to-face interaction, there is much chance for communication and its feedback through a wide variety of signs, for the damping and surging of responses, and for the emergence of homeostatic-like controls. As soon as the ride gets underway, there is a circulation of feeling among participants and an 'involvement contour' may emerge, with collective shifts in the intensity, quality and objects of involvement … And this is so even though we know that this episode of reality is tied in with the day's activity at the merry-go-round, the state of the amusement park as a whole, the park season, and the community from which the riders come. (Goffman, 1961a, p. 97)

In this description of the 'emotion work' carried out by actors on the merry-go-round a picture can be gained of how it is possible for them to embark on the ride (social encounter), at all times expertly judging what level of involvement is required. It shows how social actors move between being fully present and absent according to the signals they receive throughout encounters. In turn, these signals are interpreted and acted upon through the use of implicit 'feeling rules' which are learnt by being an active member in a 'community'.

Despite Goffman's detailed portrayals of various social encounters, it has sometimes been declared that a weakness in his work is the overemphasis on the outward 'performance' according to the 'display rules' of the particular situation (Archer, 2000; Ashforth and Humphry, 1993; Hochschild, 1979, 1983; Scheff, 1990). It is said there is no sense of the inner 'self' in Goffman's writings; 'the private "I" is simply not there'; his performances are 'acts' untouched by feeling: 'Goffman's actors actively manage outer impressions, but they do not actively manage inner feelings' (Hochschild, 1983, p. 218, 1979, p. 262). In effect, Goffman's actors merely carry out 'surface acting', they are 'psychologically absent' and can be viewed as performers who appear to present 'themselves to others in a false or manipulative fashion' (Giddens, 1987, p. 112) and, therefore, Goffman 'owes us a theory of his feisty self as a social subject' (Archer, 2000, p. 78). As Goffman himself states: 'This possibility is understandable, since no one is in quite as good an observational position to see through the act as the person who puts it on' (Goffman, 1959, p. 28). This leads the likes of Hochschild (1979, p. 263) and Harré (1990) to the conclusion that Goffman, through the alleged ignorance of the effects of social structure upon the inner self, 'under-estimates the power of the social'. The overall claim is that Goffman has a 'studied disregard' for both 'individual personality' and social structure and, therefore, does not provide a set of 'conceptual connecting tissues' between the physiological and sociological models of emotion (Archer, 2000; Hochschild, 1979, p. 261).

Yet it is possible to derive a different understanding from Goffman's writings. In presenting social actors as 'impression managers', Goffman is describing how people respond to social situations not deriding their nature. The development of an adequate theory for the sociology of emotions has, so far, relied heavily upon Goffman to introduce the 'social' into the study of emotion without ignoring 'our all too human selves' (Goffman, 1959). For him human nature may not be a very human thing but contrary to his critics' shallow reading of his work, Goffman does offer us social actors who are capable of moral commitment, who are involved with society *and* whose activities take place within multiple and layered frameworks of action that are not static cultural entities but subject to continuous change. He, therefore, offers us the link between the 'expressive order', the micro-world of social arrangements where the order of the 'proper' is meticulously observed, to the 'practical order'; 'those social arrangements by which the means of material existence are generated' (Harré, 1990, p. 354).

Take, for example, his activity on the 'merry-go-round'; this is firmly placed within the structural framework of the amusement park and the community (Goffman, 1961a, p. 97). Such concerns are also present in his example of social actors as 'pegs' whose means for producing and maintaining selves are 'bolted down in social establishments' (Goffman, 1959, p. 245). In addition, Goffman's reference to 'front and back regions' which are involved in the shaping of the 'self' (1959) goes a long way in explaining what occurs behind the public performances of 'face-work'. Such an acknowledgement can be directly compared – though is not to be equated – with Hochschild's 'surface' and 'deep' acting. Goffman says when accomplished social actors manage to convince themselves of the validity of their performances something akin to what Hochschild calls deep acting occurs: 'At one extreme, one finds that the performer can be fully taken in by his own act; he can be sincerely convinced that the impression of reality which he stages is the real reality' (Goffman, 1959, p. 28).

Nevertheless, despite his emphasis on expressive behaviour Goffman recognises, as others do not, that the concept of 'deep' and 'surface' acting (or in Goffman's (1959) terms: 'sincere' and 'cynical' face-work) gives an oversimplified impression of the socialised actor. Surely it cannot be a simple matter of either carrying out one type of performance or another. When does 'surface' acting become 'deep' acting? Where is there any room for an authentication of the self? Goffman warns of the dangers of using such divisions when discussing human conduct:

> There is a vulgar tendency in social thought to divide the conduct of the individual into a profane and sacred part, ... The profane part is attributed to the obligatory world of social roles; it is formal, stiff, and dead; it is exacted by society. The sacred part has to do with 'personal' matters and 'personal' relationships – with what an individual is 'really' like underneath it all when he relaxes and breaks through to those in his presence. It is here, in this personal capacity, that an individual can be warm, spontaneous, and touched by humour .... And so it is, that in showing that a given piece of conduct is part of the obligations and trappings of a role, one shifts it from the sacred category to the profane, from the fat and living to the thin and dead. (Goffman, 1961a, p. 152).

The use of the term 'deep' acting to describe when actors' feelings match outward demeanour, implies that it always takes hard emotion work to bring feeling and face together. In other words, the hard work that is entailed in 'deep' acting moves it into the public world of the 'formal, stiff, and dead'. Yet, quite often, when actors are comfortable with the situation or a particular event is merely a habitual ritual, it takes very little effort to shape feeling. Every social actor manages emotion but different situations require varying degrees of work. As Archer usefully suggests:

> Because of their situational and relational character as imports, our emotionality is regarded as a continuous running commentary (that is something we are never

without) and therefore it is only in sudden or urgent contexts that we are aware of a specific emotion. (Archer, 2000, p. 197)

An over-concentration on the occasions when 'deep' acting is required tends to leave little room for the acknowledgement of the importance of the 'sacred' part of the self. Those moments when actors are unaware of the rules which help them prepare the proper face; when preparation is hardly necessary as they are a mere fraction away from expressing their true feelings.[1]

Role analysis

Goffman's (1961a) concept of 'role analysis' is useful here. He offers a 'realist' account of role in that he proposes that the focus of study is not the individual but the individual carrying out a 'bundle of obligatory activity' within a system of social action (Goffman, 1961a, p. 86). Each role is recognised as having specific characteristics and there are certain expectations as to how the role will be enacted. As Goffman states, roles have particular qualities associated with them which 'provide a basis of self-image for the incumbent and a basis for the image that his role others will have of him' (Goffman, 1961a, p. 87). However, Goffman does not offer a portrayal of role incumbents who are passive followers of the dictates of 'role'. It is a basic assumption of Goffman's role analysis that each individual is a sort of 'holding company'. In Archer's terms, Goffman offers us a 'person of sufficient depth to monitor his appetites ... he also needs to be of sufficient breadth to execute his roles creatively' (Archer, 2000, p. 78). Social actors may be involved in more than one situated social system and will, therefore, have several selves and all the obligations of activity this entails. 'We do not take on items of conduct one at a time but rather a whole harness load of them and may anticipatorily learn to be a horse even while being pulled by a wagon' (Goffman, 1961a, p. 87). It is not, however, necessary for the individual to be attached to each and every one of their multiple roles. It is possible to enact some of the obligatory activity whilst feeling quite distant from the overall image of the role. As Goffman usefully states 'roles may not only be played but also played at' (Goffman, 1961a, p. 99).

Rather than defining the actor's performances as being either 'deep' or 'surface' acting, or describing the actor as being 'psychological present' or 'absent', the concept of 'role' allows a view of the actor as being 'present' at all times but to differing degrees and for varying reasons: 'While actively participating in an activity system, he is, nevertheless, also obliged to engage in other matters, in relationships, in multi-situated systems of activity, in sustaining norms of conduct that crosscut many particular activity systems' (Goffman, 1961a, p. 139). Such a concept acknowledges the extremes of 'deep' acting, in that it recognises how actors may 'embrace' a role, whilst also accepting that they may be emotionally detached from the role that is being performed. Goffman would refer to this 'surface acting' as 'role distance' and offers us an understanding that it is possible to maintain a distance from the 'virtual self' that is implied in the role (Goffman, 1961a and b).

This gives a more comprehensive understanding of what it is to carry out 'emotion work' – when actors must work on their emotion to either present a 'cynical' face (which differs from their 'real' feelings) or a 'sincere' face (when their feelings match face). Goffman's idea of 'embracing the role' (indicating acceptance of it) or 'role distance' (which can display 'disdainful detachment' from an allocated role) indicates that actors are capable of 'sustaining norms of conduct that crosscut many particular activity systems' (Goffman, 1961a, pp. 106, 110, 139). On the other hand, Hochschild presents emotionally inadequate actors who have either to give an empty performance and deceive others or become emotionally 'present' and deceive themselves. Granted, some occasions do require harder work than others and actors may not always be spontaneously 'sincere' or able to automatically present 'ceremonial behaviour' (Goffman, 1967). It can take extra effort to present a genuinely 'sincere' face by changing existing deviant feelings. This is when Hochschild's idea of working on emotion as a 'gift' can be useful: 'we may offer a tribute so generous that it actually transforms our mood and our thoughts to match what others would like to see' (Hochschild, 1983, p. 83).[2]

An acknowledgement of how actors can choose whether or not to embrace a role counters the grim portrayal of actors subjugating themselves to the feeling rules of an organisation. The concept of 'role' avoids the mistaken division between the public and the private selves; what Goffman (1961a) describes as the 'profane' and 'sacred' parts. It shows how people do not switch themselves on and off but glide from one performance of face-work to another, sometimes matching feeling and face with situation and at others merely maintaining face but at all times an element of self is present. In other words, whilst acknowledging the 'minor traffic rules' required for a particular role (Goffman, 1967), actors also (often unaware) follow feeling rules which guide them and inform them about when they should feel happy, sad or amused. These feeling rules are acquired during a lifetime's experience in how to 'codify, appraise, manage and express feeling' (Hochschild, 1990, p. 124) and are a part of their 'emotional culture'. Actors carry this knowledge with them, even when they 'embrace' a given role (thereby taking on new feeling rules) some of the old rules remain and have influence over their actions. Rarely can it be said, no matter the level of self-identification, that a person is wholly dedicated to one role in life. Goffman charmingly illustrates this:

> Perhaps there are times when an individual does march up and down like a wooden soldier, tightly rolled up in a particular role. It is true that here and there we can pounce on a moment when an individual sits fully astride a single role, head erect, eyes front, but the next moment the picture is shattered into many pieces and the individual divides into different persons holding the ties of different spheres of life by his hands, by his teeth, and by his grimaces. (Goffman, 1961a, p. 143)

When studying organisations it is necessary to recognise organisational actors as skilled emotion workers and, despite criticism of Goffman's descriptions of encounters existing in limited frameworks, his ideas help to further an understanding of the depth and scope of actors' performances. Goffman's emotion workers are highly flexible; they are able to carry out the performances required for an organisationally allocated role whilst also holding onto their own sense of identity. There may be occasions when various realities coerce actors into behaving in different ways than they otherwise might but just because actors learn to abide by organisationally prescribed rules 'we must not conflate the attempt with a successful outcome' (Archer, 2000, p. 218). If many essential elements of organisational life are not to be missed it would be a mistake to divide the private and the public worlds of emotion management and we should be wary of moving organisational actors from the 'fat and the living to the thin and the dead' (Goffman, 1961a, p. 152).

Conclusion and implications for an understanding of emotion in organisations

This chapter has so far established organisational actors as accomplished social actors and managers of emotion. It is argued that to understand what is occurring in organisational life it is necessary to draw on two sources of ideas and insight. First there is interactionist, though arguably with a realist slant, work such as Goffman's detailed accounts of social action. Second there is the labour process and a realist analysis of the service encounter. The latter demarcates the context within which the former is operative. But the interest of this combination is written in terms of the failure of the controllers of labour processes to reach inside and directly manipulate the emotions of their employees. They may prescribe allowed or preferred expressions of emotion but they do not control them. The realist account of emotion presented throughout this chapter suggests that social actors already control and regulate emotion as an important part of organisational life. In this way actors, as active and knowledgeable subjects, have been brought back into organisational analysis.

Thus, as a matter for theorising we require a way of integrating the structural determinants of the employment relationship derived from LPA with insights drawn from Goffman's insights into the interaction order. It is necessary to understand how – and to what extent – the structures that constitute a capitalist system act to shape, coerce and control employees as a means of extracting surplus value from their labour. It is also important to see that the extent of this will be limited by the variability of human character and the creative capacity of employees not only to conform to organisational rules, but also by their capacity to resist and re-shape the very rules which confine them. In an obvious sense, LPA is the basic framework within which action and activity systems are located. This is because such structures are logically prior to any given local activity system or framework of roles. However, as this chapter has argued, no labour process can determine the shape of organisational emotionality. At present the spaces that formal management would manage are already extensively managed by social actors themselves and the capacity of any newly formulated feeling rules to alter this are likely to be severely limited. Tracing out the contours of the struggle over the management of emotions, concern for the structural relations of production can therefore be usefully supplemented by an analysis of the intricacies of organisational action.

Clearly LPA is an essential vehicle for understanding the productive potential of actors' emotion management performances. The main concern of LPA lies with the capacity of the capitalist system to transform an individual's labour power into a commodity. Following on from this, their 'core theory' contains four elements: the capital–labour relation is the main focus of analysis; there is a logic of accumulation which constantly seeks to improve the production process; there is a control imperative and the employment relationship is based on contradictory elements of conflict and co-operation (Thompson, 1989, p. 244). However, such an analysis does not preclude recognition of the limits and peculiarities of the managerial regimes through which control has been exerted. The fact is that for significant periods of recent historical time managerial regimes have typically left out the control of employees' emotions. If they now wish to control this aspect of behaviour management faces the creative capacity of employees who operate within their own 'emotional cultures'.

It will be argued in later parts of this book that it is necessary to recognise the precise ways in which management attempts to extend control of emotions and emotionality at work if the likely outcomes of such projects are to be understood. By 'redrawing the boundaries of analysis' (Thompson, 1989) it is proposed that LPA should be used to theorise the context in which much emotional work takes place both in and outside the capitalist production process. Concern over political and economic factors, which are embedded in a capitalist society, situates the labour process into a wider framework which, in turn, helps to explain the changing nature of work over the past two decades. Unlike many other perspectives, the labour process understanding of the uneven power relations at work allows a theorisation of conflict in the workplace. In this way actors are not portrayed as cultural dopes, controlled by a system they know nothing of, but as knowledgeable agents who are able to consent, comply or resist and who also have the potential to collectively alter the balance of power. All of these factors are valuable analytical tools that can be usefully applied to both public and private sector organisations. However, as previously noted, LPA is strong on structure and weak on action and 'the "missing subject", or the absence of a theory of subjectivity informing the labour process debate, is a major problem' (Thompson, 1989, p. 249).

Previously in this chapter it was noted how Goffman usefully contributes to an understanding of how social actors use their emotion management skills in day-to-day encounters. He shows how, as members of society, actors learn to manage different situations with the use of the appropriate 'face-work'. Often, these learnt social skills become habitual and standardised practices and require very little effort on behalf of actors. Social actors are able to comply effortlessly with the 'rules' of each situation or what Goffman (1967) would call the 'minor traffic rules of interaction': 'it is the rules of the group and the definition of the situation which determine how much feeling one is to have for face and how this feeling is to be distributed among the faces involved' (Goffman, 1967, p. 6). However, unlike constructionism, the interactionist approach allows that these 'rules' are not somehow obligatory. Goffman offers us 'sentient-sensible' (Crossley, 1995) social actors who are able to modify and adjust the 'rules' depending on their own reading of the situation. In Goffman's writing actors are capable of being either 'sincere' or of presenting a 'face' in order to convince people that they are playing according to the 'rules' (Goffman, 1959).

It would be wrong, however, to suggest that the interactionist interpretation of work behaviour is all that is needed. If the foregoing analysis is correct, in both the private and the public sectors, management has an interest in extending control in new directions. This will inevitably intrude on areas in which, until recently, the individual conscience has reigned supreme. The problem for most interactionists is that the context of action is poised to 'bite back' in a way that their analysis is incapable of conceiving. They do not recognise any forces that may serve to coerce employees into behaving in ways other than they might wish. There is no recognition that new feeling rules might be constructed and imposed. So far it has been argued that Goffman is something of an exception to the interactionist rule in that he holds 'society to be first in every way' (Goffman, 1974, p. 13). He is very clear in his proposition that mechanisms such as day-to-day interaction are embedded in structures and are, indeed, structurally dependent, whilst remaining analytically independent. Whilst constantly referring to issues of hierarchy, status and power in the 'face-to-face' domain, he does not systematically explore the larger structures of social life. Nevertheless, his repeated allusion to two domains of analytically separable structure displays how this potential is waiting to be realised and Goffman successfully offers us the means to forge the link between the micro- and macro-worlds with his emphasis on both the power of the ties and the importance of the separation. He does this via his recognition of layers of reality that can be distinguished and analysed at different levels. Contrary to popular readings of Goffman, he does not offer us one level of reality – a 'depthless ontology' – but shows us how phenomena such as class, capitalism and patriarchy are manifested differently at each level because they are structured in different, often contradictory, level-specific ways (Brante, 2001). It appears, therefore, that labour process analysis and Goffman can more than complement each other.

This chapter argues for an approach to an understanding of emotion that is constrained and channelled by external forces. In particular there is a need for recognition of attempts by management to impose new feeling rules and re-draw the boundaries around arenas where employees have traditionally managed the expression of emotion in organisations. However, there is also a need to recognise employees' reactions to these attempts. The following chapter will attempt just such an understanding by examining in greater detail the performances, feeling rules and associated motivations which make up the emotional life of an organisation.

Notes

1. Social constructionists such as Harre (1986) would state that 'true' feelings are mere social constructs; if we feel spontaneous joy it is because we have been socially conditioned to respond in this manner at certain moments. However, whilst accepting that 'joy' can mean different things to different social groups, and be expressed in different ways, the concept of 'deep' acting appears to negate the opportunity of ever being spontaneously joyful.
2. See Chapters 5 and 7 for a more detailed analysis of emotion as a 'gift'.

5

Introducing a typology of workplace emotion

Introducing clarity

So far the book has set out the fundamentals of a general approach to the sociology of emotion in the workplace and offered a critical review of existing work concerning the emotional aspects of organisational life. In this and the next two chapters some detailed concepts are offered which, through effective application to a consideration of everyday life in contemporary organisations, will introduce an understanding of the variability of human conduct and the rich texture of people's working lives. This further develops the theory introduced in the previous chapter which utilises Goffman's insights into the creation, maintenance and presentation of self. This offers a portrayal of an active knowledge agent who is a skilled social actor and manager of emotion who operates within institutionalised boundaries and frameworks of action which can be both constraining and enabling. The following analysis also suggests that in portraying the organisational actor as a multi-skilled emotion manager the ideas presented in this chapter, and further explicated in Chapters 6 and 7, are more useful than many currently in use which offer a limited and lifeless portrayal of the world of work.

As a review of the literature in Chapter 3 and an examination of various perspectives on organisations in Chapter 2 reveals, the power and importance of the management of emotion in the workplace remains inadequately understood. An interest in the use of emotion in organisations continues to expand and yet it is as if in the rush to re-emotionalise organisations insufficient care has been taken when conceptualising emotion management in the workplace. Many commentators use (and equally often misuse or misapply) Hochschild's (1979, 1983) initial concepts of 'emotional labour' and 'emotion work' in what might be described as an 'emotional labour bandwagon'. Hochschild's work concerning the 'managed heart' is a seminal contribution that has opened up the debate on emotion in organisations in positive directions. However, whilst Hochschild's ideas are powerful, their applicability and usefulness is questionable. Her conception of organisational actors as managers of emotion is not without problems and is in need of elucidation and development. Hochschild clearly has distinctive ideas about the inability of individuals to evade what might be described as the colonisation of their mind by managerially designed feeling rules. For her there is a reality of external control because, beyond a certain point, the individual cannot sustain psychological distance from organisational feeling rules and their emotions become 'transmutated' by the capitalist labour process (Hochschild, 1983, p. 19).

In a similar vein a post-structuralists view portrays organisational actors as being passive objects of management's desires. The post-modern employee searches for a secure identity through work and is therefore open to management influence and the imposition of organisationally prescribed feeling rules. Unlike Hochschild's actors however, the post-modern employee does not have to go through a lengthy period of 'deep acting'. Their search for ontological security in an unstable world means that they quickly internalise the new feeling rules. Whether it be persuasive management discourse, seductive symbolism or technically and socially engineered panopticans, the employee is seduced into believing in corporate values and continually self-discipline themselves so that they present the prescribed 'face' with little emotion work required. As McKinlay and Starkey (1998, p. 11) state 'individuals lose themselves in regimes of power, but, paradoxically, they are created as subjects/other-selves by these same regimes'. This re-created subject has no other identity than that which the company has given her. Therefore there is little room for detachment from an organisation's feeling rules through the device of 'surface acting'. Arguably, the 'Foucauldian' feel that the term 'emotional labour' carries with it undervalues the vitality and independence of outlook that participants bring to organisations. It neglects their ability to carve out 'space for resistance and misbehaviour' (Thompson and Ackroyd, 1995) and to produce the 'unmanaged organization' (Gabriel, 1995).

It could be argued that at least post-structuralist accounts of the emotional organisation attempt to theorise agency, even if it becomes lost in the maelstrom of indefinable power networks. Whereas the functionalist perspective barely acknowledges the social actor at all – only in so far as they are organisational actors to be wholly influenced via various management prescriptions. Prescriptive management texts have barely changed over the last century in their belief in the leader's ability to 'define organisational reality' and confidence that aspiration will always match outcome – if it does not then it is to be accounted for in the pathology of individual workers who simply refuse to 'fit in' (Kotter, 1996; Senge, 1999). Though these writers often speak of 'emotional energies', the 'wow' and 'x' factors and the notion of 'happy' workers, this is set within a systems view of how these motivational factors can be integrated into the organisation structure (Deal and Kennedy, 1999; Peters, 1987, 1995). To the functionalists, organisational actors have no agency, they are robotic, hollow figures who are moulded and manipulated until they fit into the tidy box assigned to them. There is no place in their analysis for a skilled social actor who might actually resist management's manipulative practices.

And, of course, there is a whole body of work that displays a serious humanist concern for how emotion in organisations is, or should be, managed. New concepts and ideas are earnestly explored and the effects of management practices upon workers' well-being, customers' satisfaction and levels of production, are closely monitored (Ashforth and Humphrey, 1995; Kinnie et al., 2000; Peccei and Rosenthal, 1997; Rafaeli and Sutton, 1990). Whilst offering much more than the average pop management text, their analysis of the performance of emotion work and the day-to-day reality of organisational life barely moves out of the functionalist framework. Despite the well-meaning nature of these studies, their conception of human nature rests firmly within a behaviourist framework which ultimately assumes the worker to be a manageable resource.

The main purpose of the following chapters is to add to the current debates on organisational emotionality and offer a multidimensional approach which has the potential of bringing some clarification to the analysis of emotion in organisations. Unlike many current focuses on emotion in organisations, this analysis will be based on the conception of the organisational actor as a skilled social actor. Focusing upon what might be described as the 'emotional labour process' the book so far has suggested that labour process analysis (LPA) is able to make a vital contribution to an appreciation of the worker as an emotive subject. Combining LPA's interest in the structural relations of production with Goffman's ideas concerning 'the presentation of self' it is argued here that, although clearly there are forces shaping and channelling both emotions and expressions of emotionality, to a large degree, the individual actor retains a sense of him or herself as being in control of emotion.

Building on this social view of workplace emotionality, the next section of this chapter will introduce a typology which distinguishes four distinct types of emotion work/emotion management. Two of these, *pecuniary* emotion management and *presentational* emotion management , may be compared to Hochschild's (1979, 1983) terms 'emotional labour' and 'emotion work'. They denote the commercial use of emotion in organisations whilst recognising that the social actor brings the necessary skills into the organisation through a lifetime's training in 'the presentation of self'. On the other hand, it is also suggested that there are in fact two other types of emotion management: these will be designated *prescriptive* and *philanthropic* emotion management. Unlike Hochschild's term 'emotional labour', *prescriptive* emotion management allows a detailed analysis of public sector organisations, where an employee's emotion management may be closely prescribed but not necessarily for commercial gain. *Philanthropic* emotion management displays how an employee may not only follow organisational prescription but decide to give that 'little extra' during a social exchange in the workplace.

Taken as a whole the analysis suggests that it is helpful to distinguish four types of emotion management and that various combinations of the four types may be found within organisations. A typology such as this gives practical insights into the contemporary workplace. It shows that actors are able to draw on different sets of feeling rules according to context and their individual motivations to do so. This allows, where the use of the term 'emotional labour' does not, that it is not always the organisation which defines the emotional agenda.

A new agenda

Putting the subject back into organisational analysis acknowledges the emotional life of an organisation and its multifaceted nature. It is proposed that a recognition of four different types of emotion management in the workplace will help to deconstruct the complex subject of emotion in organisations. In order to affect varied performances the organisational actor must draw upon different sets of feeling rules of which the typology broadly distinguishes four classes: commercial, professional, organisational or social feeling rules (Table 5.1).

Of course, the use of the notion of 'rules' does not assume the existence of rule-bound behaviour. The concept of rules has frequently been used to analyse organisational life. From bureaucratic rules (Weber, 1947) to 'social regulative rules' (Clegg, 1981) there is the recognition that rules are not hard and fast 'social facts' but are the result of continual interpretation and negotiation which produces an ever-shifting framework for action (Salaman, 1983). Nevertheless, as Chapter 4 explores in some detail, feeling rules may be negotiated and changed and new feeling rules created by organisational actors but feeling rules also stand over and above them informing and shaping the emotional life of an organisation.

Table 5.1 A typology of workplace emotion

	Pecuniary	Prescriptive	Presentational	Philanthropic
Feeling rules	Commercial	Professional Organisational	Social	Social
Associated motivations	Instrumental	Altruism Status Instrumental	Ontological Security	Gift
Performance	Cynical Compliance	Cynical/sincere Consent/ commitment	Sincere/cynical Commitment/ consent	Sincere Commitment
Identity	Imposed/self	Professional/ self	Self	Self
Consequences	Alienation	Professional identity	Stability	Stability Satisfaction
	Contradiction Conflict Resistance	Contradiction		

In the context of the typology of workplace emotion offered here, the classification of feeling rules offers a multidimensional approach to the management of emotion and offers insights into the possible motivations behind various performances. A central feature of the typology is a recognition of what motivates organisational actors to enact feeling rules in distinct ways. These are motivations that are firmly embedded in social situations and relationships which, in turn, are wedded to broader frameworks of action that include an acknowledgement of institutionalised practices, hierarchical power relationships and social positioning. Frequently, when seeking to understand emotion and employees' performances of emotion management in organisations there is a sole concentration on the prevailing feeling rules, especially those imposed by the organisation. But without an attempt to understand the motivations that lie behind employees' performances only a 'depthless' picture of working life emerges. Because an employee acts out a prescribed performance, even appearing to offer a sincere presentation of self, unless the motivations attached to such a performance are also recognised it will always appear that the employee happily enacts organisationally imposed feeling rules and that management always knows best. Or worse, the employee colludes in their own exploitation and/or are fooled into believing themselves to be autonomous subjects (Fleming and Spicer, 2003; Hopfl, 2002; Willmott, 1993). This typology offers an alternative, more rounded, picture of organisational life and allows that there are a multitude of possible motivations behind each and every emotion management performance. It also allows that motivations are constantly emerging and changing through the process of interaction and, therefore, always have the capacity to transform it. Hence, a worker who successfully presents the organisationally prescribed demeanour may invest their performance with feeling or they may not according to a complex web of socially embedded motivations. As such, the type of feeling rules and associated motivations can be seen to impact upon the presentation of self, one's own sense of self and have consequences for the social world around us.

Pecuniary emotion management

If one were to perform *pecuniary* emotion management in the form of front-line customer service according to commercial feeling rules imposed by the organisation, then this would be instrumentally motivated – a matter of survival in the labour market and a capitalist economy that demands we are both producers and consumers. Commercial feeling rules and instrumental motivations can be most readily equated to the emotional labour process. As displayed by the typology, such externally imposed feeling rules can result in cynical performances. There is ample evidence to suggest that workers, though fully aware of the demands made upon them, detach themselves from the prescribed role. To dis-identify with a prescribed role and its associated feeling rules, however, does not mean that the role will not be enacted effectively. Many occupations requiring *pecuniary* emotion management demand routine compliance with display, rather than feeling, rules. Interaction with customers is so brief and the business at hand so tedious that investment in the performance is hardly necessary. A perfunctory politeness will fuel such brief interludes toward successful completion. Customers neither want nor expect to enter into the game of social interaction and front-line service workers answer telephone queries about bank balances whilst also thinking about calling in at the supermarket on the way home and they serve children their 'happy meals' with a smiling face but are all the while planning their own happy pursuits later in the day.

Where an investment of feeling is required, the instrumental motivations which lie behind service encounters are likely to lead to an alienating form of social interaction. A combination of aggressive marketing and the elevation of the consumer to a sovereign being raise customer expectations but the front-line service worker has limited scope to manage customer interaction. The demands of the market mean that the achievement of quantifiable targets is a priority. The meeting of predetermined standards of customer service receives enthusiastic rhetorical endorsement but not much material investment – displayed in the way service providers are barley rewarded above the minimum wage. In demanding an investment of feeling into customer service, without the recognition that it requires a careful balancing act of everyday social interaction, management preclude the opportunity for a mutual exchange. The customer gets irritated, the worker gets frustrated and a 'cycle of unease' occurs (Goffman, 1967). The front-line service worker does not have the autonomy (or the will?) to rectify the disturbed and disturbing act of customer service which, in turn, tends to breed contradiction and resistance in the emotional labour process.

In situations such as these, working at a cynical distance can actually take the form of 'micro-emancipation' (Sotirin and Gottfried, 1999). Or, just as frequently, workers re-interpret relatively rigidly prescribed feeling rules and re-shape the form of interaction that takes place. For instance, Leidner's (1996) fast-food workers use scripted interaction as a shield against any form of emotional involvement with customers, whereas Callaghan and Thompson's (2002) tele-sales agents empathise with the needs of many customers and complex motivations lay behind their performances. Either way, by maintaining some form of control over the emotional labour process, workers can preserve a sense of dignity and self-esteem. Indeed a sense of self.

Prescriptive emotion management

On the other hand, forms of *prescriptive* emotion management contain many of the instrumental motivations of *pecuniary* emotion management but has the potential to be far more complex. If the feeling rules are dictated via membership in a professional body then motivation is rarely purely instrumental but connected to ideas of social status. One may enjoy the status of the title of doctor or lawyer and the social recognition and benefits this brings, thus a great deal of emotional investment will go into living up to the requirements of professional roles and their associated idealised images. One may also be genuinely motivated to care for or serve people in a public service profession thus indicating the possibility of multiple, even contradictory, motivations. Professionals have often to balance the feeling rules of their profession against the instrumental demands of public policy, or the dictates of the public bureaucracy which offers them employment. This, of course, has further impact upon the types of performances to be expected. It would seem that there is far more likelihood of a sincere performance of *prescriptive* emotion management resulting from professional feeling rules with altruistic or status motivations than the instrumentally motivated feelings rules of *pecuniary* emotion management. Though this cannot be counted on to be a straightforward process as various motivations may come into conflict. Battles to maintain status overcome the 'caring' motivations of many professionals and we often hear of 'crooked' accountants, abusive nurses and profiteering doctors (Lee-Treweek, 1997; Lipsky, 1980; Strauss, 1975).

Prescriptive emotion management does not only apply to the professions. Long service with one particular employer means that certain feeling rules become taken for granted prompters of action – they are adhered to with little or no thought. It is simply the way 'we do things around here'. Recent reports highlight the aggressive culture embedded in the city of London investment banking sector (Guardian, 2001). Practical jokes, a manic level of humour and frenetic activity, seemingly informal, is actively encouraged by management as a means of maintaining a 'high-energy' working environment and is seen as the norm to those who have spent most of their working lives in this, or similar, sectors – it should be noted that these institutions are dominated by the white, middle class, British born male. For those who do not fit this model, or who are newly appointed, the feeling rules appear alien, and in many cases oppressive, even frightening. Some will adjust. Many do not. Different companies have different characters and often a decision to join or leave a company is based less on the job description and more on how the organisational feeling rules are perceived. For instance, is it a formal milieu, with a rigid dress code and formal modes of interaction, that is, 'morning Mr P.', rather than 'hi there, Pete'? Do employees socialise in and out of work? Is it a place that values diversity or does it appear to have a particular mono-culture as some of the traditional British financial institutions mentioned earlier?

Much of contemporary management literature has been concerned with the design and implementation of organisationally prescribed feeling rules – now commonly referred to as corporate culture (Deal and Kennedy, 1999; Peters and Waterman, 1982; Peters, 1994). The abiding hope of management is that feeling rules can be gently imposed via various integrating mechanisms such as team-working, quality initiatives and collective mission statements so that employees will internalise company values. In these cases the desired objective is that organisationally prescribed feeling rules become the automatic norm and this is often described by critical writers as the ultimate form of control as employees can no longer think or feel for themselves. There is, however, ample evidence to suggest that employees react to prescribed feeling rules in a myriad of ways. Some obviously enjoy the close community and sense of belonging created by a carefully crafted corporate culture and feel a genuine sense of involvement in organisational life on company terms. Others appear to enthusiastically perform *prescriptive* emotion management but are materialistically motivated, with their eye on a promotion, bonus or new company car. Yet others maintain a distance from such forcefully applied feeling rules offering cynical performances, just enough to 'get by' and survive organisational life and at the same time escaping into pockets of activity where particular forms of social, rather than organisational, feeling rules would apply.

Presentational and *philanthropic* emotion management

Presentational and *philanthropic* emotion management rely on social feelings rules and all of the complex motivations associated with this. Together, these forms of emotion management are derived from the notion of the mainte-nance of the 'interaction order' involving a moral commitment to maintain rituals of deference and demeanour which offer a sense of stability and onto-logical security to participants. This sense of stability might be created through the formation of sub-cultures, cliques, or informal work groups where workers can establish new, or fit in with existing, ways of being in the organisation. Though seemingly informal, with much of the activity occurring in these 'spaces' taking shape as 'misbehaviour', socially motivated feeling rules form a large part of organisational life in many cases becoming an institution-alised characteristic. Nurses congregating in the toilet for a sneaky cigarette and to exchange words of comfort (Bolton, 2002); game playing on the shop floor to relieve the monotony of a Fordist regime (Roy, 1973; Burawoy, 1979); petty pilfering according to strict, though invisible, rules (Ditton, 1977) and tele-sales agents gathering round the coffee-machine to let off steam (Korcynski, 2002) all indicate significant amounts of emotion work taking place which, though prompted by the rigours of organisational life, is carried out according to social feeling rules. And, just as in everyday life, not all of this emotion work is invested in maintaining the 'ceremonial order' of interaction. Often game-playing activity in organisations is less of a game and more of a cruel test of endurance of new-comers or perceived 'outsiders'. How many times do we hear discriminatory remarks described as 'only joking' or cases of sexual harassment dismissed as a 'bit of a laugh'?

Nevertheless, many emotion management performances in organisations according to social feelings rules do offer succour to colleagues or even kind-ness to customers. The case of *philanthropic* emotion management shows how it is possible to offer that little extra – an unusual effort at carrying out emo-tion work that may be described as a 'gift' (Hochschild, 1983; Titmus, 1970). Hochschild (1989b) illustrates how vital this concept is for social life in her description of it as an 'economy of gratitude', indicating that the giving and receiving of *philanthropic* emotion management helps to maintain or restore a sense of stability and even one's sense of self, not to mention establishing a precedent of reciprocity.

A tidy typology?

Looking at the table it can be seen how it is possible for all forms of emotion management to be performed by organisational actors for a wide variety of reasons: legitimacy, conformity, economic and empathy. Also according to differing rules: organisational regulations, professional norms and social guidelines. The following examples show how organisational actors appear to effortlessly move from one performance to another. During a social encounter within the workplace they may well perform *presentational* emotion management. Whilst dealing with a client or colleague they are capable of deciding whether to offer *philanthropic* emotion management as an extra 'gift'. Employees' training and socialisation as organisation members or as part of a professional body dictate when to perform *prescriptive* emotion management. Finally, in direct face-to-face contact with a customer of the company they may be expected to perform *pecuniary* emotion management as a means of producing 'customer contentment'.

The typology of emotion management displays how boundaries are continually being crossed. It is never a case of categorising organisational actors as performing only one form of emotion management or belonging to formal or informal aspects of organisational life. Feeling rules and motivations bleed into one another ensuring that organisational life can never fit into a tidy typology and this is certainly not the intention here. Indeed, the very function of an organisation ensures that huge amounts of organisation and management effort is invested in ensuring that emotion in the workplace is either channelled in order to meet the organisations aims and objectives or excluded as an interference in goal-oriented activity. As Van Maanen and Kunda usefully point out: 'organizational life is structured to channel, mold, enhance, sustain, challenge, and otherwise influence the feeling of organizational members – toward the organization itself, others in the organization, customers of the organization, and, crucially, themselves' (Van Maanen and Kunda, 1989, p. 43). Nevertheless, the purpose of this typology is to show in fine detail how actors, whilst constrained by organisational structures, are still capable of possessing 'multiple selves' (Goffman, 1967). It shows how they are able to draw on different sets of feeling rules and sources of motivation in order to match feeling with situation or merely to maintain face. This, however, is not to suggest that the multi-skilled emotion manager is a mere performer on the organisation stage. As seen in Chapter 4, the skilled social actor is more than capable of calibrating their performances and judging how much feeling there should be behind the face. From this it can be seen just how skilled organisational actors are when considering how they balance conflicting demands and are still able to effect polished performances.

Moving on from the 'Managed Heart'

The recognition of four types of emotion management makes it clear that emotion within organisations cannot be simplified and condensed into one category. As a consequence the conceptual ideas presented in this chapter differ markedly from the well-established topic of Hochschild's 'emotional labour'. Because Hochschild's (1979, 1983) work has been so seminal, it will be helpful to reiterate her basic ideas which are dealt with in detail in Chapter 3, as a means of further highlighting the conceptual framework presented here.

Her initial concepts distinguish between 'emotional labour' and 'emotion work'. Their importance – and much of their elemental power – derives from the contrast that they establish between the incursion of management into the area of emotion (emotional labour) and the pre-existing ability of employees to control themselves (emotion work). Hochschild, therefore, contributes a fundamental insight into the conflict of commercial and social feeling rules that explains much of the tension concerning the expression of emotion in the contemporary workplace. The most important idea is that actors already have considerable capacity to manage their emotions and that such capacities derive from basic socialisation.

The distinction Hochschild makes between 'commercial' and 'social' feeling rules and the motivations of the individual to control emotions are indeed valuable. However, there is insufficient recognition of the variety of possibilities. She does not make any distinction concerning feeling rules in the workplace that are not commercially motivated. It is now widely recognised that commercial feeling rules are produced and imposed by managers. As a novel development in management strategy this needs to be seen as an extension of the control processes involved in the commercial labour process. Nevertheless, the prescription of feeling rules in the workplace is by no means novel or distinctive in other ways. It is common for employees to undergo secondary socialisation where they become involved with and committed to a distinct set of feeling rules. Examples would be the feeling rules that inform professional codes of conduct in occupations such as nursing, where it becomes necessary to distinguish professional codes of conduct from commercial feeling rules that New Public Sector Management (NPM) now wish to impose.

Therefore, as well as the possibility that new commercial feeling rules might be in tension with pre-existing social motivations, it is also the case that they may be in tension with other externally imposed prescriptive norms that are regarded as being more legitimate. It is argued here that in addition to Hochschild's notion of commercial emotion management the possibility of other prescriptive bases for emotion management must also be considered. In general it is perhaps most useful to distinguish externally imposed rules of conduct that have been developed mainly out of commercial motivations, identified here as *pecuniary* emotion management, from other kinds of *prescriptive* emotion management.

In addition to making these clear distinctions concerning workplace emotionality, the basic social regulation of emotional expression and its relationship with work is also more clearly explicated. As we have seen here, Hochschild's basic concept is 'emotion work'. This she thinks of mainly in terms of the sharp contrast it can offer with motivations in the commercial sphere. However, she also uses the term to indicate that social actors are able to calibrate how much effort they invest in their emotion management performances depending on what they believe is 'emotionally due' to another person.

Unfortunately the use of the term 'work' tends to imply that all emotion management performances in the social realm take conscious effort. The perceived capacity that the individual has to exert special efforts in the management and presentation of emotion is an important special case in the management of emotion and, in this account, the notion of *philanthropic* emotion management has been retained to take account of it.[1] But the philanthropic attitude is not the typical outlook of individuals in the regulation of their conduct. As explored in the last chapter, primary socialisation is effective enough that social actors enact many social encounters routinely. Actively working on emotion should be distinguished from the framework of assumptions that are usually operative. Goffman (1959) would call the routine compliance with social feeling rules the 'presentation of self' and it is suggested here that actors' abilities in presenting socially desirable performances are better thought about in terms of *presentational* emotion management, with *philanthropic* emotion management being distinguished as a special case.

Using a typology that recognises four types of emotion management performances as an alternative to Hochschild's term 'emotional labour' has major implications. It recognises that only a small proportion of feeling rules and associated motivations come under the 'sway of large organizations' and are governed by a corporation's profit motive. This allows practical insights into contemporary organisational life that other conceptual approaches do not. For instance, it shows that organisational demands for *pecuniary* emotion management do not negate employees' individual subjectivities. Actors continually seek spaces in organisations where they can be their 'authentic' selves and perform *presentational* or *philanthropic* emotion management according to the social rules with which they are so familiar. The acceptance of the view of organisational actors as active, knowledgeable agents indicates just how tenacious primary socialisation is and how resistant actors are to organisational demands that they must 'buy in' to organisational values. Organisational actors are able to achieve convincing performances through their compliance with commercial feeling rules. Nevertheless, these perform-ances are materialistically motivated; they tend to be empty of feeling and, as such, are relatively impotent as a means of mapping new identities onto work-ers. There are some occupations, however, where actors are not only finan-cially motivated but abide by professional feeling rules due to status or altruistic motivations. These actors attain a new dimension to their identity; they give sincere performances and become committed to the feeling rules of a profession.

The 'Juggler and Synthesiser'

The four types of emotion management introduced in this chapter (*prescrip-tive, pecuniary, presentational* and *philanthropic*) can be used to highlight the blurring of boundaries, the blending of different roles and the contradictions this can bring into people's lives. For instance, when does workplace humour stop acting in the interests of organisational efficiency (Fine, 1988) and begin to be seen as a means of challenging the 'status quo' (Collinson, 1992)? When do a nurse's personal feeling rules interfere with the carrying out of *prescrip-tive* or *pecuniary* emotion management according to the dictates of New Public Sector Management (NPM) (Bolton, 2002)? When does the plastered on smile of a front-line service worker indicate emotional absence (Kahn, 1992)? And when do tele-sales agents' kindly ministrations to 'needy' cus-tomers interfere with the achievement of quantifiable targets (Callaghan and Thompson, 2002; Wray-Bliss, 2001)? Mills and Murgatroyd would describe such situations as 'moments of truth'. When actors question organisational rules those rules then become contested and 'conflict (becomes) as much a part of the game of organizational life as is institutionalization and stability' (Mills and Murgatroyd, 1991, p. 170). The possibility of such contradiction emphasises how there can never be a black and white, clean-cut divide between emotion management carried out in the private sphere of actors' lives and the emotion management that is performed within organisations. Why can the telesales agent not offer *philanthropic* emotion management and still do a proficient job—even if it is not according to management prescription? Or, as we have seen with the previous discussion of cynicism, service providers can 'absent' themselves from organisationally prescribed roles and still fulfil their work obligations.

These examples display how 'unmanaged spaces' remain available in organisations for 'moments of truth' to occur. Such spaces can take individualised or collective forms, may be temporally or spatially segregated, or may be almost wholly integrated into the moment-by-moment conduct of work. For instance, in some organisations so-called informal spaces can actually dominate the organisation of work. As in the case of the slaughtermen who have their own distinct (and it must be added effective) ways of doing things so that management became mere observers rather than controllers of the labour process (Ackroyd and Crowdy, 1992). In this way, the informal occupational culture of the slaughtermen becomes the formal organisation of work – motivations, boundaries and feeling rules are all blurred beyond the scope of categorisation. And, of course, this is often the aim of many intensive corporate culture programmes that seek to ensure that the employee wants what the organisation wants. In other cases, and even within the strongest of corporate cultures, spaces may only be fleeting moments where workers have an opportunity to express their disdain for organisational prescription, this is often done with the use of ironic humour, expressed both verbally and physically (Ackroyd and Thompson, 1999; Bolton, 2004b). A put down comment, a secret smile – these are small, but important, moments. They have negotiative potential offering important intervals in organisational control for the maintenance of workers' identities.

Examining both feeling rules and their motivations introduces the useful concept of contradiction which, in turn, highlights how the provision of distinct categories within the typology do not suggest that only one form of emotion management may be performed by organisational actors at any one time. This would be to duplicate the error of those who describe a solid divide between the public and private (Hochschild, 1983, 1989b; Van Maanen and Kunda, 1989). Rather, the typology should be used to display how there are 'multi-situated systems of activity'. Organisational actors may apparently comply with an organisation's 'rules' whilst performing *prescriptive* or *pecuniary* emotion management but they are not wholly defined by the official definition of the situation (Goffman, 1961a). For instance, a nurse may genuinely empathise with a patient rather than present the face of a detached personal carer within the service-provider/customer relationship (James, 1989, 1992, 1993). A debt collector may show a more sympathetic face to a client rather than the prescribed aggressive one (Sutton, 1991) and an air-stewardess may retain some autonomy in how she/he provides customer contentment and gains satisfaction from providing that 'little extra' (Bolton and Boyd, 2003; Hochschild, 1983; Tyler and Taylor, 1998). These organisational actors perform *presentational* and *philanthropic* emotion management in addition to *prescriptive* or *pecuniary*. This is not to say their private feelings have been 'transmutated'. Rather it is the case that their skills are so fine-tuned they are capable of mixing and managing all forms of emotion management according to 'rules' other than those solely controlled by the organisation. The way the nurse and the debt collector are able to re-define the situation through their emotion management skills highlight how 'action logics' are being mixed (Flam, 1990a). It is possible for organisational actors to have 'multiple identities' (Goffman, 1961a; Gerth and Mills, 1954; Mills and Murgatroyd, 1991). As Goffman states:

> The image that emerges of the individual is that of a juggler and synthesizer, an accommodater and appeaser, who fulfils one function while he is apparently engaged in another; he stands guard at the door of the tent but lets all his friends and relatives crawl in under the flap. (Goffman, 1961a, p.139)

Conclusion and implications for an understanding of emotion in organisations

For many, the nature of work has dramatically changed in the contemporary organisation. It becomes increasingly difficult to theorise such changes using existing theoretical perspectives which are tuned into a different industrial era and using descriptive terms (such as 'emotional labour') which take to extreme the notion of capitalism's appropriation of a worker's soul. What is needed is a sociology of workplace emotion that recognises both the structural constraints of the capitalist labour process and also social actors as knowledgeable agents. As previously mentioned in Chapters 3 and 4, a theoretical partnership – labour process analysis and Goffman – have been brought together in order to offer just such a sociology of emotion suitable for the contemporary workplace. LPA firmly places organisational actors within a capitalist system and displays how political and economic constraints act to shape action. Goffman presents a detailed examination of socially skilled actors and shows how they can be 'jugglers and synthesisers' and fulfil many roles.

Building upon these basic theoretical assumptions, the typology offered here acts as a more meaningful way of understanding organisational emotionality. The four categories contained in the typology – *presentational*, *philanthropic, prescriptive, pecuniary* – offer the possibility of creating a portrait of the multifaceted nature of organisational life. The aim is to display the different 'action logics' present in an organisation and how it is not always management 'logic' which defines the situation. There are many variables that will affect how emotion is managed within an organisation and, in turn, affect how the four types of emotion management can be applied. It is through the recognition of variables such as the nature of work and type of clientele, professional status, length of service to the organisation and personal life histories, that it can be seen how the performance of emotion management within organisations is the result of many intersecting influences. The types of emotion management used are dependent upon these variables. Some occupations using only two types where others, such as professional 'carers' who work in the increasingly marketised public services, may use all four types in any one working day.

It can be seen from the preceding discussion that each type of emotion management included in the typology has distinct characteristics. The most obvious differences are the associated motivations and the amount of available opportunity between the social and rational demands of organisational life for 'spaces' to emerge. However, one similarity between all four types is the requirement for organisational actors to enact skilled performances, continually adjusting how much 'emotion work' or 'face work' is necessary according to the rules of the particular situation. As Goffman highlights: 'Thus rules of conduct transform both action and inaction into expression, and whether the individual abides by the rules or breaks them, something significant is likely to be communicated' (Goffman, 1967, p. 51).

It is this 'significant something' the typology introduced here aims to capture. Examples of skilled emotion management performances, such as those given by the hairdresser, the debt-collector, the air-stewardess or the nurse leads to the realisation that although 'human agency is bounded' there are limits to the success of organisational efforts to control employees' emotions. Contrary to some commentators, it is not solely management who control the emotional life of an organisation. The typology of workplace emotion recognises that organisational life cannot be treated as a homogenous entity. Employees have diverse, varied and multiple ways of enacting an organisation's rules and the difficulty lies in attempting to unravel the meanings behind their actions. Such a typology does not imply a 'sovereign subjectivity which can take off on its Quixotic adventures with no regard for the power practices of organizations' (Gabriel, 1995, p. 498). It does, however, acknowledge that an organisation's rules are constantly re-contested and re-negotiated through the actions of its members. And in doing so, such an analysis can contribute to broader debates concerning agency and organisational control and transcend 'border skirmishes' involved in the understanding of emotion in organisations.

Actors bring personal baggage when they enter an organisation. A sense of self who has hopes, dreams and aspirations that cannot be completely over-written by the disciplining demands of the organisation and the project for the researcher should be an attempt to uncover these realities. Introducing conceptual clarity will prove particularly useful as a means of highlighting an organisation's increasing use of employees' emotion management skills for commercial purposes and how *pecuniary* emotion management can vary considerably from *prescriptive* emotion management; especially in the British public services. Something which will be explored in more detail in Chapter 6. A new conceptual tool, such as the typology of emotion management introduced in this chapter, allows the different dynamics involved in the management of organisational emotion to be better understood.

The remainder of the book will explore in more detail the four sets of feeling rules introduced as part of the typology of workplace emotionality. First the commercial, professional and organisational feeling rules which organisations attempt to impose to engender *pecuniary* and *prescriptive* emotion management performances. Second, those implicit social feeling rules that result in *presentational* and *philanthropic* emotion management and serve to form an employees' enduring identity. In this way insights are given into the motivations and, therefore, the limitations of certain feeling rules to control employees' emotion management performances.

Note

1. The category of 'philanthropic' emotion management borrows directly from Hochschild's (1979) ideas concerning the concept of working on one's emotion as a 'gift' in order to present the 'correct' face to another in social exchange. However, it differs greatly in that Hochschild does not allow this to be part of organisational life, believing that the 'gift' of emotion management belongs solely in the 'private realm of feeling'.

6

Prescriptive and *pecuniary* emotion management

Commercial, professional or organisational feeling rules?

As the typology presented in the previous chapter shows, there are broadly four classifications of feeling rules which may be identified in organisations. When considering the area of organisational life that focuses on goal-orientated activity then commercial, professional and organisational feeling rules come into play. These are at their most obvious where certain attributes and even ways of being are attached to particular organisational 'roles' and there are 'official expectations as to what the participant owes the establishment' (Goffman, 1961b, p. 267). This tends to conjure up images of explicit job description but feeling rules attached to organisational roles encompass much more than that. The implicit nature of many organisational feeling rules show how an essential part of the complex mix of rules, roles and obligations are assumptions about the character of the employee and a tacit understanding that the employee has the capacity to discharge organisational demands in particular ways. Of course, the definitional power of these feelings rules vary depending on the motivations that lie behind compliance with them and, as will be shown throughout this chapter, these motivations can vary greatly between organisational, commercial and professional feelings rules.

Actors are able to successfully comply with organisational prescription and hence fulfil their given organisational roles by performing *prescriptive* and *pecuniary* emotion management. As the typology of workplace emotion shows, though both *pecuniary* and *prescriptive* emotion management are seen to fulfil organisational demands this can be achieved in different ways. Goffman distinguishes between a sense of commitment to certain obligations where they may be enacted efficiently but with little sense of allegiance to the organisation or they may be enacted with enthusiasm displaying a sense of attachment. Thus the social actor will find her/himself 'with obligations: some will be cold, entailing alternatives forgone, work to be done, service rendered, time put in, or money paid; some will be warm, requiring *him* to feel belongingness, identification, and emotional attachment' (Goffman, 1961b, p. 159).

This commitment and attachment may be understood in terms of *pecuniary* or *prescriptive* emotion management. *Pecuniary* emotion management can be most readily equated with Goffman's ideas concerning 'obligations', indicating a cynical distance and emotion management performances absent of feeling. It is interesting to note how often Goffman refers to actors distancing themselves from organisationally prescribed roles or how he suggests that it is not only possible, but very probable, that employees will absent themselves from externally imposed feeling rules which, as the typology introduced in the last chapter suggests, is closely related to the expected consequences of the performances of *pecuniary* emotion management. Whereas *prescriptive* emotion management may entail 'obligations' but, due to its different motivations, may also indicate 'identification' creating sincere performances and a sense of involvement with an organisation or professional body. Employees may embrace the role and offer both commitment and attachment to the demands made by the organisation. In effect they immerse themselves into a prescribed role taking on a new identity (Goffman, 1961a, p. 87). However, rarely does an organisational actor simply embrace or distance themselves from either set of feeling rules. For instance, whilst embracing some professional feeling rules, public sector caring professional groups may distance themselves from some organisational rules and continually attempt to evade commercial feeling rules. Yet others may be purely materially motivated and comply with commercial feeling rules but never really 'fit in' and embrace the organisationally prescribed feeling rules. There are many variations on this theme, highlighting the complexity of working life and the convoluted network of motivations that fuels the emotional life of an organisation.

The rest of the analysis in this chapter will explore the peculiarities of the three types of feeling rules, organisational, commercial and professional that lie behind the performances of *prescriptive* and *pecuniary* emotion management within the framework of contemporary debates and issues in organisational life, such as the growing army of front-line service workers and the commercialisation of public services. In this way the motivations, enactment and consequences of these differing modes of the presentation of self can be explored within the confines of organisational prescribed feeling rules, especially the differences between those that may be purely instrumentally motivated and those that have social status or altruistic dimensions attached to them.

Organisational feeling rules

Being a member of an organisation

Many organisationally prescribed feeling rules are much more implicit than those professional or commercial feeling rules found to be attached to specific roles, though no less demanding of certain characteristics of the employee or less influential upon the employee's character. Each organisation has different expectations of employees' conduct and organisational feeling rules provide a constant set of expectations as to how the employee, as well as others, should act. Feeling rules are but one dimension of organisational life; one of a combination of many rules at play at any one time. There are policies, hierarchies, contracts, divisions of labour and status positions but feeling rules impact upon all of these arrangements affecting how even the most rigid of organisational rules will be enacted. Even in places that may be classed as informal areas of organisational life, such as the staff canteen, or organised 'outings', implicit feeling rules encourage stable modes of conduct.

Of course, hardly any employee will know all the organisational rules, the situations to which they apply or whom. Some rules are ignored, some forgotten, some never called upon and many are so implicit as to be hardly recognised as rules at all. As Strauss notes, 'areas of action covered by clearly enunciated rules is therefore really very small' (Strauss, 1975, p. 201). It is less a matter of concrete rules than shared understandings which provide stable prompters of action as the rules, however implicit, provide a set of symbols which people draw upon in a sense-making process (Blumer, 1969). Organisational feeling rules act as a script. Like all scripts they offer interpretive schemes, resources and norms that enable a course to be steered through a particular social world. That is, it offers a clear path that can be followed. The language becomes familiar, there are certain norms of conduct associated with certain occupations or social groups and certain expectations that one knows one must fulfil. In this way the individual can not only plan their path but feel a sense of belonging as they take on the identity of a certain occupation or organisation.

Through this progression employees discover how to be an active member of the organisation. Chicago sociologists speak of this as a combined process involving the objective notion of institutionalised practice and the 'concrete' elements of organisation structure shared with organisational actors' interpretations of these structures. Involvement in an organisation consists of a series of 'status passages' – that is those ritual occasions when an individual's being is publicly transformed in the eyes of a particular culture (Strauss, 1970). A status passage not only connotes a temporally staged shift from one social role to another but also a fundamental change in an individual's identity, an alteration in the person's conceptions of self. The social actor learns to live up to the organisation's expectations about their character, not just their enactment of a formally prescribed role but also their presentation of what is assumed to be their 'true' self. Goffman successfully fuses the objective and subjective elements of this process in his following statement: 'Built right into the social arrangements of an organization, then, is a thoroughly embracing conception of the member – and not merely a conception of him qua member, but behind this a conception of him qua human being' (Goffman, 1961b, p. 164).

The interpretive shift that attends the transition into a new organisation involves more than simply 'learning the ropes' it also entails appropriation of what C. Wright Mills calls a 'vocabulary of motive'. This is a language, a libretto, typical of the occupants of a specific status, occupation, profession or organisation. This is how different groups will view the same situation differently, but very much the same within the group. The transition however takes time and human interaction and Strauss usefully summarises this:

> Passage from one (status) to another involves not only changes of action and demeanour, but of the verbalised reasons that are associated with them. Indeed the stability of a given social structure rests largely upon a preparation of these sequential steps. Motivations appropriate to earlier status must be sloughed off and transmuted, and new ones added or substituted … At any step of this complicated drama of progression, things will go awry if the actors lag behind or speed up unduly in their action or rationale. (Strauss, 1970, p. 73)

It is precisely because the enactment of organisational feeling rules is such a 'complicated drama' that they can never be classed as universal prescriptions. As the next chapter will show, employees become adept at evading the various forms of organisationally imposed feeling rules and create 'spaces' where they may escape. Rules are interpreted, negotiated and stretched. This may amount to forms of misbehaviour but just as often are related to a genuine desire to get the job done in the best possible way (Zimmerman, 1971). In fact, concerns about overly rule-bound behaviour in the form of the 'bureaucratic personality' (Crozier, 1964) have ensured that some interpretation of organisational feeling rules is to be expected, if not welcomed.

Recent management prescription encourages loosely defined rules, relying on a more holistic approach in the form of corporate culture where there are no feeling rules, only internalised and thus barely recognised guides to action. The assumption being that employees will embrace organisationally defined ways of being, enacting *prescriptive* and *pecuniary* emotion management with enthusiasm and offering sincere performances. It would seem that it is not only impression rules that are being bureaucratised, but companies are attempting to also bureaucratise the spirit (Goffman, 1959). Recent prescriptive management literature shows how there now appears to be a more complicated management agenda. Organisations have much higher aspirations where the workforce is concerned. Organisations now call for employees to love the company, to love the product and to feel motivated through their empowerment in the workplace. With increasing competition in 'this marketing of bonhomie' (Parkinson, 1991) the perspicacious customer expects to be satisfied and is liable to 'pounce on trifling flaws as a sign that the whole show is false' (Goffman, 1959, p. 235). Organisations require their employees to do more than 'surface act'; they want them to invest their performances with feeling, becoming 'sincerely convinced that the impression of reality which he (she) stages is the real reality' (Goffman, 1959, p. 28).

The organisation will find it much easier to involve employees in 'sincere performances' if they set out, when recruiting, to select the ones whose 'human nature' is pre-disposed toward organisational values. Huge amounts of resources are invested into selecting employees who fit person, rather than job, specifications. If people with the 'right attitude' are brought into the organisation it is thought that the process of 'learning the ropes' will be a much more complete and less painful process, thus ensuring that any interpretation of organisational rules will remain within the organisational framework for action. For instance, Parkinson (1991) found when researching hairdressing work that those who are successful in jobs which call for large amounts of personal contact already possess the necessary interpersonal skills which can be put to work in the service encounter. Grey (1994) notes that accountants recruit only in their own image – white, male, middle-class – thus excluding the possibility of discord with professional norms. Townley (1994) believes the intensive processes of selection ensure the employee becomes objectified and therefore, more amenable to manipulation and normative control. And Callaghan and Thompson (2002) note that there are certain prerequisites expected of tele-sales agents. In all of these scenarios it is assumed that through careful recruitment and selection processes, the way in which employees enact their organisational role corresponds closely to how they would deal with situations outside of the work context.

In addition to the organisation attempting to carry out a process of 'natural selection', upon entering the organisation, actors undergo a process of socialisation. As already mentioned, many companies now go to great lengths to inculcate employees into the values of the company. They foster both formal and informal practices,[1] thereby ensuring that organisational actors fully 'embrace' their work role. It is hoped the natural self will be moulded into the organisational self, with organisational rules becoming implicit prompters of action rather than explicit prescriptive guides to action. Goffman portrays the company's ideal when he describes how a role may be fully embraced: 'To embrace a role is to disappear completely into the virtual self available in the situation, to be fully seen in terms of the image, and to confirm expressively one's acceptance of it. To embrace a role is to be embraced by it' (Goffman, 1961a, p. 106).

Just how successful these training and socialisation practices are remains a matter for continued conjecture and debate (Collinson, 1992; Rose, 1990; Thompson and Ackroyd, 1995; Thompson and Findlay, 1996; Willmott, 1993). Far from internalising company values employees provide a 'cynical' performance: 'they smile less broadly, with a quick release and no sparkle in their eyes, thus dimming the company's message to the people. It is a war of smiles' (Hochschild, 1983, p. 127). The danger in any discussion concerning rules and organisational control mechanisms is the assumption that a standardised product will be the result. Yet, when organisational life is examined, a constant reminder is found that daily interactions between organisational actors or during face-to-face interaction with 'customers' of the company are not based on a mute consensus. Each actor interprets situations differently and reacts in a variety of ways. The re-interpretation of rules by individuals inevitably leads to differences of opinion and the possibility of conflict arises. This leads back to the realisation that *presentational* emotion management prepares actors for the performance of *pecuniary* or *prescriptive* emotion management. This gives organisational actors the ability to mix and match feeling rules according to the needs of the situation whilst also allowing them to create 'spaces' into which they may 'escape'. The perceived need to escape will ultimately depend upon the motivations which lie behind the enactment of various feeling rules. As mentioned previously, employees have various ways of enacting prescribed feeling rules. Whether they are commercial, professional or organisational, feeling rules will always offer the potential to be 'stretched, negotiated, argued, ignored, or applied at inconvenient moments' (Strauss, 1975, p. 189) and the problem faced by organisations who attempt to instil a new set of feeling rules into their employees is neatly summarised by Berger and Luckman:

> The formal processes of secondary socialization are determined by its fundamental problem: it always presupposes a preceding process of primary socialization; that is, that it must deal with an already formed self and an already internalized world ... This presents a problem because the already internalized reality has a tendency to resist. (Berger and Luckman, 1966, p. 160)

Organisational feeling rules offer generalised models of conduct that guide employees' actions. In large-scale bureaucratic organisations rules may be clearly determined and sanctioned, though they more usually act as symbolic anchors. They are the ropes that new organisational members learn as the 'way things are done around here' thus ensuring they are able to fit in and become an active member of the organisation. Commercial and professional feeling rules tend to be much more explicit – offering official and publicly stated, ways of being with intensive periods of training and socialisation though, as the rest of this chapter will show, their enactment is not any less of an exquisite or complicated drama than organisationally prescribed feeling rules.

Commercial feeling rules

Pecuniary emotion management and front-line service

Pecuniary emotion management and commercial feeling rules can most clearly be linked with the increasing army of front-line service workers where a growing interest has revealed several recurrent, not to say paradoxical, themes. The focus of many studies is on the actual interaction between worker and customer, whether this is face-to-face or voice-to-voice. Service work has its own peculiarities, in that it is intangible, perishable, variable and inseparable (Korczynski, 2002, pp. 5–6). It is the only form of work where the customer is directly involved in the process of production and increasingly seen to control it. The service interaction relies upon front-line workers presenting a desirable demeanour and creating an alluring emotional climate. To achieve this they work on their own emotions and seek to manipulate those of the customer working within the commercial feeling and display rules set by the organisation. Whilst 'quality service' is often cited as a main source of competitive advantage in an increasingly service-based economy, its qualitative features are very hard to define, though it is commonly accepted that it relies on extensive amounts of emotion work performed by service providers. The interaction between customer and service provider is often seen as the 'moment of truth' (Carlzon, 1987) and management exert considerable energy in trying to capture and routinely replicate that special moment.

Close communication with customers requires that service workers carry out *pecuniary* emotion management in order to present the desirable corporate image and create the profitable product of customer satisfaction. It is the emotional tone of the interaction between customer and service-provider that has become something of a talking point. Of particular interest for the analysis of *pecuniary* emotion management are the 'emotional proletariat' (MacDonald and Sirianni, 1996), those who are engaged in front-line interactive service work which can be variously described as mundane, routine, low-skilled and, most importantly, tightly controlled. These are the workers who make up the 'have-a-nice-day' culture where 'niceness' is routinely delivered: faceless service workers dealing with faceless customers.

Though the emotional proletariat come low in the status hierarchy of knowledge work, they are in fact a major, if not the only, means of a company differentiating in a highly competitive sector. The front-line service worker is frequently the only contact a customer has with an organisation making the quality of interaction with customers a major criterion by which the organisation can be judged. Little wonder that this particular segment of the labour force and this type of emotion work are the focus of so much attention. Whilst management practitioners express concern over service quality and their difficulties in controlling a course of action that involves simultaneous production and consumption (Bowen and Lawler, 1992; Heskett *et al.*, 1997), academic studies reveal the exploitative potential and the detrimental effects upon workers' emotional well being (Hochschild, 1983; MacDonald and Sirianni, 1996; Morris and Feldman, 1996). Though very different in content, these studies share a concentration on the outcomes, rather than the processes, of production. That is, contradictory combinations of performance targets, surveillance mechanisms, recruitment and selection procedures and high commitment human resource practices are all seen as having a significant impact upon both the producer and consumer of 'service' (Kinnie *et al.*, 2000; Pitt *et al.*, 1995; Schneider and Bowen, 1995). Underlying this, however, is a persistent reliance on the routinisation of service delivery, via scripts and prompts, with predictability and reliability being the desired aim.

In many routine face-to-face service jobs a bureaucratisation of the rules governing organisational emotionality are at their most obvious. In the interests of efficiency, the organisation requires that work routines are predictable and continually correspond with predetermined standards. In other words, the organisation needs to be able to rely on its employees to give a homogenous performance on every occasion. When these performances involve face-to-face interaction with customers companies try to ensure that such interaction does not differ from the set guidelines by attempting to make employees' emotions 'solidified and permanent' (Flam, 1990b; Goffman, 1959). Organisations such as Walt Disney and McDonald's give explicit training and issue handbooks and guides that instruct employees to convey 'positive' emotions to customers (Van Maanen, 1991). For example, in one particular American supermarket chain counter-staff receive spot prizes for 'expressively' greeting customers (Rafaeli and Sutton, 1987). In this way the organisation establishes norms of conduct that dictate only certain emotions should be expressed. Organisational actors are asked to assume a particular identity which helps them to perform their work role more efficiently. In effect, employees are being paid to laugh, smile or be 'caring' and the taking-on of this organisationally prescribed 'mask' often entails actors absenting parts of their 'natural' selves that would not conform to the given role. Goffman succinctly sums up this process:

> The cultural values of an establishment will determine in detail how the participants are to feel about many matters and at the same time establish a framework of appearances that must be maintained, whether or not there is feeling behind the appearances. (Goffman, 1959, p. 234)

By binding emotional labourers to scripts, imposed rules of interaction and unachievable production targets management are actually distorting and unbalancing this achievement. The constrictions imposed by the demands made for the performance of *pecuniary* emotion management mean that workers are unable to calibrate their performances according to the social rules of interaction, the ceremonial order is disrupted, and irritation and disaffection are the result. This is the result of an over-concentration on the outcome rather than the process of customer service and an apparent neglect of customer interaction as social interaction. Of course, some of the motivations involved in providing customer service will differ from those involved in day-today social interaction – but not all. The differences are exacerbated by the focus on the satisfaction of only one of the parties involved in the encounter – that is the customer – rather than the reciprocal obligation involved in social interaction.

Current (mis)representations of customer service

With the rising number of service workers an analysis of their work has necessarily included a third party in an understanding of the employment relationship and shaped perceptions of how *pecuniary* emotion management is to be performed – that is, the customer. Unsurprisingly, the 'customer' comes in many guises: sovereign consumer, co-producer, emotional vampire, citizen, rebel, management accomplice and as an ever shifting discursive product (Gabriel and Lang, 1995; Rosenthal *et al.*, 2001). Equally, for every representation of the customer there is an accompanying understanding of the character of the service-provider: automaton, enterprising individual, servant and, most of all, performer. Analyses of 'customer-relations' are wide and varied coming from both prescriptive and critical sources but sharing a focus on the important role played by the 'sovereign consumer'.

For some, the dominant discourse of enterprise has become the 'primary image informing representations of economic life' (du Gay, 1996, p. 80). The 'cult(ure) of the customer' (du Gay and Salaman, 1992) necessarily informs the organisation of work, most especially that of the front-line service worker. In the unreliable, fragmented conditions of consumer capitalism consumption and production are inextricably linked and the boundaries between the public and private blurred. People are in search of a sense of coherence and meaning and the world of production offers a stable platform where identities can be confirmed and people can take their rightful place in the world of consumption. In this way the 'sovereign customer' becomes the 'moral centre of the enterprising universe' (du Gay and Salaman, 1992, p. 622) and paid employment becomes a means of enterprising self-actualisation (Rose, 1990). Producers and consumers therefore share a common identity based on the 'enterprising self' (du Gay, 1996). In such an analysis it is assumed that the front-line service worker offers 'quality' service to customers because they have been seduced by the discourse of enterprise, which not only informs managerial control of *pecuniary* emotion management but actually replaces it. Workers, therefore, internalise the notion of the sovereign customer and perform *pecuniary* emotion management with barely any need for closely defined feeling rules.

A harmonious, though differently constructed, relationship with the customer is also portrayed by writers from the new service management school (Bowen and Lawler, 1992; Heskett *et al.*, 1997). In their analysis the customer is a bundle of needs, desires and preferences that can be partially shaped by the marketing function, whilst the soft techniques of people management will recruit and subsequently develop the empowered, self-actualising front-line service worker who is then able to provide quality service. A culture of service excellence pervades the organisation creating a win:win:win situation in that customers, workers and managers equally benefit (Korczynski, 2002). This agreeable combination is achieved through the prescriptions of the new service management school, which are almost indiscernible from those of the excellence management literature resting, as they do, upon the same unitarist framework and customer-orientation where front-line workers readily perform *pecuniary* emotion management according to carefully prescribed commercial feeling rules.

The normalising tendencies of customer relations are also represented in the sinister connotations of the customer as both disparaging audience and management spy (Rosenthal *et al.*, 2001). In these accounts conflict is an accepted part of relations between management, service-provider and customer. However, various normative control devices obscure the conflict and even the more empowered workers become self-disciplining service providers. Mystery shoppers and employee development programmes serve to transform social interaction and *pecuniary* emotion management is performed on company terms (Fuller and Smith, 1991; Hochschild, 1983). As Hochschild observes of the airline cabin crew she studied: 'her have-a-nice-day smile is not really her smile but is an indirect extension of the company smile' (Hochschild, 1989a, p. 440). It is suggested that this is achieved via customer care programmes which propose that front-line service workers should actively alter their perceptions of aggressive customers and imaginatively give them characteristics with which they can personally identify, such as frightened children (Hochschild, 1983; Sutton, 1991). By 'pretending deeply' service workers can alter their emotional state and more easily match feeling with face, thus offering a convincing performance of customer care. (Hochschild, 1983). In this way *pecuniary* emotion management is enacted as a sincere performance displaying what Goffman might describe as 'attachment' to the role of service-provider.

At worst, if practices of 'deep acting' do not have the desired affect the worker will at least comply with the display rules and present a desirable performance for fear that their audience, the discerning customer, will make a complaint to the management. Once again the customer takes command as management can rely on receiving accounts of the service customers have experienced which, in turn, indicates precisely employees who are not abiding by the company feeling rules. This apparent abdication of control by managers obfuscates power relations in the workplace, as employees find management 'blameless' for the increasing demands made upon them by the 'sovereign' customer: As Fuller and Smith note:

> the power to control workers and mid-level managers may appear to be removed from upper management's hands and redistributed to a company's clients, customers, patients, etc. In fact, however, feedback from consumers strengthens employers' hold over the workplace by providing them with an additional source of data they can use for control, evaluation and discipline. (Fuller and Smith, 1991, p. 10)

Management are not quite so absent, however, when considering direct control strategies of performance targets, surveillance and scripted interaction. The sovereignty of the customer is, of course, never doubted but speed and predictability are necessary prerequisites in the mass market of service provision. Quality service requires efficiency provided in an empathetic and assuring manner (Parasuraman *et al.*, 1991). The five dimensions of service quality: reliability, responsiveness, assurance, empathy and tangibles surrounding service (Pitt *et al.*, 1995) are a contradictory combination of the 'hard' and the 'soft'. The 'dual logics' of quantity and quality in the organisation of front-line service work are aptly described by Korczynski (2002) as the 'customer-orientated bureaucracy':

> This concept of the customer-oriented bureaucracy captures the requirement for the organisation to be both formally rational, to respond to competitive pressures to appeal to customers' wishes for efficient, and to be formally irrational, to enchant, responding to the customers' desire for pleasure, particularly through the perpetuation of the enchanting myth of customer sovereignty. (Korczynski, 2002, p. 64)

This becomes particularly apparent in management accounts of the empowered front-line service worker where worker autonomy is carefully proscribed and only available to the rare elite. Whilst berating the routinisation of service-work these writers merely advocate different standardised practices which may, or may not, include some 'soft' management touches such as 'time out' for stressed workers, teamwork and yet more customer service training (Bowen and Lawler, 1992; Kinnie *et al.*, 2000; Pitt *et al.*, 1995). High commitment management practices often prove 'to be a thin and temporary veneer' for the reality of tightened control and further routinisation of interaction with little material reward (Callaghan and Thompson, 2002; MacDonald and Sirianni, 1996, p. 19). It is notable how the performance of *pecuniary* emotion management is rarely described as satisfying or rewarding work.

Though the ontological assumptions of the 'sovereign consumer' may not be shared by all, the basic notion of the customer as a figure of authority and definer of service workers' identities most certainly is. In the management–worker–customer triangle, there seems little doubt that the customer reigns supreme. The result being that 'customer relations' are now privileged over 'industrial relations' (Wray-Bliss, 2001, p. 46) and social relations. Even though, upon closer examination, the customer can be seen as something of a 'mythical sovereign' (Korczynski, 2002). The various images of customer relations offer a portrait of docile service workers interacting with sometimes aggressive but otherwise not much more agential customers. The consumers are discursively produced as sovereign beings and front-line service workers are mere simulations, offering depersonalised care and attention (Ritzer, 1999). Little wonder customer relations and the related performances of *pecuniary* emotion management in late capitalism have been described as a form of 'abuse' to both producer and consumer (Hopfl, 2002).

The efficacy of *pecuniary* emotion management

Despite extraordinary efforts to define and achieve 'quality' customer service via the prescribed performance of *pecuniary* emotion management there is little evidence of satisfaction with the results. The gap between customer expectations of service and perceptions of the service received continues to grow and, increasingly, concern is expressed about the detrimental effects upon workers in what can only be described as a no-win situation. Customer service is a potentially fragile accomplishment, its success dependent upon the service worker meeting the expectations of the customer. Needless to say, interactions between customer and service-provider do not always proceed according to management prescription and both customers and workers are adversely affected by the experience.

The potentially damaging effects of the 'marketing of bonhomie' (Parkinson, 1991) have not gone unnoticed. Management academics continually strive to find the cause of these dissatisfactions and the individual personal weaknesses of the front-line service workers have become the focus of analysis. So much so, that it is recommended that the most reliable way to reduce the potential for disruption of the service encounter is to employ 'self-monitors' and 'extroverts' who 'will be more inclined to comply with organizational display norms' (Morris and Feldman, 1996, p. 1005; Rafaeli and Sutton, 1987). In this way, some autonomy may be allowed in the emotional labour process as long as the organisation introduces tactics whereby emotion can be 'neutralized, buffered, prescribed and normalised' so that it may contribute to organisational effectiveness (Ashforth and Humphrey, 1995).

A different approach suggests that presenting a desirable demeanour to customers can be classed as hard and demanding labour that invades the worker's sense of self (MacDonald and Sirianni, 1996). There are, of course, ample examples that serve to undermine conclusions concerning workers' fragile identities. The recalcitrant front-line worker develops many methods, often very subtle and barely detectable by management, of registering their refusal to be defined by organisational feeling rules. As Goffman (1967, p. 87) highlights: 'in scrupulously observing the proper form he may find that he is free to insinuate all kinds of disregard by carefully modifying intonation, pronunciation, pacing, and so forth.' Some episodes of 'misbehaviour' (Ackroyd and Thomspon, 1999) may be classified as coping mechanisms others as acts of resistance and defiance against the obligatory rituals of deference that deny interactants the basic right to dignity (Hodson, 2001). Paules' (1996, p. 266) study of waitresses highlights how they refuse to be denied 'the courtesies of personhood':

> Though constrained to comply with the interactive conventions of master and servant, while clad in a domestic's uniform, the waitress does not internalize an image of service as servitude and self as servant. In times of stress she sees her work

as war and herself as soldier. In times of peace she sees her work as a private enterprise and herself as entrepreneur. (Paules, 1996, p. 284)

As Goffman states, very often there is an absence of 'feeling behind the appearances' and it should be noted how organisationally prescribed performances can be an 'exquisite drama'; a way of enacting the organisation's 'display rules'. The performances are in fact a mask donned by employees and therefore require only 'face work' or 'surface-acting' (Fineman, 1993; Goffman, 1967; Hochschild, 1983).[2] That is, actors may remain emotionally detached from the performance acting out their role obligations without ever 'buying-in' to the norms set by the company. As a sample of trainee hairdressers state 'you plaster a false smile on your face, grin and bear it' (Parkinson, 1991, p. 430) and similarly a Delta Airline stewardess describes her job as being an 'illusion maker' (Hochschild, 1983). This style of impression management indicates a cynical detachment from the work role, displaying how the public and private selves have not become 'fused' (Wouters, 1989b). *Pecuniary* emotion management becomes less a result of emotion work and more associated with face work where employees merely act out various performances in order to produce the profitable product of customer satisfaction.

Customer service as abuse

An examination of *pecuniary* emotion management highlights that the source of abuse in the service encounter is not the recalcitrant, fragile or alienated worker, it is not even the obnoxious customer, it is the imposition of management controls upon the emotional labour process that continually reproduce the concept of sovereign customer and subjugated service-worker. Interaction between customer and service-provider is essentially a social process which is violated by commercial feeling rules and the associated control imperative that demands emotional labour power be transformed into a profitable product. The continued emphasis on speedy transactions enhanced with routinised 'niceness' actually constitutes a form of 'misinvolvement' (Goffman, 1967, p. 117). Neither service-provider or customer truly participate in the encounter as, unlike everyday conversation that has a life of its own (Goffman, 1967), the service encounter is a fabricated performance with faceless actors. The 'socialized trance' (Goffman, 1967, p. 113) of spontaneous involvement will never materialise as the imposed script deprives interactants of their involvement obligations. As Goffman states of successful interaction ritual:

> the individual must phrase his own concerns and feelings and interests in such a
> way as to make these maximally usable by the others as a source of appropriate

involvement; and this major obligation of the individual qua interactant is balanced by his right to expect that others present will make some effort. (Goffman, 1967, p. 116)

Commercial feeling rules do not offer the service-provider and customer opportunities for 'appropriate involvement'. Speed and standardisation are of the essence and the script presents limited scope for any form of deviation. Often this works very well, a straightforward query over the telephone dealt with in an effective manner without any obvious need for the spontaneous involvement of the social encounter. In fact, many workers are said to feel the benefit of this as they are able to offer 'empty performances' (Goffman, 1961a), using the script as a shield against any personal involvement with customers (Leidner, 1996). However, even in these fleeting moments the customer is aware that the 'whole show is false' and the fragile order of the service encounter begins to be threatened: 'When the individual senses that others are insincere or affected he tends to feel they have taken unfair advantage of their communication position to promote their own interests; he feels they have broken the ground rules of interaction' (Goffman, 1967, p. 122). The perspicuous customer expects to be satisfied and does not anticipate any leakage that may intimate they are not receiving personalised service. But more than this, the *customer* as a *person* feels discomfited and alienated from the interaction when *pecuniary* emotion management is the order of the day. Feelings of uneasiness concerning the 'misdemeanour' are directed toward the service-provider at the expense of the customer's own sense of obligation to the encounter. So a cycle is created where uneasiness becomes a 'contagious disease' (Goffman, 1967, p. 126). This unease may materialise as open aggression, a sense of awkwardness or a vague sense of disquiet but, in whatever form, the social accomplishment that is the interaction ritual has been disturbed with very real consequences for those involved. Goffman usefully summarises the effects of such a 'failure':

> When the encounter fails to capture the attention of the participants, but does not release them from the obligation of involving themselves in it, then persons present are likely to feel uneasy; for them the interaction fails to come off. A person who chronically makes himself or others uneasy in conversation and perpetually kills encounters is a faulty interactant; he is likely to have such a baleful effect upon the social life around him that he may just as well be called a faulty person. (Goffman, 1961a, p. 135)

The service encounter is a minor event, one episode among many. However, in consumer capitalism it is an event that accounts for an increasing amount of day-to-day social interaction. Thus, commercial feeling rules set the tone for social encounters far more than social feeling rules. It is important, therefore, that it is recognised that when the interaction order is disrupted both selves and society are at stake (Schwabe, 1993).

Professional feeling rules

Prescriptive emotion management and the professions

There are certain occupations that entail a much more intense period of professional training and socialisation. Each professional discipline has its own set of 'implicit feeling rules' which represent what they claim to be their unique mission (Strauss, 1975). The recruits accept these 'rules' as a normal pattern of behaviour. Professional occupations are not seen as 'just a job' but a lifetime's career and a way of life. Many have high social status, material reward, public service or caring ideals attached to them and new recruits enthusiastically sublimate their whole life in pursuit of careers as professionals. They begin to envisage themselves according to new standards and in terms of their professional title. Actors undergo what Berger and Luckman (1966) refer to as 'secondary socialisation' and develop a new 'perspective', a new way of seeing things and a new set of feeling rules to guide them. This attachment to the image of a role is a major element of Goffman's role analysis and would be more closely associated with the performance of *prescriptive* emotion management associated with professional codes of conduct:

> The self-image available for anyone entering a particular position is one of which *he* may become affectively and cognitively enamoured, desiring and expecting to see *him*self in terms of the enactment of the role and the self-identification emerging from the enactment. (Goffman, 1961a, p. 89)

The impression of a professional is one who actively engages in *prescriptive* emotion management. They appear to willingly internalise the professional feeling rules in order to meet the expectations of their colleagues and the public concerning the 'right' image of a professional. Whether it be a lawyer, accountant or doctor all have established notions concerning the presentation of self and to maintain a certain demeanour is an essential part of being a professional. It is not surprising to note that many professionals describe this as a 'mask' that must not slip otherwise the image of the profession would be damaged. This often entails hard emotion work and is employed to maintain distance between the professional and client. For instance, though caring professionals are expected to show compassion in their interactions with clients they must not express emotion and nurses, social workers, and doctors all express horror at the thought of crying in front of clients, stating that they would feel a sense of shame and humiliation for letting the professional mask slip (Bolton, 2001; James, 1992; Smith, 1992). Public sector professionals experience frustration and anger at the resource limitations they face every day when attempting to offer services to their clients but work very hard not to show it (Lipsky, 1980). And lawyers are extolled to feel passionately involved in the legal cases with which they deal but must maintain their distance from the people involved (Lively, 2000). The maintenance of the professional façade through the performance of *prescriptive* emotion management is often described as hard work and would seem to be an unbearable burden for the professionals involved. Various accounts tell us that this is not so for two central reasons. First, professional feeling rules have the capacity to act as a shielding mechanism, the mask is a protective veneer that protects the self from the emotional demands of the job. Second, the professional is so sincerely attached to the image of the professional (and its associated benefits) that the extraordinary effort involved in maintaining this image is hardly seen as hard work at all but an integral, and mostly invisible, part of the job (Bolton, 2001; Lively, 2000).

Clearly there are powerful influences which mould professionals into behaving in the manner expected of them. These influences begin early in a professional's career – in many cases before their career formally begins. For example, Grey (1994, p. 485) found that those who are recruited into the accountancy profession tend to be a homogenous group predominantly consisting of the 'white, male, middle class and young'. It is believed such a group will already have the required personal characteristics to fit in with the norms of the profession. It can be seen how in some cases careers start very early so that by the time the recruitment procedure begins, and the organisation seeks to select the right person for a job, the person, with the help of existing ideological images attached to certain occupations, has already selected the job and organisation for them. This is never more important than in the professions where the mutual selection process ensures that the 'right' candidates enter into the complex professional value system (Salaman, 1974). New recruits actively seek to match the idealised image of their chosen profession; sober accountant, dynamic lawyer, caring doctor, and 'are already constituted as certain sorts of subjects' so that the transition to a professional persona is a relatively simple one (Grey, 1994, p. 485). This not only encompasses the formal content of their education but also their day-to-day contact with fellow professionals which give constant clues on ways of being. It is an orientation toward the much publicised idealised image and other members of the profession, rather than toward explicit professional feeling rules, that act as a control mechanism over professionals' actions. Every medium – fictional romance, media sensationalism, soap operas – bombard us with images of various professionals who possess seemingly desirable qualities.

So powerful are these feeling rules that they leak into the day-to-day routines of occupations who are closely coupled with professional groups, what might be described as associate professionals. Though these occupational groups do not undergo lengthy periods of formal training and socialisation, they borrow and develop the 'folk symbols' of an established profession to construct their own mode of professionalism (Becker, 1970). For instance, we find legal clerks and nursing auxiliaries enacting *prescriptive* emotion management according to feeling rules of the legal and nursing profession. This is not just emulating behaviour but an organising principle as the feeling rules they borrow define the way they think about themselves, their position as an occupation and their mode of presentation (Lee-Treweek, 1997; Lipsky, 1980; Lively, 2000). These 'paraprofessionals' lack the autonomy or the socially recognised depth of knowledge to become part of the established professions and whilst some strive to attach themselves to a 'master' profession others will never hope to have the title fully recognised but still think and act as 'professional nonprofessionals' (Ritzer, 1971).

As powerful as professional feeling rules are, the process of socialisation is never total and is 'never anything like a passive imprinting upon each individual' (Berger and Luckman, 1966; Giddens, 1979, p. 129). Professional groups are far from homogenous, split as they often are into formal specialities but also into emergent groupings which Strauss usefully describes as 'segments' as part of his 'process model' of the professions: 'there are many identities, many values, and many interests. These amount not merely to differentiation or simple variation. They tend to become patterned and shared; coalitions develop and flourish – and in opposition to some others' (Strauss, 1975, p. 10). This model allows that professional feeling rules are open to interpretation, meaning that *prescriptive* emotion management is performed in particular ways by different members of the same profession. The establishment of particular feeling rules is not always agreed upon and the past tells us that professional codes of conduct are often the 'historical deposits of certain powerful segments' (Strauss, 1975, p. 19). This is particularly the case when considering the varied relationships professionals have with clients where divisions of emotion work within each profession are often segregated along the lines of seniority and/or gender. For instance, it is assumed that the female doctor will be more willing and able to share difficult moments with patients or that the female nurse, as the lesser being in the medical division of labour, will mop up the emotional mess left by the doctor who is less adept at carrying out emotion work or who sees his professional feeling rules and his standing as a skilled expert in the technical realm, as allowing him to remain completely distant from the client, even when imparting tragic news (James, 1993; Lively, 2000; Strauss, 1975). This shows how professional feeling rules, like other feeling rules in operation in organisational life, cannot be divorced from societal structures that reproduce the notion of women being the more adept emotion workers or that assigns values to certain forms of knowledge. Often to the extent that emotion work is not recognised as a form of knowledge work at all. It is notable how the more senior a professional, the more the feeling rules appear to condone emotional distance from clients, even colleagues, as the acceptable form of *prescriptive* emotion management. However, when a woman maintains her emotional distance as a senior professional she is described as 'unnatural' or a 'hard bitch' (Wajcman, 1998).

Professional groups may appear to be founded upon tradition and unchanging in their ways but this would be an overly simple portrayal. The different 'segments' involved in the enactment and development of professional feeling rules not only ensure their continual renewal but also their renegotiation so that often feeling rules emerge in an altered form and new understanding and ways of being are formed. One only has to look at the changing image of the senior nurse: from the formal matriarchal battle-axe figure of the matron to the more informal and dynamic picture of a technically proficient professional carrying out the duties of a junior doctor. Though it must be added that the notion of the 'feminine' or 'semi-professional' (Etzioni, 1969; Lorentzon, 1990) firmly remains with little hope of change as long as the gendered ideology of 'caring' lives on and the image of the nurse continues to reside with the 'angel of mercy'.

It is also the case that professional feeling rules are not always adhered to. As with any traffic rules of interaction there are the 'heroes and the villains' (Goffman, 1959). For every nurse who may be described as an angel of mercy there will be one who is either a bully or who is simply too tired to invest the level of effort required to perform *prescriptive* emotion management according to professional feeling rules. For every doctor who attempts to maintain dignified encounters with vulnerable patients there will be one who abuses this trust – feeling rules are either blatantly ignored or again, the pressures of an under-resourced system do not allow the time to invest in the degree of emotion work necessary to carry out successful *prescriptive* emotion management. In these cases it is often the system that is the villain, rather than the individual professional, as undue pressures prevent the adherence to professional feeling rules or even the emergence of undesirable feeling rules devised as a means of circumventing an oppressive or failing system. As Lipsky found of the street level bureaucrats he studied, rules are continually twisted and turned in order to survive the rigours of public service in what he describes as a 'neat paradox':

> Lower level participants develop coping mechanisms contrary to an agency's policy but actually basic to its survival. For example, brutality is contrary to police policy but a certain degree of looking-the other way may be necessary to persuade officers to risk assault. Street-level bureaucrats have a role interest in securing the requirements of completing the job. (Lipsky, 1980, p. 19)

And, of course, management also have an interest in work related targets etc. Though a defining feature of professional groups is the amount of autonomy and discretion they enjoy in the carrying out of their work, many professionals face the dual demands of both professional and organisational feeling rules. For many public sector professionals they are partly professionals and partly bureaucrats (Lipsky, 1980) with all of the dilemmas and contradictions this brings. This is especially the case with the public service professions where commercial feeling rules are being increasingly introduced in the interests of efficiency and effectiveness.

Public service workers: *pecuniary* or *prescriptive* emotion management?

For many occupations, there is little to differentiate the categories of *pecuniary* and *prescriptive* emotion management. As can be seen when looking at jobs that belong in the private service sector[3] there is very little difference between the categories of *pecuniary* and *prescriptive* emotion management. Quite simply, the organisation prescribes the way employees should perform emotion management as part of the labour process and these performances are instrumentally motivated. The implication being that this will produce the profitable product of customer satisfaction. In other words, these workers perform 'emotional labour'. However, not all occupations perform a combined version of both *pecuniary* and *prescriptive* emotion management. To assume that they do risks missing the many different zones within an organisation's emotional architecture. Many writers apply the concept of 'emotional labour' to public service professionals such as nurses or traditional professions such as barristers (James, 1989, 1992, 1993; Smith, 1988, 1992; Harriss, 2002). Whereas others would say that professional groups are exempt from performing 'emotional labour' in that they retain discretion and autonomy in the interpretation of professional feeling rules (Hochschild, 1983). For instance, when looking at the British public services, distinct differences can be identified between the categories of *prescriptive* and *pecuniary* emotion management, the associated feeling rules and motivations. Though there may be materialist motivations behind a performance of *prescriptive* emotion management, in the case of public sector professionals there is also a complex web of ideas concerning their role as part of a professional group and the adherence to associated modes of conduct along with the ideology of being a public service provider with all the related dilemmas this brings. We may find public sector workers working hard on the presentation of self, particularly with clients, but this is often to create a stable emotional climate and maintain poise for the carrying out of 'dirty work' such as body care, disturbing behaviour, or imparting bad news (Dent *et al.*, 1991; Goffman, 1961b; James, 1993; Lawler, 1991; Strauss, 1970) or it may be devoted to concealing a lack of resources and responsiveness of a particular public service (Lipsky, 1980). During these encounters a new order is achieved, with consideration shown to clients' vulnerability and the service providers' professional status. Many comment that this new order represents professional dominance in interactions with clients rather than the dominance of the customer in other service-providers' interactions. It would seem that p*ecuniary* emotion management with its purely instrumental motivations and servility toward consumers does not play a part in the working lives of public sector professionals.

However, there are early indications that the introduction of an internal market and the 'culture of the customer' into the public sector services is having far-reaching effects. Accompanying changes in work organisation, whereby greater numbers of patients are treated whilst using broadly the same amount of resources, premises, technology and labour, there has also been a transformation of managerial beliefs and values. 'New' public sector management (NPM) philosophy clearly reflects an ideological shift, beginning in the early 1980s with the proposed marketisation of many public services and continuing today with the current government, toward newly valued entrepreneurial attitudes and behaviours (du Gay, 1996). More importantly, 20 years of emphasising the sovereignty of the customer (du Gay and Salaman, 1992) has also altered the perceptions of the general public and redefined patients and service-users as 'customers' and 'consumers'.

The 'cultural crusade' (du Gay, 1996) of the NPM includes an increasing focus on issues of quality service and there have been direct attempts to imbue health service employees with a new deference to the needs of consumers. It is unlikely that promises of an efficient, quality service could ever be fully matched with the necessary resources. This means that the target of financial efficiency remains at the heart of management reform. Of course, public sector management have always been 'constrained to act as capitalists'

(Cousins, 1987) in that they must purchase labour power and harness its productive creativity. Nevertheless, though management in the public service does take a distinct form, in that their paymasters are central government rather than the market, the imposition of efficiency quotas and performances measurements, along with the enterprise discourse of 'consumer as King', has meant that public service work no longer represents a liberation from the 'commodity form' (Cousins, 1987). Though public sector professionals' labour is not conducted for the creation of profit, their labour process is now organised and controlled as if it were and public service management can no longer be as clearly differentiated from its commercially motivated counterpart.

This aspect of managerial change involves the imposition of new instrumentally inspired feeling rules into the nursing labour process; feeling rules which are commonly thought to be alien to the ideals of public service. There is little doubt that the working lives of public health professionals have been deeply affected by recent reforms. Public sector workers now find themselves having to present the calm and caring face of the public service professional whilst also having to present a smiling face to clients who now behave as demanding customers. It could be argued that the increasing emphasis on efficiency, cost-cutting and, most especially, consumer satisfaction has transformed how public sector professionals manage their emotions at work and added new dimensions to their roles as service providers. It will be argued that the increasing emphasis on efficiency, cost-cutting and, most especially, consumer satisfaction has transformed how nurses manage their emotions at work and added new dimensions to their role as public health care professionals.

This means the performance of *pecuniary* emotion management will become more probable. However, the nature of professionals' work is more emotionally complex than that of the 'emotional proletariat' involved in routine front-line service work in the service sector, air-stewardesses or telesales agents and is supported by entirely different motivations. This makes it highly unlikely that their emotion management performances could ever be neatly labelled under one heading. Even if certain professional groups are explicitly 'paid to smile' (Phillips, 1996) and asked to perform according to commercial feeling rules as a means of producing 'customer' satisfaction, they will still also comply with professional and social feeling rules.

When pecuniary meets prescriptive: conflicting feeling rules

It is hardly surprising that there are instances when we may witness *pecuniary* and *prescriptive* emotion management in direct conflict. Obvious examples abound within the public services where front-line workers feel they can no longer fulfil their drive to meet their role obligations due to altruistic motivations. For instance, medical professionals state that the demands for *pecuniary* emotion management mean that they can no longer spend time with clients as they would wish offering care and support. Their time with clients according to professional feelings rules is, as Bone so aptly describes it, reduced to 'nano-second emotionality' (Bone, 2002, p. 141). The demands of quantifiable targets such as student achievement levels and apprehended criminals means that street-level bureaucrats such as teachers and police officers cannot respond to their 'clients' in a fully human way (Lipsky, 1980). Even in those occupations where the performance of *pecuniary* emotion management assumes paramount importance, workers have a different view of their role. For instance, airline cabin crews are very conscious of needing to adhere to professional safety and service standards even though the work has intensified, the physical conditions deteriorated and the customers are ever more demanding (Bolton and Boyd, 2003).

Similarly, managing irate and abusive customers may be thought of as part of the job (according to purely commercial feeling rules), while engaging with this type of customer interaction may conflict with employees' expectations of what is involved in their job (according to professional feeling rules). Negative feelings concerning the reinvention of public service clients as customers and the reduction of seemingly professional work to routine compliance with commercial feeling rules frequently surface and workers comment how their faces often 'ache with the effort of smiling all day' (Bolton, 2002) or workers suffer a state of 'emotional numbness' (Boyd, 2002). Just as social feeling rules will conflict with commercial, organisational or professional feeling rules and create spaces where workers re-shape or even escape from such demands and perform *presentational* emotion management there is a special case where the demands for *pecuniary* management will be ignored and professional feeling rules will win the day. Professionals are expert at performing *prescriptive* emotion management and are fully committed to the maintenance of a particular 'face'.

Public sector professionals are especially resistant to management efforts to add further commercial values to their work and offer empty performances of *pecuniary* emotion management. In their view of themselves as 'professional' service providers many occupations in both the public and private sectors are quite clear that placating abusive customers is not part of their professional role and that they undertake this task reluctantly with barely concealed contempt. Sometimes this comes in the form of an over played performance and much like the emotional proletariat who use *pecuniary* emotion management as a protective shield professionals will make it quite clear that their performances are skilled acts and not displays of genuine concern. In this way they feel they have gained control of the interaction and actually gain some pleasure from knowing they have subtly shown their disregard for the recipients of public sector services who act as a 'customer'. At other times they quite simply refuse to perform the 'smiley face' routine. Many public sector professionals share the feelings as expressed by this National Health Service nurse:

> Do you know some days I just can't be bothered with this 'patient as customer' business. What a load of rubbish it is. I go to extraordinary lengths to avoid having to be nice to them when they are getting up my nose. I'll even pretend that there is a major emergency in another part of the ward rather than stand around pandering to them. It's ridiculous really. The energy I've used in setting up the little act to avoid them is probably much less than I would need to deal with them, but they're such a pain sometimes. And what really annoys me are the times when other less demanding patients really do need you but these people who have decided it is their 'right' to demand your attention take up all your time. (Staff Nurse, cited in Bolton, 2002, p. 136)

Comments form nurses, doctors, cabin crew and a wide-range of 'street-level bureaucrats' (Bolton, 2002; Lipsky, 1980; Lively, 2002) show that the introduction of new feeling rules has not altered their identities as professional service providers.

Conclusion and implications for an understanding of emotion in organisations

From the review of organisational, commercial and professional feeling rules presented in this chapter it can be seen how organisational life is a combination of compliance, commitment and resistance resulting in both sincere and cynical performances of *pecuniary* and *prescriptive* emotion management. This highlights the complex motivations which lie behind each performance and how they are not always as dutifully enacted as management may prefer. Unlike Hochschild's (1983) air-stewardesses the organisational actors portrayed using the typology of workplace emotion presented in Chapter 5 have not internalised organisationally imposed feeling rules. Most especially in the case of *pecuniary* emotion management the commercial feeling rules are actively converted into display rules offering only empty performances. The next chapter explores in more depth the means by which workers express distance from and resistance to various feeling rules. In their capacity to create 'spaces' workers have a means of escape where they may be their authentic selves, performing both *presentational* and *philanthropic* emotion management according to social feeling rules. The performances which occur in these spaces have much more potential to be sincere, further emphasising the emptiness of *pecuniary* emotion management acts. This aids in an understanding of the contradictions that workers face in their everyday working lives, whether a member of the growing army of front-line service workers providing routinised 'niceness' to customers or public sector professionals who are faced with ever demanding 'customers' in the face of every decreasing resources these workers clearly have mixed feeling about their work roles and the emotion work they must invest into it.

Notes

1. Flam (1990b, p. 226) mentions how 'mandates often translate into formal and informal norms requiring that the individuals working for an organisation to manage their emotions in specified ways'. Rafaeli and Sutton (1987, p. 27) point out how 'perhaps more powerful than formal socialisation practices are lessons about emotional display learned through the informal organization. The stories told and actions taken by role models provide opportunities for social learning.'
2. Hochschild (1983) uses the terms 'surface' and 'deep' acting to differentiate between the times when an actor merely presents a 'face' without feeling attached to it and other occasions when they 'work' on their emotions to make sure not only face but also feelings fit the situation.
3. Such as the air-hostess, the hairdresser, the double-glazing salesman, the debt-collector, fast-food server, i.e. those who have direct face-to-face contact with the public and whose responsibility it is to keep the customer satisfied.

7

'Presentational' and 'Philanthropic' emotion management

Spaces for being human

This chapter deals with *presentational* and *philanthropic* emotion management. That is emotion management which is not controlled by an organisation's feeling rules but by the implicit traffic rules of social interaction. A basic premise of the discussions throughout the book is that organisational actors are highly efficient emotion managers who are able to present themselves in an appropriate manner according to the often implicit rules of the situation. It could be said, therefore, that *presentational* and *philanthropic* emotion management represents the basic socialised self, drawing as it does on social feeling rules. When entering into organisational life, although unaware of the particular rules of the game, actors are already prepared with a basic understanding of how the game will be played. In other words, social actors can manage their emotions in order to fit into the accepted 'conventions of feeling' (Hochschild, 1979, 1990). A lifetime's social guidance prepares actors with the 'traffic rules of social interaction', giving what Goffman would refer to as a 'universal human nature'.[1] A necessary attribute if actors are to become 'self-regulating participants in social encounters', enabling them to 'stay in the game on a proper ritual basis' (Goffman, 1967, pp. 45–91).Without the basic skills acquired as socialised beings organisational actors would be unable to comply with any of the rules necessary for the performance of other types of emotion management so essential for the smooth running of organisations.

As the previous chapter has shown, organisational, commercial and professional feeling rules dominate a large part of organisational life. So influential are some of these 'rules' that many observers conclude that there is, or should be, little room for any forms of conduct other than that dictated by the organisation. Rules, roles and associated modes of conduct and imputed conceptions of the self are, of course, an everyday part of organisational existence but, as Mills and Murgatroyd (1991, p. 22) usefully point out, 'the deliberately formulated rules of an organisation only form part of a given reality'. One only need observe much of the conduct in organisations, either as an employee, customer, or researcher, to see that the variability of human conduct cannot be wholly captured by organisationally prescribed feeling rules. When a situation arises where specific prescriptive organisational rules do not apply, or when they are significantly relaxed, an 'unmanaged space' may be created. That is, organisational actors find 'spaces between (organizational) rules' (Mills and Murgatroyd, 1991) where they create their own form of organisational reality. They are able to create 'emotional zones' (Fineman, 1993); 'back regions' (Goffman, 1959) or even only 'nooks and crannies' (Giddens, 1987) where they feel comfortable and are allowed to take shelter. As Gabriel observes: 'within every organization there is an uncolonized terrain, a terrain which is not and cannot be managed in which people, both individually and in groups, can engage in all kinds of unsupervised, spontaneous activity' (Gabriel, 1995, p. 478).

This is not to say that such 'off-stage settings are emotion free ports' (Fineman, 1993, p. 3). Emotion is managed in these spaces just as in other areas of organisational life, the difference being that to fulfil the role obligations which occur in these spaces the rules are often much more familiar and the motivations quite different. 'Spaces' 'back regions' or 'zones' are not necessarily created as actual physically delineated areas where agents may congregate – whether officially in places such as the staff canteen or unofficially whilst sneaking a cigarette in the toilet. Though some informal spaces in organisations are both spatially and temporally dominant, as with certain occupational cultures, others may only be fleeting moments, an exchanged smile or a small nudge, which indicate how actors are able to be both present and not be present on certain occasions. As Goffman (1967, p. 87) highlights: 'in scrupulously observing the proper form he may find that he is free to insinuate all kinds of disregard by carefully modifying intonation, pronunciation, pacing, and so forth'.

Within the spaces where *presentational* and *philanthropic* emotion management is performed it is possible to be many things to many people: close friend, casual acquaintance, colleague, adversary, father/mother-figure, practical-joker, bully, authority figure. We form friendships in organisations, romantic relationships and lasting bonds that inform many other aspects of our lives. It is possible to derive great pleasure from the social side of organisational life, feeling bound to the organisation not out of a desire to fulfil their work role but in their role as supportive colleague and friend. Some of these roles may demand quite hard emotion work – not all of it can be described as *philanthropic* emotion management but including this type of emotion work in an analysis of organisational life adds considerably to the richness and texture of the analysis.For example, employees may be forced to work closely as a team with colleagues whom they actively dislike. Of course, much of the team interaction may be controlled by the organisation as it is now deemed necessary to treat fellow team members 'as-if' they were customers. Nevertheless, there is a vast difference in the interactions between employees and the external customer and those between so-called 'internal' customers. When working as a team there are ample opportunities for unmanaged spaces to occur and team members can become close personal friends, relieving tensions through shared banter or they may become bitter adversaries, constantly resisting the urge to thump each other. It is more likely encounters within the team would be managed according to the implicit social rules that govern the *presentational* emotion management category, rather than explicit organisational guidelines that control *prescriptive* or *pecuniary* emotion management.

The notion of spaces captures the ability of organisational actors to evade organisationally prescribed feeling rules and allows an examination of a 'special kind of absenteeism, a defaulting not from prescribed activity but from prescribed being' (Goffman, 1961b, p. 171). Many forms of activity takes place in these various spaces according to social feeling rules and people in organisations use them to create and maintain familial bonds, to relieve anger and anxiety, to register their resistance to demands made of them by management and to take time to offer extra emotion work as a gift to colleagues or customers and clients. The rest of the chapter will attempt to capture the performances of *presentational* and *philanthropic* emotion management in their many guises, within spaces for resistance and misbehaviour, spaces for the gift exchange, spaces for occupational communities, spaces for a bit of a laugh, spaces for violations, and spaces for the creation and maintenance of identity. In other words, this, along with the previous two chapters, enables a view of the best and worst of organisational life.

Spaces for resistance and misbehaviour

With the decline in overt, collective episodes of resistance it is easy to assume that the 'gap' in the employment relationship has been successfully bridged. That is, worker effort equals management demand. A combination of right-wing political ideology, the changing nature of work and the introduction of forms of normative control through HRM practices serve to support this assumption. There are, of course, some quarters in organisational analysis that do not recognise any form of conflict at all. Such approaches tend to link a relationship between environment, structure and behaviour with people cast as passive adapters. This is underpinned by a systems or functionalist perspective which assumes an underlying consensus and interdependence of the parts of the organisation. The emphasis is on equilibrium with structure being the determining factor for successful management. The messy reality of conflict in the employment relationship is absent as there is hardly ever a gap to be filled. Organisational theorists who operate within a behavioural framework do recognise various forms of conflict and resistance but reduce it to something that can be understood and therefore managed. What some authors describe as 'unconventional practices' can be dealt with in conventional ways – through communication, structures, planning and control, and the provision of a means through which employees can express their voice and leadership style:

> Managers in industry should provide the foundation for the creation of the appropriate workplace culture in which only the least disruptive and damaging forms of discontent are promoted, rewarded and are naturally adopted as the logical response to situations of discontent. (Analoui and Kakabadse, 1993, p. 58 cited in Ackroyd and Thompson, 1999, p. 19)

This style focuses on the individual and recognises not a basic conflict of interest between employer and employed but a pathological 'deviance' in the employee which can be managed. We see both of these views underlying much of the recent HRM and general management prescriptive literature. The basic problem with these approaches is that they simply do not recognise the capacity for self-organising which employees have. In both of these accounts conflict is conceived as individual, irrational, marginal or temporary.

There are writers who recognise the inherently conflictual nature of the employment relationship but go so far as to declare that the final frontier of control has been crossed. This approach, in a different way to those mentioned earlier, particularly believes in the power of new HRM practices to inculcate employees with a fierce loyalty to the company, wherein they become self-disciplining and, to borrow Foucault's term, docile bodies. This is said to be achieved through powerful discourse and cultural control. Willmott (1993), for instance, compares modern organisations with *Orwell's 1984* where organisational culture is something from which we cannot escape, but more importantly we do not feel we want to escape. Therefore we 'willingly reproduce prevalent relations of domination and exploitation' (Willmott, 1993, p. 520). Similarly, Deetz describes how we, as employees, 'strategise our own subordination' and 'the disciplined member of the corporation wants on his or her own what the corporation wants' (Deetz, 1992, p. 42). And Townley (1994) discusses how recruitment and selection processes and performance management systems render the subject as object, producing a worker that is readily calculable to management in every way. This literature portrays a 'velvet cage', which is soft and subtle and irresistible.

There are problems with all of the approaches which suggest that the gap in the employment relationship has been bridged, through one means or another. There are plenty of accounts of work from a variety of sources to show that for the vast majority of employees the organisations they experience day by day are still authoritarian, rule bound and punitive (Thompson, 1993). This displays that organisations have many continuities with the past, with forms of management based on low-trust regimes where direct control or Taylorism is far from dead and gone. As the analysis of *prescriptive* and *pecuniary* emotion management in the last chapter shows, commitment to 'soft' HRM practices and normative control regimes is often only a 'surface' act; a cynical embracement of organisational or commercial feeling rules that, on many occasions, are experienced as alien to the employees who are asked to enact them. Finally, whilst recognising the basic conflict of interest inherent in the employment relationship that results in a continuous emotional effort-bargain (Callaghan and Thompson, 2002), it should also be recognised how various organisational rules are continually re-negotiated, highlighting how the trickle down effects of prescribed feeling rules means that the message becomes re-interpreted within the frame of social feeling rules and emotion management performances are not always enacted as management might wish.

As far as bending organisational feeling rules are concerned, this can come in both individual and collective forms. Individuals offer empty performances and work groups evade and re-interpret prescribed feeling rules finding the necessary space to create their own group specific 'ways of being'. There are various ways of describing these activities but Ackroyd and Thompson's concept of 'misbehaviour' is particularly useful to illustrate these everyday, often barely noticeable, acts of resistance precisely because it encapsulates the variability of human conduct and in their words 'bends the methodological and theoretical stick away from all-seeing, all-knowing management, back towards self-aware, self active labour' (Ackroyd and Thompson, 1999, p. 162).This also supports Edwards' *et al.* (1996) findings from an empirical study which 'suggest that conflict at workplace level is not so much being removed as re-organised and expressed in new ways' (Edwards *et al.*, 1996, p. 284).

This is not to say that misbehaviour is a new phenomenon. The recalcitrant worker has long been the subject of research and workers have always reacted to prescribed feeling rules in a myriad of ways. But under the more recent regimes of normative control the recalcitrant worker takes on a new meaning and Ackroyd and Thompson (1999) suggest that the traditional pattern of organisational misbehaviour is changing; away from the familiar, traditional examples of soldiering and absenteeism and toward more subtle kinds of behaviour that are in many ways more difficult for managers to handle. This is a welcome alternative view of contemporary organisations as it is increasingly assumed that the informal aspects of organisational life can be captured and its energies harnessed to meet capitalism's veracious demands. As Ackroyd and Thompson (1999, p. 27) usefully point out 'The view of the employer and manager – that the employee will be willing to identify with their company – is no more nor less than a startling piece of wishful thinking.'

As the last chapter shows, resistance to organisationally prescribed feeling rules can be very subtle. Workers are able to distance themselves from the role prescribed to them and offer empty performances of *pecuniary* or *prescriptive* emotion management that serve a multitude of beneficial functions to the employee. Some episodes of 'misbehaviour' may be classified as coping mechanisms, others as acts of resistance and defiance against the obligatory rituals of deference that deny interactants the basic right to dignity (Hodson, 2001). Often spaces are created where the status quo can be challenged and, however gradually, ultimately changed. These small spaces of resistance and misbehaviour do not promise grand revolution or an immediate disruption of organisational hierarchies but every organisation has its spaces, its 'damp corners' as Goffman describes them, where the demands of work are mediated, where resistance 'breeds and starts to infest the establishment' (Goffman, 1961b, p. 268). Within these dark corners workers can protect their sense of self from the invasive demands of commercial feeling rules, they can build their own communities at work forming relationships and offering support to each other, they can use display, rather than feeling, rules as a protective mechanism and they can subtly adjust interactions with customers or demanding colleagues re-interpreting the rules as they enact them. Goffman beautifully summarises the wealth of activity that arises once rules are prescribed:

> Whenever we look at a social establishment, … we find that participants decline in some way to accept the official view of what they should be putting into and getting out of the organization and, behind this, of what sort of self and world they are to accept for themselves. Where enthusiasm is expected, there will be apathy; where loyalty, there will be disaffection; where attendance, absenteeism; where robustness, some kind of illness; where deeds are to be done, varieties of inactivity. We find a multitude of homely little histories, each in its way a movement of liberty. Wherever worlds are laid on, underlives develop. (Goffman, 1961b, p. 267)

Indeed, underlives do develop but are not confined to the 'damp corners' of organisational life. Resistance and misbehaviour comes in a myriad of forms and it continually crosses formal, temporal, spatial and hierarchical organisational boundaries, often with surprising consequences. As will be seen from the investigation of 'spaces for humour' presented later in this chapter, humour can cause mischief in organisations but it is also a means of letting off steam and, as such, can contribute to getting the job done in an effective manner. And, in what Ackroyd and Thompson (1999) describe as 'the complicity of management', management find some forms of misbehaviour are a fruitful means of maintaining manageable levels of conflict and 'turn a blind eye' to a bending of the rules, or they are involved with resisting organisational rules themselves.

It should also be recognised that not all forms of resistance manifest as what might typically be seen as misbehaviour. Where people in organisations resist the prescribed feeling rules spaces are opened up for *presentational* and *philanthropic* emotion management to be performed according to a variety of motivations: extraordinary efforts at emotion work are offered as a gift, occupational communities or communities of coping are created which help to buffer organisational actors from the ravages of organisational demands, playful practices relieve boredom and ease strained situations whilst also being used as a powerful negotiative device, relationships are formed and broken, and violence, bullying and harassment are suffered. The rest of this chapter will explore all of these spaces within and between organisationally prescribed feeling rules in all of their variance and complexity.

Spaces for a gift exchange

Even within the social side of organisations there may be occasions when actors have to carry out hard emotion work; times when responses are not habitual reactions to implicit rules. At these moments, when actors become aware of a discrepancy between how they actually feel and how they think they ought to feel, they are in a position to consciously decide how much effort is put into making their own feelings match the socially prescribed face. The freedom to 'give that little extra' comes under the category of *philanthropic* emotion management and is a special case in that it denotes extra effort has been invested into offering a sincere performance as a gift to those around us. As Hochschild (1979, 1983, 1989b) states, some gestures in social exchange 'seem more than ample others less'. She describes this concept as a 'gift exchange' and points out that 'the most generous gesture of all is the act of successful self-persuasion, of genuine feeling and frame change, a deep acting that jells, that works, that in the end is not phoney' (Hochschild, 1979, p. 274).

The rigours of organisational life do not preclude this gift being offered as an everyday occurrence. As Frost *et al.* (2000, p. 26) suggest 'organisations are sites of everyday healing and pain' and, therefore, the ability to give emotion management as a gift is a vital part of both social and organisational life. Without this social actors would appear to exist in a cynical world of self-concerned agents, when in fact much of social interaction is centred around not only saving actors' own faces but also those around them (Goffman, 1967). This is especially the case where close working communities exist or the emotional labour process is particularly gruelling and colleagues offer performances of *philanthropic* emotion management in mutual support. In addition, like the category of *presentational* emotion management, organisational actors can be found drawing upon this as part of their work role; expanding the emotional labour process beyond the scope of the dictates of *prescriptive* or *pecuniary* emotion management. This highlights how care-giving and the giving and receiving of compassion is interwoven in working lives (Kahn, 1998). It might be suggested that it is *philanthropic* emotion management that represents everyday humanity in the workplace.

Perhaps one of the most obvious occupational groups that might be expected to offer their emotion work as a gift are caring professionals (Bolton, 2000b; Bone, 2002). In an era when 'creative altruism' is increasingly rejected in favour of a 'market mentality' (Titmus, 1970, p. 245), caring professionals nonetheless allocate themselves the time to offer extra emotion work as a gift to consumers of care. Though there are many studies that show how caring professionals frequently offer extra emotion work to each other, this is more of an equal exchange (Bolton, 2000b; Meerabeau and Page, 1998). As part of a stable community they are givers and takers of the gift which continually helps to create, maintain and heal the bonds of kinship. This is unlike the emotion work caring professionals offer to clients, which is given with little or no expectation of a return on their investment – other than the satisfaction they derive from being able to 'make a difference' (McQueen, 1997; Titmus, 1970). Nevertheless, though they may empathise deeply, they cannot truly share their feelings whilst at work as they must always maintain the professional face (Bolton, 2001). They offer a little extra and become deeply involved in clients' situations and also have to work extra hard to enact professional feeling rules and present the image of the professional carer. In this way caring professionals must work doubly hard on their emotions. They not only perform *prescriptive* and, increasingly, *pecuniary* emotion management within the confines of the emotional labour process, but also offer extra emotion work as a gift in the form of authentic caring behaviour. As Richard Titmus (1970, p. 212) points out in his examination of the gift relationship, what caring professionals offer to consumers of care is special because, unlike the concept of a gift exchange, it carries with it no explicit or implicit demand for a return gift.

Performances of *philanthropic* emotion management for the benefit of customers would be less expected from front-line service workers who have little autonomy or room for manoeuvre in the emotional labour process. We frequently hear of call-centre workers, waitresses and fast-food workers resisting the strictures of enforced customer interaction; either by setting out to deliberately disrupt the carefully preserved emotional climate of servitude or, more subtly, withdrawing their emotion work and only ever presenting a hollow smile, if a smile at all (Hopfl, 2002; Leidner, 1996; Paules, 1996). However, the category of *philanthropic* emotion management within the typology of workplace emotion shows very clearly that not all acts of defiance will have a detrimental effect upon the service encounter; on the contrary, a refusal to abide by commercial feeling rules has the potential to improve the quality of customer relations, though it may have negative connotations for the achievement of objective targets. A call-centre worker expresses this tension very well:

> We get a lot of people who are on their own, they're pensioners. They ask for a balance, and then they will want a chat – 'what's the weather like?' I'm quite happy to chat to them, but it's always in the back of your mind, got to watch my average handling time. I think you're setting a better example for the bank. (Customer Service Representative cited in Callaghan and Thompson, 2002, p. 250)

This call-centre worker, though aware of the material demands made of her via the demands for *pecuniary* emotion management, re-interprets encounters with customers depending upon context and different motivations. Represented in this way, service workers cease to be self-disciplining subjects or sufferers of emotional dissonance. Whilst they have little influence over the setting of the stage on which they must carry out their work role they are, nevertheless, an active and controlling force in the service encounter. The pensioner is a person to whom the CSR relates both socially and morally (Wray-Bliss, 2001), therefore, for both participants in the encounter the exchange of social niceties creates and sustains a 'moral order'.

A particularly good example of this are air cabin crew, where first aid emergencies are common and crew may have to comfort and assist passengers who are unwell (Bolton and Boyd, 2003). They may feel empathy and compassion and due to this attunement decide to go beyond professional feeling rules attached to their health and safety duties or the commercial feeling rules so eloquently represented in Hochschild's (1983) study of Delta airline cabin crew. As in social life, the cabin crew do this in order that they may reassure others of 'genuine' motives and commitments. A member of cabin crew describes an incident involving an elderly passenger:

> As I walked past the toilet an elderly passenger fainted. I crouched down to assist and she immediately vomited over both of us. I had to help her to clean her clothes and try to calm and reassure her. It was very traumatic for both of us but I did not mind. (Cabin Crew cited in Bolton and Boyd, 2003, p. 299)

This cabin crew member did not merely adhere to professional feeling rules in restoring order and dignity to the situation; neither did she concentrate solely on producing 'customer contentment' according to commercial feeling rules. She worked hard to mask feelings of distaste and offered 'deference and demeanour' (Goffman, 1967) to care for the elderly passenger as a fellow social interactant, not merely as a customer of the airline.

Spaces for a bit of a laugh

The significant part humour plays in organisational life has long been recognised. For instance, Roy's (1973, p. 215) classic study of shop floor workers brought attention to the way apparently inane banter between organisational actors is a vital form of communication in that it offers a form of structure and meaning and gentles the 'beast of boredom' to the 'harmless kitten'. More recent ethnographic studies, carried out in a variety of workplace settings, confirm the important role of play and laughter. They note that humour crosses organisational boundaries, it may subvert, support or accommodate social forms (Linstead, 1985) and serves many purposes: conformity (Ackroyd and Crowdy, 1992; Thompson and Bannon, 1985); opposition (Collinson, 1988; Westwood, 1984); relief from boredom (Burawoy, 1979; Collinson, 1988; Roy, 1973) or 'letting off steam' (Fine, 1988).

Workplace humour is a particularly good example of how emotional activity may cross organisational boundaries. Typically play and work are seen as polar opposites, fun and humour belong in the hidden, unmanaged spaces in organisations. However, recent research shows instances when humour in organisations is not only in the interests of 'group conformity' or can be construed as 'inherently oppositional' (Collinson, 1992) but can also act as a means of relieving boredom (Collinson, 1992) or 'letting off steam' (Fine, 1988). Management has been swift to recognise its positive effects and note that 'workplay' need not always undermine performance. Humour can create a sense of involvement (Ashforth and Humphry, 1995; Barsoux, 1993; Duncan and Feisal, 1989) and, in the interests of encouraging employee consent to the rigours of the labour process (Burawoy, 1979), management often ignore, tolerate and even actively encourage playful practices. As Fine found in his study of restaurant workers:

> I suggest that play in the kitchen reinforces work in four ways. First, kitchen play fits into the workday in such a way as to diminish the likelihood of boredom. Second, play, like work, builds collective cooperation. Third, the existence of expressive behaviour at work serves to maintain the worker's allegiance to the workplace and prevents turnover. Fourth, one may play at work, and add 'joy' to one's occupational requirements. (Fine, 1988, p. 12)

In this example informal rules, which generally inform humorous episodes at work, do not stand in opposition to formal organisational rules. That is, they do not create a contradictory relationship but rather have the unintended consequence of furthering organisational goals.

Humour can indeed add 'joy' to work but it can also have a serious point to it and may not always be seen as beneficial to all participants. Many accounts show how teasing and practical joking amongst colleagues can be harsh and destructive (Ackroyd and Crowdy, 1992; Burawoy, 1979; Collinson, 1988). 'Applied' humour such as this is often used to reorder the hierarchical positions of members of informal work-groups by testing the vulnerability of various group members. Humour used in this way demonstrates the multifaceted nature of joking relationships. Play and laughter may serve to bind an occupational community together and give relief from the monotony and pressures of work but it can also create long-standing and deep-seated conflicts.

Despite recognition of both the creative and 'dark-side' of humour (Collinson, 1988, p. 198), and its power to alter informal relationships, it is rare that play, joking and laughter are seen to have any transformative power. In general, humour is underestimated as a form of resistance at work, despite various accounts showing that it can become a critical resource and a powerful means of social control (Ackroyd and Thompson, 1999). During social interaction humour is often employed to deal with difficulties encountered in hierarchically structured situations where the division of 'definitional labour' (Goffman, 1959, p. 21) is not equal. The 'unreal' nature of humour means that actors may attempt to influence the conduct of others in order to upset the established 'working consensus' (Goffman, 1959). The power of humour as an effective form of covert resistance lies in the way apparently innocuous banter is able to define and redefine 'non-play' activity (Linstead, 1985). Frequently employees' light-hearted comments are actually of a deeply subversive character and have a 'serious intellectual content' (Ackroyd and Thompson, 1999, p. 111) that is used to register criticism, defiance or discontent concerning certain persons, practices or situations. As Emerson states 'for the very reason that humour officially does not "count" persons are induced to risk messages that might be unacceptable if stated seriously' (1973, p. 269). Thus, under the guise of humorous discourse, the delicate balance of human interaction is disturbed and the once dominant party finds they have lost control of the exchange. They are left feeling 'unruled, unreal and anomic' (Goffman, 1967, p. 135) and unable to reassert their authority without losing further face. Even where humour may not be directly aimed at those in authority, joking and laughter are ways in which employees delineate their identity and maintain a sense of self separate from the workplace. Teasing, practical joking and general exchange of light-hearted banter between organisational actors creates spaces where organisational prescription may be evaded and from which management are firmly excluded.

The evidently meaningless character of much of organisational humour often leads to the conclusion that humorous discourse, whilst creating some temporary discomfort for those who are its target, is a futile form of resistance. The framework of interaction may be momentarily disrupted through the use of applied humour but the structures of power and control remain firmly intact (Collinson, 1988; Mulkay, 1988). To dismiss the use of humour as a mode of resistance, however, is to neglect its negotiative potential. Humour plays on contradiction. Applied humour, especially, identifies weaknesses and creates ambiguity. It upsets the status quo in subtle ways, blurring and obfuscating power relationships. It creates interpretive loose ends that can be picked up time and time again in order to continually reassert dissent. Whilst the use of humour as a mode of resistance makes no claim to over throw structures of power and domination, each interaction which successfully unsettles the working consensus is a micro-revolution (Douglas, 1975) where the 'unreal' of joking and laughter creates the possibility of changing very real hierarchically ordered relationships.

Spaces for occupational communities

Occupational communities come in many forms; ranging from work-groups who are recognised as having a distinctive identity to those who form sub-cultures within a larger organisational culture, to communities of coping where organisational actors come together from a definite need to offer mutual support. Just how much of organisational life is taken up in these spaces varies a great deal and depends very much upon occupation, organisation structure, and spatial and temporal constraints. Whatever their form and degree of institutionalisation, occupational communities are generally recognised as a by-product of formal organisational life; as small reservoirs of social life that are classed as peripheral to the formal organisational structure. They are either ignored or tolerated as an element of the human side of enterprise that will, as an automatic reaction to management intervention in the formal processes of work, be pulled into line with organisational prescription. As Goffman (1961b, p. 280) notes of this particular approach to understanding people in organisations 'the simplest sociological view of the individual and his self is that he is to himself what his place in an organisation defines him to be'. Yet occupational communities contribute a great deal to the fabric of the organisation and not just as places to evade organisationally prescribed feeling rules. Work is such a large part of people's lives that it is relatively safe to assume that organisational actors 'seek a feeling of connection with one another, a feeling of belonging, and a feeling of being cared for and respected' (Frost *et al.*, 2000, p. 26), thus, occupational communities offer a source of friendship and support, in many cases providing the only basis of pleasure in work (Abrams, 2002; Westwood, 1984). On the other hand, they can exert a form of control and be the source of violations far more powerful than the organisation is able to impose (Ackroyd and Crowdy, 1992; Collinson, 1992; Ditton, 1977).

Spaces for occupational communities, sub-cultures and communities of coping are created, re-created and continually strengthened through the spontaneous communication of painful experiences (Korczynski, 2002); through common frustrations concerning the rigours of the labour process (Westwood, 1984); through endless 'chatter' and 'bitching' about everyday life (Sotirin and Gottfried, 1999), via banter that often creates unique methods of identification for individuals in the community (Bolton, 2002) and game playing where the rules are somehow known but never available for scrutiny (Collinson, 1992; Roy, 1973). In this way, shared meanings are created by members of occupational communities through the subscription to implicit feeling rules that act as a frame (Goffman, 1959) for social interaction that gives a unique character. What Frost *et al.* (2000, p. 35) refer to as an 'emotional ecology'. Within occupational communities social feeling rules are drawn upon to offer empathy or humour as a gift to colleagues in the form of *philanthropic* emotion management and the order of interaction is maintained in the form of *presentational* emotion management.

Ackroyd and Crowdy's (1992) research concerning slaughtermen show how occupational communities can dominate almost to the exclusion of any managerial intervention. The slaughtermen have their own accepted patterns of behaviour, their own very particular feeling rules that, though appearing barbaric to those outside of their 'space', are everyday ways of being for those involved. The slaughtermen can be classed as a very particular example of a strong occupational community due to the nature of their work and how it is perceived by society. The specific nature of certain types of work leads it to be classified as 'tainted' (Hughes, 1958) and gives it the social distinction of 'dirty work'. As Ashforth and Kreiner (1999, p. 415) usefully point out: 'the common denominator among tainted jobs is not so much their specific attributes but the visceral repugnance of people to them.' Occupations that deal in death, dirt or undesirable aspects of society tend to create a distinctive occupational community (Ackroyd and Crowdy, 1992; McQueen, 1997; Meerabeau and Page, 1998). 'Dirty workers' become the celebrated 'Other' in relation to the socially structured notions of 'good work'. Similarly, workers who work unsocial hours feel generally out of sync with the rest of the social world. Both of these groups find it very difficult to form relationships outside of work, meaning that they rely very much on a form of collective sense-making between fellow workers which excludes outsiders thus intensifying the bonds of the occupational community.

Many professional groups can also be included in this analysis where a strong identification with particular professional feeling rules assert certain accepted ways of being that bind a community together. It is well documented how nurses work and socialise with nurses, entirely relying on support from colleagues within their communities of coping (Bolton, 2000b; Korczynski, 2002), and accountants share similar conceptions of personhood only with fellow accountants (Grey, 1994). As a result, they generate their own coping mechanisms, their own methods of letting off steam and their own ways of asserting their collective identity. In turn, a sense of belonging to a closed world within symbolic boundaries is created that serves to reinforce a sense of difference, even isolation. The very reasons why their work may be classified as different are used by those within the occupation to justify and verify its value. The lack of appreciation and understanding of the peculiar demands attached to their work from those outside of the occupation ensures that sense-making is rarely diluted and, therefore, the community is continually strengthened as it is perceived by those within that it is only they who recognise the special nature of their work.

Occupational communities are not only important to those work groups who seem to be set-apart from society. Many occupations regard teamwork and support from colleagues as 'lifelines' in coping with the various demands of the job. For instance, air cabin crew are known to rely upon a sense of camaraderie to help them deal with difficult situations, ranging from intensive work schedules to dealing with difficult or abusive passengers (Bolton and Boyd, 2003).

They use play and laughter in order to evade organisational prescription but their commitment to colleagues is also an expression of *philanthropic* emotion management – the freedom to give that little extra. Bolton and Boyd (2003) report that a main reason for cabin crew not 'calling in sick' for a flight even when ill is because they do not want one of their colleagues to be called out from standby duty.

Whatever type of space occupational communities may occupy, it is notable that it is a social arena and thus, performances of *presentational* and *philanthropic* emotion management are fuelled by social feeling rules and motivated by the needs for human contact, a sense of ontological security and an attachment to a collective identity. In the examples of nurses comforting one another and cabin crew protecting their colleagues' rights to free time from work it is notable how it is a sense of commitment to the social group at work that is the motivational force behind these generous gestures, not successful normative control regimes implemented by the organisation.

Spaces for violations

Whilst examining spaces in organisational prescribed feeling rules, where kindnesses can be offered, friendships formed and shared banter lightens the spirits, we must be careful not to get carried away with the 'nice guy' theories of social action. When talking about the social spaces in organisations, episodes of sexual harassment, bullying and physical violence clearly represent the damp and dark corners of organisational life and though it comes in many guises,[2] social interaction that includes such episodes clearly seeks to degrade, humiliate and subordinate certain organisational actors and, therefore, can be generally classified as violations (Hearn and Parkin, 2001). This acts as a harsh reminder that not all of social interaction rests upon rituals of deference and demeanour. It also emphasises that violations are social acts carried out by social actors. Too often workplace violence and aggression is neatly contained within organisational boundaries as though societal influences are of no importance (Neuman and Baron, 1998). But violations do not happen spontaneously or individually, even though this is often apparently so. They are rooted within organisational processes, which in turn form part of wider social processes. And in some spaces acts of physical violence, verbal abuse or a constant stream of sexual innuendo is seen as everyday reality. This highlights how activity within organisations cannot be easily categorised. There are overlapping violations, this is what often renders them so dangerously elusive. For instance, examples of harassment, bullying and violence can be found within the realm of spaces for a bit of a laugh in the form of abrasive humour or practical jokes; spaces for being human where sexual attraction is not reciprocal but pursued anyway; spaces for occupational communities with ritualised practices that emphasise conformism, and spaces for the creation and maintenance of identities through the imposition of particular ways of being.

Until relatively recently violations have not been a central concern of organisational analysis. Where research has taken place it has centred on the issue of sexuality and gendered power relations in organisations. For instance, studies concerning sexual harassment reveal the power of heterosexual masculinity and the associated violence in organisational life where men seek to control themselves and others as a way of affirming their male identity. Similarly, various feminist analyses show how the interpretation of social feeling rules and the performance of *presentational* emotion management clearly reflect forms of collective, institutionalised and interpersonal domination that is frequently associated with masculinity. Collinson's (1992) study of shop floor joking practices, Ackroyd and Crowdy's (1992) observances of the easy acceptance of violent acts within the community of slaughtermen, and Collinson and Collinson's (1996) portrayal of the taken-for-granted nature of sexual harassment are good examples. This is not to suggest that anger, violence or harassment is solely a male prerogative. However, powerful emotions are more usually connected with men which in turn is associated with men's more powerful position within social structures and their sense of entitlement to preserve these power inequities (Shields, 2002).

Nevertheless, it is important to recognise that not all violations are the product of gendered social relations. Spaces in organisation have their own social stages for action and occurrences of various forms of violations are embedded within other social divisions, such as race, class, disability and age. The various performances of *presentational* or *philanthropic* emotion management will reflect not only organisational actors' position in the informal hierarchies within particular occupational communities or work groups but will also be closely related to their position within the large and enduring social structures of inequality. Thus the apparent worth of organisational actors in social spaces within organisations will reflect their perceived worth in society as a whole. In turn, this will most likely not be too far away from the organisation's formal hierarchical relations and violations are frequently perpetrated, encouraged or ignored by those in positions of senior rank.

Within different organisational spaces organisational violations will be experienced differently. Recent studies show how violations directly suffered as part of the emotional labour process can be damaging to organisational actors. As the review of *pecuniary* emotion management in the last chapter demonstrates, the focus on commercial feeling rules is itself a violation of social interaction inviting customer violence to be directed at service-providers (Boyd, 2002) and exacerbating the unequal distribution of definitional labour already based on social divisions. However, what is often neglected are the means by which many front-line service workers re-negotiate their position within the emotional labour process. Filby's (1992) study of life in a betting shop show the women behind the counter use their sexuality as a form of resistance. They mercilessly verbally tease some of the customers and use sexual innuendo as a constant put-down which helps them to assert some sense of worth into a situation that positions them as worthless. Observing nursing auxiliaries working in a care home, Lee-Treweek (1997) notes how they render the elderly people they care for devoid of humanity in the way they roughly handle their bodies, talk over their heads and generally ignore their attempts at communication. No doubt the nursing auxiliaries are distancing themselves from the demands of a gruelling labour process but in doing so they are violating the people in their care. Though the nursing auxiliaries come low in organisational and social hierarchies, within the distribution of power and resources within social divisions they are still higher on the status scale than the elderly in their care.

Spaces for the maintenance and creation of identity

Much of the activity described in the social spaces illustrated in this chapter are small gestures, in many cases barely discernable. So slight that they can hardly be conceived of as resistance as they may cause barely, if any, disruption to the organisation. In fact, performances of *presentational* and *philanthropic* emotion management continually cross boundaries in such a way that they have the unintended consequence of working in the organisation's favour. Kindness shown by call-centre workers and air cabin crew leave customers with favourable impressions of the company and letting off steam with the use of a manic form of humour actually serves to get the job done during periods of frenetic activity and heightened emotions. Even where organisational actors escape into spaces in order to actively resist organisational feeling rules, for instance where workers withdraw and offer only empty performances according to the dictates of *pecuniary* emotion management and the small resistances involved in ironic humour, they can hardly be said to cause an obvious and disruptive effect on hierarchical relations in the organisation. Yet these spaces are very important, nevertheless. Important because the ability to escape into these spaces allows organisational actors to protect their sense of self from the invasive demands of organisationally prescribed feeling rules. Goffman describes just how vital apparently insignificant activity can be:

> To forgo prescribed activities, or to engage in them in unprescribed ways or for unprescribed purposes, is to withdraw from the official self and the world officially available to it. To prescribe activity is to prescribe a world; to dodge a prescription can be to dodge an identity. (Goffman, 1961b, p. 170)

Commercial, professional and organisational feeling rules not only demand routine performances of *prescriptive* or *pecuniary* emotion management. Prescribed feeling rules bring with them assumptions concerning the 'nature' of those involved in the emotion management performances and it is these assumptions that organisational actors attempt to resist. Paules' (1996, p. 266) study of waitresses highlights how they refuse to be denied 'the courtesies of personhood':

> Though constrained to comply with the interactive conventions of master and ser-vant, while clad in a domestic's uniform, the waitress does not internalize an image of service as servitude and self as servant. In times of stress she sees her work as war and herself as soldier. In times of peace she sees her work as a private enterprise and herself as entrepreneur. (Paules, 1996, p. 284)

Increasingly organisations seek huge amounts of emotional investment from their employees. The organisation attempts to prescribe when organisational actors should feel happy or sad, when they should feel enthusiastic and commit-ted. However, even those who profess to enjoy their work, feel some loyalty to the organisations they work for and generally are seen as 'good' employees, find many ways in which they assert and continually re-affirm their sense of self. Goffman (1961b, p. 280) suggests that it is only 'against something that the self can emerge' displaying how it is the various social spaces within an organisation where *philanthropic* and *presentational* emotion management is performed that actually constitutes the heart and soul of organisational life. It also shows how performances of emotion management continually cross organisational bound-aries, leaking into even those performances which adhere completely to organi-sational prescribed feeling rules and preventing a wholesale invasion of self:

> Without something to belong to, we have no stable self, and yet total commitment and attachment to any social unit implies a kind of selflessness. Our sense of being a person can come from being drawn into a wider social unit; our sense of selfhood can arise through the little ways in which we resist the pull. Our status is backed by the solid buildings of the world, while our sense of identity often resides in the cracks. (Goffman, 1961b, p. 280)

The small measures of resistance that take place within the spaces discussed in this chapter could, therefore, be described as the largest gestures of all.

Conclusion and implications for an understanding of emotion in organisations

The presence of *presentational* and *philanthropic* emotion management helps to avoid an overly deterministic picture of organisational life and enables the reader to 'capture the agency, and knowledgeability of subjects, the dynamic, interpretative and interwoven character of everyday organizational relations' (Collinson, 1992, p. 45). Even though the categories of *presentational* and *philanthropic* cover a myriad of emotion management performances, the labelling of these various performances under easily recognisable categories serves to highlight the intrusion of the 'social side' of organisational emotionality into that directly policed by the organisation. It also allows us to see how various forms of organisational emotionality continually cross boundaries. Some forms of *presentational* and *philanthropic* emotion management may prove to be disruptive to the order of organisational life, much of it is not – as we see from tele-sales agents offering their *philanthropic* emotion management to elderly customers or groups of workers forming 'communities of coping'. Whether through sharing their distress or through various forms of humour these performances, rather than being troublesome, actually enable the organisation to run smoothly. Often management are not slow to recognise this and on many occasions informal practices are adopted by organisations; what were once emotion management performances according to social feeling rules become dictated by organisational rules. As Goffman notes with some irony: 'Domestic establishments are not the only ones in which there is a regularization through marriage of previous living in sin' (Goffman, 1961b, p. 178). For instance, Royal Automobile Club (RAC) has implemented time out sessions at their call-centre so that staff may have formally sanctioned space where they can escape from the rigours of tele-sales work, service management literature now extols companies to allow workers to deviate from an imposed script and 'be themselves' with customers and nurses are given an official 'smoking' area so that they no longer have to hide away in a cramped toilet cubicle, even offering official break-times. It is, however, interesting to note how new spaces continually emerge and new forms of 'underlife' do indeed continually come to life. In other words there are, in one form or another, spaces for a gift exchange, spaces for occupational communities, spaces for having a bit of a laugh and, giving consideration to the darker side of organisational life, there are spaces where the structured inequalities of social life are represented as individual violations.

Notes

1. It should be noted that Goffman does not view 'universal human nature' as a 'very human thing', rather he sees it as a societal construct 'built up not from inner psychic propensities but from moral rules that are impressed upon him from without' (1967, p. 45).
2. Which include intimidation, interrogation, surveillance, persecution, subjugation, discrimination and exclusion.

8

Mixed Feelings

Exploring the emotional organisation

The book has so far fulfilled several objectives: it has brought conceptual clarity into an otherwise ambiguous and unclear area of study; it adds to a sociological understanding of workplace emotionality and finds a place for the subject in organisational analysis; it introduces concepts which allow close examination of the emotional life of organisations and it offers insights into people's everyday working lives. The introduction of a typology of workplace emotionality brings the emotional life of an organisation into focus so that a picture of the emotionally skilled actor emerges throughout the book.

In contrast to many recent accounts concerning the emotional organisation, the approach to organisational emotionality presented here acknowledges the potential transformative power of human action whilst also recognising forces which inhibit conduct. The important contribution to the present understanding involves drawing on both symbolic interactionism and labour process analysis. The core insight is that human interaction is set firmly within a structural framework. The use of Goffman allows an understanding of how organisational actors have the necessary skills which enable them to comply with management demands for performances of 'emotional labour'. His 'frame analysis' shows many of the constraints that surround social actors in what might be described as a framework for social action that contains layers of reality, as opposed to the criticism sometimes levelled at his work as consisting of 'fractured islands of reality' (Hochschild, 1983). However, even though Goffman often refers to the importance of 'society', once removed from the level of the local his analysis becomes more limited. It is LPA which complements Goffman's accounts of social action, especially when attempting to place action in the frame of a capitalist labour process.

Labour process analysis is essential to an understanding of the 'discourse of enterprise' (du Gay and Salaman, 1992): the political, economic and managerial processes that have contributed to recent organisational change. The decline in traditional manufacturing industries and the rise of the service sector have created the need for entrepreneurs in the workplace: flexible and multi-skilled workers who enable companies to compete in volatile markets. An integral part of the so-called enterprise culture is the idea of consumer sovereignty. Political rhetoric concerning the rights of consumers has been particularly effective in transforming clients of British public services into demanding customers. This has added commercial dimensions to the duties of public sector employees and has opened up their work to LPA.

An analysis of structural constraints such as these emphasise management's need to mobilise worker consent, and even commitment, rather than attempt direct control. After all, if management require workers to offer 'commercial love' to customers, how much more effective the performance will be if the worker is committed to the aims of the enterprise. Whilst Goffman analyses the intricacies of social action, it is LPA which highlights that interaction which occurs as part of the capitalist labour process is a distorted form of social interaction. For instance, the perspicacious customer demands satisfaction and the balance of interaction in a service encounter is not achieved through reciprocal obligation. The exchange becomes unequal and employees are supposedly compensated with a wage. In effect, capitalism has appropriated an employee's emotion management skills as a means of creating surplus value and yet this type of work is barely, if at all, recognised as hard and demanding labour or given the status and material reward of skilled work.

The skilled emotion worker

The book has sought to address some of the conceptual confusions around the notion of emotion work by highlighting the dynamic and multi-dimensional nature of organisational life. Unfortunately this highlights, rather than addresses, the contradiction in the way that emotion work is seen as a core competence but attracts little material reward unless tied to a recognised technical skill (Green, 1999). Despite the growing recognition of the importance of emotion work or emotional competencies (Goleman, 1998a), and concern over a shortage of key skills in the British labour market (DfEE, 2001), employees who successfully carry out emotion work may not be acknowledged as skilled workers at all. Rather, they are said to have certain types of personality, to possess particular character traits or have natural caring qualities. Whilst communication skills and interpersonal skills are frequently mentioned as essential qualities in the workforce (DfEE, 2000a and b, 2001), such competencies are not easily measured or certified. Instead companies rely on recruiting 'self-monitors' and 'extroverts' who 'will be more inclined to comply with organizational display norms' (Morris and Feldman, 1996, p. 1005; Rafaeli and Sutton, 1987). Recognised only as 'personal attributes' (DfEE, 2001) emotion work remains a shadowy and ill-defined form of knowledge work.

Emotion work, of course, is an integral part of everyday social and organisational life, and has always been a vital part of many labour processes. Increasingly, however, the emphasis in the labour market is on creativity, rather than rule-bound behaviour, with communication, team-working, customer care, individual initiative and self-reliance seen as key skills (Brown *et al.*, 2001; DfEE, 2000a, 2001). Emotion workers are far from homogenous, with some occupations involved in the production of material goods or requiring complex technical knowledge; while others, such as the front-line service worker, invest the full capacity of their labour power in presenting the desired corporate image and creating customer satisfaction. Occupations involving emotion work can be found in different positions within a skills hierarchy with large differentials in status and material reward between the 'emotional proletariat' who deliver routinised 'niceness' (MacDonald and Sirianni, 1996) and the caring professions who are deemed to be 'angels of mercy' (Salvage, 1985).

It is not clear that the distinction between technical skills and innate qualities is helpful, particularly given the growing demand for a new model worker able to employ 'soft', 'generic' or 'key' skills (DfEE, 2001). An over-concentration on formal education and qualifications neglects the fact that skill acquisition and utilisation is not a technical formality but a social act. Occupations which require large amounts of emotion work, such as the increasing array of front-line service jobs, rely almost wholly on the embodied capacities of the worker. Capacities that, though they share many of the common features of skill – discretion, variety and experience – are rarely formally recognised. More fundamentally, the emphasis on emotion work as an individualised innate quality actively contributes to the making and re-making of inequalities thus ensuring that it remains a 'non-skill'.

A social stage

A social view of emotion, which forms the core of analysis throughout the book, recognises that emotion work does not exist in a symbolic realm but requires a social stage for its production. Utilising insights into the 'interaction order' (Goffman, 1959, 1967, 1974) it seems that the ritual of every day social interaction is something of a feat. It is a social process that relies upon participants monitoring and regulating their own and others' conduct in order to achieve the 'socialized trance' (Goffman, 1967, p. 113) of spontaneous involvement. There is much emotion work involved in achieving the 'order' of interaction. Similarly, the service interaction relies on emotion workers presenting a desirable demeanour and creating an alluring emotional climate. To achieve this they work on their own emotions and seek to manipulate those of the customer or client, within the feeling and display rules set by the organisation. A successful episode is a fragile accomplishment requiring high levels of skilled emotion work. There is nothing particularly 'natural' about this achievement, yet the illusion remains that certain 'types' of employees are able to carry it off with ease.

For instance, the natural qualities of 'people skills' are seen to be the same as feminine qualities and therefore require no other definition than 'women's work', along with the lack of status this implies. A particularly clear example is the emotion work carried out by caring professionals which is acknowledged as an important aspect of providing a quality service, yet in female dominated occupations the relational skills used in achieving high standards of care are seen as 'womanly qualities'. As such, they are neither acknowledged as essential technical skills nor rewarded in financial or professional terms (Davies and Rosser, 1986; Phillips, 1996). Within the public sector caring professions it is a 'gift' which is nurtured but, outside of this community, it is neither understood nor valued. It is simply something that women 'do'.

The social stage upon which emotion work is preformed also shows how the everyday social process of emotion work, both in and out of organisational life, ensures that it plays a large part in the continual creation and re-creation of social inequalities. The status of participants will be a defining feature of how emotion work is to be carried out: considerations of gender, class, race, occupation and, increasingly, vast material inequalities alter the 'rules of the game' and effect how face-saving activity will be distributed. In fact, it is the structured inequalities of social interaction that provides much of its predictability. Rules of engagement include or exclude social actors on a variety of terms and distribution of 'definitional labour' (Goffman, 1959, p. 21) is far from even. Once again, gender is a defining feature of these interactions where it is often assumed that women will work much harder at face-saving activity in order to maintain the status quo – neither expecting or demanding the deference and demeanour that other social actors, who would be deemed as equal participants in the exchange, would be accorded.

One of the greatest strengths of a social view of emotion is that it is able to include issues such as social class in its analysis. For too long this has been a neglected dimension of the analysis of social interaction, most especially when investigating organisational emotionality where the behavioural approach to emotion management does not recognise that a lack of skills in the area of emotion work is less a personal failure but due to limited embodied dispositions, borne of a limited, class-specific, condition of existence (Charlesworth, 2000; Hochschild, 1989a; Witz *et al.*, 2003, p. 41). Including class in the analysis highlights how some social actors are unable to play according to the company's rules of social interaction and hence suffer exclusion from opportunities in the growing service economy. Leading to the paradoxical situation where there is a growing shortage of 'soft' skills in the labour market but large swathes of the working population are excluded as training and development is offered in objectively measured skills such as Information Technology but not in the 'presentation of self' (Nickson *et al.*, 2003; Thompson *et al.*, 2000).

Customer service

Throughout, the book has argued that emotion work is indeed skilled work and that it has never before been so important to a capitalist economy. Trends in work, growth in interactive service work and the re-imagining of the consumer, of both public and private sector goods and services, as a sovereign customer has meant that emotion workers have had to develop a greater awareness of their social skills and an adaptability in how and when to deploy them (Thompson *et al.*, 2000, p. 128). It is the only form of work which involves simultaneous production and consumption, it is the central ingredient of 'quality service' and team-work and it is viewed as a core competence offering competitive advantage to those companies who successfully utilise it. In consumer capitalism producers' creative capacities are harnessed to serve the needs of capital so emotion work becomes hard and demanding labour requiring skill and control in the regulation of feeling and the presentation of one's self. Yet because it is intangible, immediately perishable, and open to variation, its qualitative features are hard to define rendering emotion work an 'invisible' skill which, though deemed to be a magic ingredient of many occupations, is barely recognised and poorly rewarded.

These paradoxical themes are rooted in the neglect of the social embeddedness of emotion work. In an economy that values skill on the basis of technical formality, the view of emotion as a natural, taken-for-granted quality leads to many mistaken assumptions. Companies go to great lengths to recruit the right 'attitude' (Callaghan and Thompson, 2002) searching for potential employees who possess certain personal characteristics and the ability to 'deal with people'. But ultimately when the customer is sovereign control is inherent in the emotional labour process. Management will impose various control strategies, such as performance targets, surveillance and scripted interaction, in order to regulate the 'natural' qualities of service providers and mould their emotion work into a routinised and predictable performance. This is described in the typology of workplace emotion management presented in Chapter 3 of the book as *pecuniary* emotion management.

Though companies desperately seek sincerity from their front-line service workers' interactions with customers, the social process of customer service is essentially violated by the control imperative. The continued emphasis on speedy transactions enhanced with routinised 'niceness' according to purely commercial feeling rules actually constitutes a form of 'misinvolvement' (Goffman, 1967, p. 117). This is particularly relevant in consumer capitalism as producers' creative capacities are harnessed to serve the needs of capital and make it difficult to sustain the sacredness of the self. The economic interests that tightly control the interaction between service provider and customer disrupt the interaction order that normally serves to 'buffer the self from the direct ravages of inequality' (Schwabe, 1993, p. 342) and help to maintain an element of dignity for all involved.

As previously mentioned, the untoward effects of such controls upon workers' well-being is now well recognised and there are ample studies that recognise the benefits of granting autonomy to front-line service workers (Weatherly and Tansik, 1992; Wharton, 1996). However, such privilege is only ever granted to workers with the 'right attitude' who can be relied upon to express 'real feelings' in the interests of creating the right emotional climate and, hence, improving customer service. This then is not autonomy at all but rather self-rule in line with the organisational regime and the source of blame for any 'improper' behaviour is found within the personalities of the service-provider. There is little recognition of the actual process of the social order of interaction, typical of one-dimensional views of emotion work which neglect that organisational emotionality comes in many forms which all contribute to the emotional life of an organization. As a result, there is little trust that any form of order can be maintained without management intervention. It is the neglect of the social embeddedness of the service encounter that leads to its violation. Enforcing interaction with customers and clients of the organisation into the narrow confines of *pecuniary* emotion management means that neither service-provider or customer truly participate in the encounter as, unlike everyday conversation that has a life of its own, the service encounter is a fabricated performance with faceless actors. Little wonder then that customer relations in late capitalism have been described as a form of 'abuse' to both producer and consumer (Hopfl, 2002).

Care-work

The alienating effects of routinised front-line service work are well documented but what of the changes in the work of public sector professionals who provide a caring service to the public? Emotional investment is increasingly acknowledged as an essential, although often under-valued, element of public sector caring professional's work. Descriptive terms such as 'emotional labour' and 'sentimental work' are used as a means of stressing its importance (James, 1989, 1992, 1993; Smith, 1988, 1992; Strauss *et al.*, 1982). However, 'care-work', just as many other types of work, requires different forms of emotion management and as Chapter 3 shows, the use of a label such as 'emotional labour' tends to underestimate its complexity. Throughout a working day caring professionals, using their emotion management skills, are able to present a variety of faces. The differentiation of various forms of emotion management presented in the typology, as well as an acknowledgement of the underlying forces which currently act to shape 'care-work', helps to display its multifaceted nature. It shows how professional carers' skills lie not only in the accomplishment of technical tasks, but in the creation of the 'correct' emotional climate.

Since the introduction of a markets and managerialist rationality into the public services, work for public sector professionals has dramatically intensified and they are increasingly asked to perform according to commercial feeling rules that they see as alien to their public service ethos (Ackroyd and Bolton, 1999; Phillips, 1996). Caring professionals experience a discrepancy between their professional definition of quality care and the one being imposed by management as perpetual attempts are made to meet customer requirements at the lowest costs (Bolton, 2004a). Further tensions are introduced as patients, who have been re-invented as customers by the 1980s political rhetoric of the enterprise culture, demand to have their unrealistically raised expectations met. In effect, caring professionals are being asked to perform according to the alien feeling rules of *pecuniary* emotion management in an attempt to maintain customer satisfaction in the face of unmet expectations. Nurses, teachers, and social workers find themselves unable to offer what they see as a truly 'quality service'. The time available when they could offer their authentic self to patients, pupils and clients has been restricted.

Time that in the past proved to be mutually beneficial and not only bolstered caring professionals' morale but also led to consumer satisfaction (Issel and Kahn, 1998; Scott *et al.*, 1995). What caring professionals now offer are empty performances. The measured facework of *pecuniary emotion* management is no substitute for authentic *philanthropic* emotion management given as a gift.

Increasing numbers of citizens placing heavy demands upon the public services mean that caring professionals are becoming ever more efficient at presenting the professional face in order to mask their exhaustion and frustration. It could be said that it is their performance of *prescriptive* emotion management which helps to 'paper over the cracks' of an under-resourced service and it is their gift of *philanthropic emotion management* which actually enables genuine quality care (as perceived by the consumer of the service) to be delivered.

There is little doubt that public sector caring professionals are at the front line of care and their emotion work does make a difference to how consumers view the care received. If they were to withdraw their *philanthropic emotion management* and only perform *prescriptive emotion management* half-heartedly, then clearly this would be of great cost to the consumer. By recognising the complex nature of caring work and how service providers and consumers are increasingly affected by over 20 years of market reform it becomes possible to ask 'who benefits and who pays?' At whose cost, the empty performances of *pecuniary emotion* management? The introduction of a typology of workplace emotion makes it conceivable that something so subjective, and often elusive, as organisational emotionality can be opened up to systematic analysis and further an understanding of how actors' emotion management skills can become valuable organisational commodities. Only by recognising how caring professionals are able to move deftly from one form of emotion management to another can it be understood how valuable a contribution their emotion work really is. As this analysis shows caring labour is multifaceted and requires various skilled performances; some the source of great satisfaction, whilst others are the cause of resentment and painful feelings. Caring professionals continue to juggle their mixed feelings in order to provide health care to ever increasing numbers of 'customers'.

The restoration of dignity?

If emotion work is recognised as a multidimensional social accomplishment, and interaction with customers and clients of the organisation accepted as social interaction, emotion workers could then be conceptualised as multi-skilled emotion managers able to judge the type and amount of emotion work required to maintain the order of interaction. If the 'customer' is understood as a person rather than a sovereign being, then customer service can be conceptualised as a form of social encounter that is not purely instrumentally motivated and cannot be directly controlled via management intervention. Recognising emotion work as a social relationship acted out on a material stage gives the potential for worth to be restored to what is often an unequal exchange and an exclusive production process. It could also mean that the autonomy and higher rewards offered to 'skilled' emotion workers might be extended, with desirable outcomes for all involved.

Giving autonomy to front-line service workers allows for the restoration of dignity to the service encounter. The service worker does not only relate to the customer as a sovereign consumer, as expected in the enactment of commercial feeling rules in the form of *pecuniary* emotion management, but as another human being. This brings into play ritualised acts of deference and demeanour that can be found in all social encounters and more usually associated with social feeling rules and the performance of *presentational* or *philanthropic* emotion management. Goffman usefully summarises that there can never be just one unrivalled discourse as suggested with the concept of 'enterprise':

> a spate of deferential behaviour is not expressing a single relationship between two individuals active in a single pair of capacities, but rather a medley of voices answering to the fact that actor and recipient are in many different relations to one another, no one of which can usually be given exclusive and continuous determinacy of ceremonial conduct. (Goffman, 1967, p. 62)

Many front-line workers actually view the provision of customer service as 'working with people' or 'helping people' and frame this as a socially relevant activity with all the multiple interpretations and contradictions this brings (Callaghan and Thompson, 2002; Sturdy, 1998; 2000; Wray-Bliss, 2001). Amongst empirical studies of service workers in both public and private sector organisations there are ample examples of *presentational* and *philanthropic* emotion management being offered to customers wherever opportunities might arise to escape from the dictates of *pecuniary* emotion management. This is because the commercial feeling rules involved in customer orientation programmes and scripted service encounters cannot deal with the unpredictability and variability of the interaction order. And yet, commercial feeling rules are every more tightly imposed thus leaving the service-worker little space for manoeuvre if the service-encounter does not go according to the organisation's plan. Such constrains actually have the reverse effect of imposing order and force the participants from the 'circle of the proper' into a cycle of 'unease' (Goffman, 1967, p. 93).

Of course, the obnoxious customer can be a very real presence with which the service-provider has to deal but given the right to self-determination the employee can use various tactics and draw on social feeling rules to help restore the ceremonial order. They may employ 'deferential stand-off arrangements' in order to deflect aggression and anger or various forms of humour to ease anxiety. Humour, via 'playful profanation', can also be used in to make a serious point reminding the consumer of their obligations as an interactant (Emerson, 1973; Goffman, 1959, 1967). And at all times, the service provider can choose whether to invest their performance with feeling or to offer a convincing but empty performance. In this way both service-provider and customer are reminded of the negotiative nature of interaction and its important role in the maintenance of the self as a sacred object.

A cycle of unease does not have to be the essential feature of the service encounter. Service-providers are not merely 'simulacrums' (Ritzer, 1999), customers and clients are not discursively defined, neither are symbolic images but they are image makers. Every social encounter is risky as there are moments of 'decision, of resistance and of feeling' but the social order of interaction is there to minimize the risk (Goffman, 1961a; Schwabe, 1993, p. 337). That is, the service-provider and the customer can be viewed as 'creative composites' (Gabriel and Lang, 1995, p. 5) and interaction with customers and clients as a socially relevant activity. Goffman, once again, usefully situates the minor courtesies of social interaction into a larger setting showing how the conditions in which it takes place must be conducive to producing the necessary reciprocity:

> It is therefore important to see that the self is in part a ceremonial thing, a sacred object which must be treated with proper ritual care and in turn must be presented in a proper light to others. As a means through which this self is established, the individual acts with proper demeanour while in contact with others and is treated by others with deference. It is just as important to see that if the individual is to play this kind of sacred game, then the field must be suited to it. The environment must ensure that the individual will not pay too high a price for acting with good demeanour and that deference will be accorded him. Deference and demeanour practices must be institutionalised so that the individual will be able to project a viable, sacred self and stay in the game on a proper ritual basis. (Goffman, 1967, p. 91)

Despite such insightful observations, it does not require too many reminders to realise that the plea for institutionalised 'deference and demeanour practices' will largely fall on stony ground. The pressures on the army of emotion workers in the labour market to meet quantifiable targets will no doubt increase according to the demands of an increasingly vigorous capitalism (Thompson, 2003).

The social aspects of interaction will continue to be neglected; offering the necessary autonomy to workers will be seen as just too much of a risky business and attempts will continue to deprive emotion workers of their opportunity to mediate the worst excesses of the emotional labour process. Though, as the typology of workplace emotion highlights, aspiration should not be mistaken for outcome. Even if opportunities are limited, organisational actors' creative capacities will continue to turn to the formation and maintenance of spaces within, between and around organisationally prescribed feeling rules where resistance takes place, identities are protected and we are constantly reminded of the push and pull of the emotional effort bargain.

Very mixed feelings

This is the concluding chapter but not the conclusion. There can be no conclusions just more and more questions. The ideas concerning emotion management introduced in the book have highlighted the complexities involved in organisational life which necessarily raises more questions than answers. This is a frustrating state of affairs but also a productive one. Using the social view of emotion and Goffman's insights into the intricacies of social interaction the different motivations and outcomes of various forms of emotion management have been revealed. Through Goffman's role analysis it is possible to see that organisational actors may embrace their work role but they also may distance themselves and merely perform according to prescriptive display rules (Goffman, 1959). LPA widens the frames of action and allows an understanding that actors exist in a capitalist system and are therefore forced into selling their labour power. In this way it is possible to see how employees may give convincing performances but their identities remain untouched by the organisation's commercial feeling rules. By placing actors' experiences of organisational life firmly within political, economic and social structures it becomes possible to recognise the variety of means an organisation employs in order to achieve its ends whilst also acknowledging the subjective experiences of its members. Only by understanding the different ways people manage their emotions at work can they be recognised as highly competent social actors and multi-skilled emotion managers.

The constant theme throughout the book has been how emotion work continually crosses boundaries – self and society, private and public, formal and informal. The broad theoretical understanding that this book introduces presents actors as 'jugglers and synthesizers' (Goffman, 1961a). The typology of workplace emotionality shows how they are able to present many 'faces' and fit into whichever frame they find themselves. In attempting to capture the complexities of workplace emotion in the frames of commercial, professional, organisational and social feeling rules the categories of *pecuniary, presentational, prescriptive* and *philanthropic* emotion management serve to display the futility of endeavours to place emotion firmly within organisational boundaries. In fact, the typology's failure to firmly categorise organisational emotionality is something of a triumph for an understanding of emotion work. It becomes possible to acknowledge the complexities involved in organisational life and the contradictions actors experience as an inherent part of their everyday working lives. In effect, it clearly displays how organisational actors continually juggle their mixed feelings in order to both enjoy and endure the rigours of organisational life.

References

Abrams, F. (2002) *Below the Breadline: Living on the Minimum Wage*. London: Profile Books.

Abu-Lughod, L. and Lutz, C. (1990) 'Emotion, Discourse, and the Politics of Everyday Life', in Lutz, C. and Abu-Lughod, L. (eds), *Language and the Politics of Emotion*, Cambridge: Cambridge University Press.

Ackroyd, S. and Bolton, S. (1999) 'It is not Taylorism: Mechanisms of Work Intensification in the Provision of Gynaecology Services in a NHS Hospital', *Work, Employment and Society*, 13, 2: 367–85.

Ackroyd, S. and Crowdy, P. (1992) 'Can Culture be Managed? Working with "Raw" Material: The Case of the English Slaughtermen', *Personnel Review*, 19, 5: 3–13.

Ackroyd, S. and Thompson, P. (1999) *Organizational (Mis)Behaviour*. London: Sage.

Adkins, L. (1995) *Gendered Work: Sexuality, Family and the Labour Market*. Bukingham: Open University Press.

Albrow, M. (1990) *Max Weber's Construction of Social Theory*. London: Macmillan Education Ltd.

Albrow, M. (1992) 'Sine Ira et Studio – Or Do Organizations Have Feelings?', *Organization Studies*, 13, 3: 313–29.

Albrow, M. (1994) 'Accounting for Organizational Feeling', in Ray, L. and Reed, M. (eds), *New Weberian Perspectives on Work, Organization and Society*, London: Routledge.

Albrow, M. (1997) *Do Organizations Have Feelings?* London: Routledge.

Aldrich, H. (1992) Incommensurable Paradigms? Vital Signs from Three Perspectives, in Reed, M. and Hughes, M. (eds), *Rethinking Organization: New Directions in Organization Theory and Analysis*, London: Sage Publications.

Aldridge, M. (1994) 'Unlimited Liability? Emotional Labour in Nursing and Social Work', *Journal of Advanced Nursing*, 20: 722–8.

Archer, M. (2000) *Being Human: The Problem of Agency*. Cambridge: Cambridge University Press.

Ashforth, B. and Humphrey, R. (1993) 'Emotional Labor in Service Roles: The influence of Identity'. *Academy of Management Review*, 18: 88–115.

Ashforth, B. and Humphrey, R. (1995) 'Emotion in the Workplace: A Reappraisal'. *Human Relations*, 48, 2: 97–125.

Ashforth, B. and Kreiner, G. (1999) ' "How Can You Do It?": Dirty Work and the Challenge of Constructing a Positive Identity', *Academy of Management Review*, 24, 2: 413–34.

Ashkanasy, N. Zerbe, W. J. and Hartel, C. E. (2002) *Managing emotions in the workplace*, M E Sharpe, Armonk, USA.

Attwood, M., Pritchard, S., Pedlar, M. and Wilkinson, D. (2003) *Leading Change: A Guide to Whole Systems Working*. London: Policy Press.

Averill, J. R. (1994) 'Emotions Unbecoming and Becoming', in Ekman, P. and Davidson, R. J. (eds), *The Nature of Emotion: Fundamental Questions*, New York: Oxford University Press.

Bahnisch, M. (2000) 'Embodied Work, Divided Labour: Subjectivity and the Scientific Management of the Body in Frederick W. Taylor's 1907 "Lecture on Management" '. *Body & Society*, 6, 1: 51–68.

Barbalet, J. M. (2001) *Emotion, Social Theory, and Social Structure: A Macrosociological Approach.* Cambridge: Cambridge University Press.

Barley, S. and Kunda, G. (1992) 'Design and Devotion: Surges of Rational and Normative Ideologies of Control in Managerial Discourse', *Administrative Science Quarterly*, September 1992, 363–99.

Barnard, C. (1938) *The Functions of the Executive.* Cambridge: Harvard University Press.

Barsoux, J. (1993) *Funny Business: Humour, Management and Business Culture.* New York: Cassell.

Becker, H. (1970) *Sociological Work: Method and Substance.* Chicago: Aldine.

Berger, B. (1974) *Foreword to Frame Analysis*, Goffman, E. Boston: Northeastern University Press.

Berger, P. and Luckman, T. (1966) *The Social Construction of Reality.* London: Penguin Books.

Beynon, H. (1973) *Working for Ford.* Wakefield: EP Publishing Ltd.

Bittner, E. (1967) 'The Police on Skid-Row: A Study of Peace Keeping'. *American Sociological Review*, 32: 699–715.

Bittner, E. (1973) 'The Concept of Organisation', in Salaman, G. and Thompson, K. (eds), *People and Organisations*, Longman: London.

Blanchard, K. and Bowles, S. (1998) *Gung Ho! Turn on the People in any Organization.* New York: Harper Collins Business.

Blumer, H. (1962) 'Society as Symbolic Interaction' in Rose, A. M. (ed.), *Human Behaviour and Social Processes: An Interactionist Approach*, London: Routledge and Kegan Paul.

Blumer, H. (1969) *Symbolic Interactionism.* New Jersey: Prentice Hall.

Bolton, S. (2000a) 'Emotion Here, Emotion There, Emotional Organisations Everywhere', *Critical Perspectives on Accounting*, 11: 155–71.

Bolton, S. (2000b) 'Who Cares? Offering Emotion Work as a "Gift" in the Nursing Labour Process', *Journal of Advanced Nursing*, 32, 3: 580–6.

Bolton, S. (2001) 'Changing Faces: Nurses as Emotional Jugglers', *Sociology of Health and Illness*, 23, 1: 85–100.

Bolton, S. (2002) 'Consumer as King in the NHS'. *The International Journal of Public Sector Management*, 15, 2: 129–39.

Bolton, S. and Boyd, C. (2003) 'Trolley Dolly or Skilled Emotion Manager?', *Work, Employment and Society*, 17, 2: 289–308.

Bolton, S. (2004a) 'A Simple Matter of Control? NHS Hospital Nurses and New Management', *Journal of Management Studies*, 41, 6.

Bolton, S. (2004b) 'A Bit of a Laugh: Nurses' Use of Humour as a Mode of Resistance', in Dent, M., Chandler, J. and Barry, J. (eds), *Questioning the New Public Management*, Aldershot: Ashgate. pp. 177–89.

Bone, D. (2002) 'Dilemmas of Emotion Work in Nursing Under Market-Driven Health Care', *International Journal of Public Sector Management*, 15, 2: 140–50.

Bourdieu, P. (1990) *The Logic of Practice.* Stanford, California: Stanford University Press.

Bowen, D. and Lawler, E. (1992) 'The Empowerment of Service Workers', *Sloan Management Review*, Spring, 31–9.

Boyd, C. (2002) 'Customer Violence and Employee Health and Safety', *Work, Employment and Society*, 16, 1: 151–69.

Brante, T. (2001) 'Consequences of Realism for Sociological Theory-Building', *Journal for the Theory of Social Behaviour*, 31, 2: 167–95.

Braverman, H. (1974) *Labor and Monopoly Capital.* New York: Monthly Review Press.

Brown, P., Green, A. and Lauder, H. (2001) *High Skills: Globalization, Competitiveness and Skill Formation.* Oxford: Oxford University Press.

Burawoy, M. (1979) *Manufacturing Consent: Changes in the Labour Process Under Monopoly Capitalism.* Chicago:University of Chicago Press.

Burns, T. and Stalker, G. (1961) *The Management of Innovation.* London: Tavistock.

Burrell, G. (1988) 'Modernism, Post Modernism and Organizational Analysis: The Contribution of Michel Foucault', *Organization Studies*, 9, 2: 221–35.

Burrell, G. and Morgan, G. (1979) *Sociological Paradigms and Organisational Analysis*. London: Heinemann.

Butler, J. (1993) *Bodies that Matter*. London: Routledge.

Callaghan, G. and Thompson, P. (2001) 'Edwards Revisited: Technical Control and Call Centres', *Economic and Industrial Democracy*, 22, 1.

Callaghan, G. and Thompson, P. (2002) 'We Recruit Attitude: The Selection and Shaping of Routine Call Centre Labour', *Journal Management Studies*, 39, 2: 233–53.

Carey, A. (1967) 'The Hawthorne Studies: A Radical Criticism', *American Sociological Review*, 32: 403–16.

Carlzon, J. (1987) *The Moment of Truth*. Cambridge, MA: Ballinger.

Caruso, D. (2001) 'Emotionally Challenged', *People Management*, 19, April: 40–4.

Casey, C. (1995) *Work, Self and Society: After Industrialisation*. London: Routledge.

Cavendish, R. (1982) *Women on the Line*. London: Routledge and Kegan Paul Ltd.

Charlesworth, S. (2000) *A Phenomenology of Working Class Experience*. Cambridge: Cambridge University Press.

Checkland, P. (1999) *Systems Thinking, Systems Practice*. New York: John Wiley.

Clegg, S. (1981) 'Organizations and Control', *Administrative Science Quarterly*, 26: 532–45.

Clegg, S. (1990) *Modern Organizations: Organization Studies in the Postmodern World*. London: Sage.

Cockburn, C. (1983) *Brothers*. London: Pluto Press.

Cockburn, C. (1991) *In the Way of Women*. London: Macmillan Education Ltd.

Collins, J. and Porras, J. (2002) *Built to Last: Successful Habits of Visionary Companies*. New York: Harper Business.

Collinson, D. L. (1988) 'Engineering Humour: Masculinity, Joking and Conflict in Shop Floor Relations', *Organization Studies*, 9, 2: 181–99.

Collinson, D. L. (1992) *Managing the Shopfloor: Subjectivity, Masculinity and Workplace Culture*. Berlin: Walter de Gruyter.

Collinson, M. and Collinson, D. L. (1996) 'It's Only Dick . . . .: The sexual Harassment of Women Manager in Insurance Sales', *Work, Employment and Society*, 10, 1: 29–56.

Cornelius, N. (2000) *Human Resource Management: A Managerial Perspective*. London: Thomson Learning.

Cousins, C. (1987) *Controlling Social Welfare: A Sociology of State Welfare Work and Organizations*. Sussex: Wheatsheaf Books.

Craib, I. (1995) 'Some Comments on the Sociology of the Emotions', *Sociology*, 29: 151–8.

Craib, I. (1997) 'Social Constructionism as a Social Psychosis', *Sociology*, 31, 1: 6–16.

Crawford, J., Kippax, S., Onyx, J., Gault, U. and Benton, P. (1992) *Emotion and Gender*. London: Sage.

Crossley, N. (1995) 'Body Techniques, Agency and Intercorporeality: On Goffman's Relations in Public', *Sociology*, 29, 1: 133–49.

Crozier, M. (1964) *The Bureaucratic Phenomenon*. Chicago: Chicago University Press.

Dale, B., Cooper, C. and Wilkinson, A. (1997) *Managing Quality and Human Resources*. Oxford: Blackwell.

Darwin, C. (1965) *The Expression of the Emotions in Man and Animals*. Chicago: University of Chicago Press.

Davies, C. and Rosser, J. (1986) 'Gendered Jobs in the Health Service', in Knights, D. and Willmott, H. (eds), *Gender and the Labour Process*, Aldershot: Gower Publishing.

Deal, T. and Kennedy, A. (1999) *The New Corporate Cultures*. New York: Orion Business.

Deetz, S. (1998) 'Discursive Formations, Strategized Subordination and Self-Surveillance' in McKinlay, A. and Starkey, K. (eds), *Foucault, Management and Organization Theory*, London: Sage Publications. 151–72.

Delbridge, R. (1998) *Life on the Line in Contemporary Manufacturing*. Oxford: Oxford University Press.

Delbridge, R., Turnbull, P. and Wilkinson, B. (1992) 'Pushing Back the Frontiers: Management Control and Work Intensification under JIT/TQM Factory Regimes', *New Technology, Work and Employment*, 7: 97–106.

Dent, M., Burke, W. and Green, R. (1991) 'Emotional Labour and Renal Dialysis: Nursing and the Labour Process', Paper Presented to *The 9th Annual International Labour Process Conference*, University of Manchester.

Denzin, N. (1984) *On Understanding Emotion*. San Francisco: Jossey-Bass Inc.

Denzin, N. (1993) Rain Man in Las Vegas, *Symbolic Interaction*, 16: 65–77.

Derrida, J. (1981) *Positions*. Chicago: University of Chicago Press.

DfEE (2000a) *Skills For All: Proposals for a National Skills Agenda*, Final Report of the National Skills Task Force. Sudbury: Prolog.

DfEE (2000b) *Skills For All: Research Report from the National Skills Task Force*. Sudbury: Prolog.

DfEE (2001) *Opportunity and Skills in the Knowledge-Driven Economy*. Nottingham: DfEE Publications.

DiMaggio, P. and Powell, W. (1983) 'The Iron Cage Revisited: Institutional Isomorphism and Collective Rationality in Organizational Fields', *American Sociological Review*, 48: 147–60.

Ditton, J. (1977) 'Perks, Pilferage, and the Fiddle: The Historical Structure of Invisible Wages', *Theory and Society*, 4, 1: 39–71.

Douglas, M. (1975) *Implicit Meanings*. London: Routledge

Doyle McCarthy, E. (1989) 'Emotions are Social Things: An Essay in the Sociology of Emotions' in Franks, D. and Doyle McCarthy (eds), *The Sociology of Emotions: Original Essays and Research Papers. Contemporary Studies in Sociology, Vol. 9*, Greenwich, Connecticut: JAI Press Inc. pp. 51–72.

Drucker, P. (1981) *Managing in Turbulent Times*. London: Pan Books.

du Gay, P. (1994) 'Colossal Immodesties and Hopeful Monsters: Pluralism and Organizational Conduct', *Organization*, 1: 125–48.

du Gay, P. (1996) 'Organizing Identity: Entrepreneurial Governance and Public Management', in Hall, S. and du Gay, P. (eds), *Questions of Cultural Identity*, London: Sage.

du Gay, P. and Salaman, G. (1992) 'The Cult(ure) of the Customer', *Journal of Management Studies*, 29, 5: 615–33.

Dulewicz, V. and Higgs, M. (1998) 'Soul Searching', *People Management*, October 1998: 42–5.

Dulewicz, V. and Higgs, M. (1999) *Can Emotional Intelligence be Measured and Developed*, Working Paper Series, Henley Management College, Oxon.

Duncan, W. and Feisal, J. (1989) 'No Laughing Matter: Patterns of Humour in the Workplace', *Organisational Dynamics*, 17, 4: 18–30.

Duncombe, J. and Marsden, D. (1993) 'Love and Intimacy: The Gender Division of Emotion and "Emotion Work"', *Sociology*, 27, 2: 221–41.

Durkheim, E. (1938) *The Rules of Sociological Method*. New York: The Free Press.

Durkheim, E. (1971) *The Elementary Forms of the Religious Life*. London: George Allen and Unwin.

Edwards, R. (1979) *Contested Terrain: The Transformation of the Workplace in the Twentieth Century*. London: Heinemann.

Edwards, P., Collinson, D. and Della-Rocca, G. (1996) 'Workpalce Resistance in Western Europe', *European Journal of Industrial Relations*, 1, 3: 283–94.

Emerson, J. (1973) 'Negotiating the Serious Import of Humour', in Birenbaum, A. and Sagarin, E. (eds), *People in Places: The Sociology of the Familiar*, New York: Nelson. 269–80.

Etzioni, A. (1969) *The Semi-Professions and Their Organization*. New York: The Free Press.

Ezzy, D. (1997) 'Subjectivity and the Labour Process: Conceptualising "Good Work"', *Sociology*, 31, 3: 523–53.

Fayol, H. (1949) *General Industrial Management*. London: Pitman.

Fernie, S. and Metcalfe, D. (1998) '*(Not) Hanging on the Telephone*', Centre for Economic Performance, London: London School of Economics.

Filby, M. P. (1992) 'The Figures, the Personality and the Bums: Service Work and Sexuality'. *Work, Employment and Society*, 6, 1: 23–42.

Fine, G. A. (1988) 'Letting Off Steam?: Redefining a Restaurant's Work Environment', in Jones, M., Moore, M. and Snyder, R. (eds), *Inside Organizations: Understanding the Human Dimension*, Newbury Park: Sage Publications.

Fine, G.A. (1993) 'The Sad Demise, Mysterious Disappearance and Glorious Triumph of Symbolic Interactionism', *Annual Review of Sociology*, 19: 61–87.

Fineman, S. (1993) *Emotion in Organizations*. London: Sage.

Fineman, S. (2000) (2nd edn), *Emotion in Organisations*. London: Sage.

Fineman, S. (2003) *Understanding Emotion at Work*. London: Sage.

Fineman, S. and Sturdy, A. (1997) ' "Struggles" for the Control of Affect', Paper presented to the 16th *International Labour Process Conference*, Edinburgh University, March 1997.

Fineman, S. and Sturdy, A. (1999) 'The Emotions of Control: A Qualitative Study of Environmental Regulation', *Human Relations*, 52, 5: 631–63.

Flam, H. (1990a) 'Emotional "Man": I. The Emotional "Man" and the Problem of Collective Action', *International Sociology*, 5, 2: 39–57.

Flam, H. (1990b) 'Emotional "Man": II. Corporate Actors as Emotion-Motivated Emotion Managers', *International Sociology*, 5, 2: 225–34.

Fleming, P. and Spicer, A. (2003) 'Working at a Cynical Distance: Implications for Power, Subjectivity and Resistance', *Organization*, 10, 1: 157–79.

Ford, H. (1924) *My Life and Work*. London: William Heinemann Ltd.

Foucault, M. (1970) *The Order of Things*. London: Tavistock.

Foucault, M. (1972) *The Archaeology of Knowledge*. London: Tavistock.

Foucault, M. (1977) *Discipline and Punish*. Harmondsworth: Penguin.

Foucault, M (1991) '*The Foucault Reader*'. Rabinow, P. (ed.), London: Penguin.

Freidman, A. (1977) *Industry and Labour: Class Struggle at Work and Monopoly Capitalism*. London: Macmillan.

Frost, P., Dutton, J., Worline, M. and Wilson, A. (2000) 'Narratives of Compassion in Organizations' in Fineman, S. (ed.), *Emotion in Organizations*, London: Sage. pp. 25–45.

Fuller, L. and Smith, V. (1991) 'Consumers' Reports: Management By Customers in a Changing Economy', *Work, Employment and Society*, 5, 1: 1–16.

Gabriel, Y. (1995) 'The Unmanaged Organization: Stories, Fantasies and Subjectivity', *Organization Studies*, 16, 3: 477–501.

Gabriel, Y. and Lang, T. (1995) *The Unmanagable Consumer*. London: Sage.

Garrahan, P. and Stewart, P. (1992) *The Nissan Enigma*. London: Mansell.

George, J. (2000) 'Emotions and Leadership: The Role of Emotional Intelligence', *Human Relations*, 53, 8: 1027–55.

Gerstner Jnr, L. (2002) *Who Says Elephants Can't Dance?* New York: Harper Collins.

Gerth, H. and Wright Mills, C. (1954) *Character and Social Structure*. London: Routledge and Kegan Paul Ltd.

Gharajedaghi, J. (1999) *Systems Thinking – Managing Chaos and Complexity*. California. Butterworth-Heinemann.

Giddens, A. (1972) *Politics and Sociology in the Thought of Max Weber*. London: The Macmillan Press.

Giddens, A. (1979) *Central Problems in Social Theory*. London: Macmillan Press Ltd.

Giddens, A. (1984) *The Constitution of Society*. Cambridge: Polity Press.

Giddens, A. (1987) *Social Theory and Modern Sociology*. Cambridge: Polity Press.

Giddens, A. (1992) *Human Societies*. Cambridge: Blackwell Publishers.

Goffman, E. (1959) *The Presentation of Self in Everyday Life*. London: Penguin Books.

Goffman, E. (1961a) *Encounters*. New York: The Bobbs-Merrill Company Ltd.

Goffman, E. (1961b) *Asylums*. London: Penguin Books.

Goffman, E. (1967) *Interaction Ritual: Essays in Face-to-Face Behaviour*. Chicago: Aldine Publishing Company.

Goffman, E. (1974) *Frame Analysis*. Boston: Northeastern University Press.

Goffman, E. (1991) 'The Interaction Order: American Sociological Association, 1982 Presidential Address', Plummer, K. (ed.), *Symbolic Interactionism: Contemporary Issues*, London: Edward Elgar Ltd.

Goleman, D. (1998a) *Working with Emotional Intelligence*. New York: Bantam Books.

Goleman, D. (1998b) 'What Makes a Leader?', *Harvard Business Review*, 76: 93–102.

Gouldner, A. (1955) 'Metaphysical Pathos and the Theory of Bureaucracy', *American Political Science Review*, 49, 496–507.

Green, F. (1999) *The Market Value of Generic Skills*. Skills Task Force Research Paper 8. Sudbury: DfEE Publications.

Greenwood, J. D. (1994) *Realism, Identity and Emotion*. London: Sage.

Grey, C. (1994) 'Career as a Project of the Self and Labour Process Discipline', *Sociology*, 28, 2: 480–97.

Guardian (2001) 'Skull Cap Used by Race Jokers', Emma Brockes, Thursday, February, 2001, *The Guardian*.

Guest, D. (1987) 'Human Resource Management and Industrial Relations', *Journal of Management Studies*, 24, 503–21.

Handy, C. (1989) *The Age of Unreason*. London: Business Books Ltd.

Harré, R. (1986) *The Social Construction of Emotions*. Oxford: Basil Blackwell Ltd.

Harré, R. (1990) 'Exploring the Human Umwelt' in Bhaskar, R. (ed.), *Harré and his Critics*. Oxford: Basil Blackwell. pp. 297–365.

Harré, R. (1997) 'Forward to Aristotle: The Case for Hybrid Ontology', *Journal for the Theory of Social Behaviour*, 27, 2/3: 173–91.

Harré, R. and Gillett, R. (1994) *The Discursive Mind*. Thousand Oaks, California: Sage.

Harriss, L. C. (2002) 'The Emotional Labour of Barristers', *Journal of Management Studies*, 39, 4: 553–84.

Hearn, J. (1993) 'Emotive Subjects: Organizational Men, Organizational Masculinities and the (De)construction of Emotions', in Fineman, S. (ed.), *Emotion in Organizations*. London: Sage. 142–66.

Hearn, J. and Parkin, W. (1987) *'Sex' at 'Work': The Power and Paradox of Organisation Sexuality*. London: Wheatsheaf Books.

Hearn, J. and Parkin, W. (2001) *Gender, Sexuality and Violence in Organizations*. London: Sage.

Hertzberg, F. (1966) *Work and the Nature of Man*. Ohio: World Publishing Company.

Heskett, J., Sasser, W. and Schlesinger, L. (1997) *The Service Profit Chain*. New York: The Free Press.

Hirschborn, L. and Gilmore, T. (1992) 'The New Boundaries of the "Boundaryless" Company', *Harvard Business Review*, May–June, 1992.

Hochschild, A. (1979) 'Emotion Work, Feeling Rules, and Social Structure', *American Journal of Sociology*, 85, 3: 551–75.

Hochschild, A. (1983) *The Managed Heart: Commercialization of Human Feeling*. Berkeley: University of California Press.

Hochschild, A. (1989a) 'Reply to Cas Wouters's Review Essay on The Managed Heart', *Theory Culture and Society*, 6: 439–45.

Hochschild, A. (1989b) 'The Economy of Gratitude' in Franks, D. and Doyle McCarthy (eds), *The Sociology of Emotions: Original Essays and Research Papers. Contemporary Studies in Sociology,* Vol. 9, Greenwich, Connecticut: JAI Press Inc. pp. 95–114.

Hochschild, A. (1990) 'Ideology and Emotion Management: A Perspective and Path for Future Research', in Kemper, T. (ed.), *Research Agendas in the Sociology of Emotions*, New York: State University of New York Press.

Hochschild, A. (2003) *The Commercialization of Intimate Life*, Berkley, Los Angeles: University of California Press.

Hodson, R. (2001) *Dignity at Work*. Cambridge: Cambridge University Press.

Hopfl, H. (2002) 'Playing the Part: Reflections of Aspects of Mere Performance in the Customer-Client Relationship', *Journal of Management Studies*, 39, 2: 255–67.

Hughes, E. C. (1958) *Men and their Work*. Glencoe, Il: Free Press.

Huy, Q. (1999) 'Emotional Capability, Emotional Intelligence, and Radical Change', *Academy of Management Review*, 24, 2: 325–45.

Issel, L. M. and Kahn, D. (1998) 'The Economic Value of Caring', *Health Care Management Review*, 23, 4: 43–53.

Jackson, S. (1993) 'Even Sociologists Fall in Love: An Exploration in the Sociology of Emotions', *Sociology*, 27, 2: 201–20.

James, N. (1989) 'Emotional Labour: Skill and Work in the Social Regulation of Feeling', *Sociological Review*, 37, 1: 15–42.

James, N. (1992) 'Care = Organisation + Physical Labour + Emotional Labour', *Sociology of Health and Illness*, 14, 4: 488–509.

James, N. (1993) 'Divisions of Emotional Labour', in Fineman, S. (ed.), *Emotion in Organizations*, London: Sage. 94–1117.

James, W. (1950) *Principles of Psychology*. New York: Holt.

Kahn, W. A. (1992) 'To Be Fully There: Psychological Presence at Work', *Human Relations*, 45: 321–49.

Kahn, W. A. (1998) 'Relational Systems at Work', in Staw, B. and Cummings, L. (eds), *Research in Organizational Behaviour*, Vol. 20, Greenwich: JAI Press. pp. 39–76.

Kanter, R. (1990) *When Giants Learn to Dance*. London: Routledge.

Kemper, T. (1990) 'Themes and Variations in the Sociology of the Emotions' in Kemper, T. (ed.), *Research Agendas in the Sociology of Emotions*, New York: State University of New York Press.

Kinnie, N., Hutchinson, S. and Purcell, J. (2000) 'Fun and Surveillance: the Paradox of High Commitment Management in Call Centres', *International Journal of Human Resource Management*, 11, 5: 967–85.

Kirshenbaum, M. (2003) *The Emotional Energy Factor*. New York: Delacorte Press.

Knights, D. (1990) 'Subjectivity, Power and the Labour Process', in Knights, D. and Willmott, H. (eds), *Labour Process Theory*, London: Macmillan. 297–335.

Knights, D. and McCabe, D. (1999) '"Are There no Limits to Authority?": TQM and Organizational Power', *Organization Studies*, 29, 2: 197–224.

Knights, D. and Vurdubakis, T. (1994) 'Foucault, Power, Resistance and All That', in Jermier, J., Knights, D. and Nord, W. (eds), *Resistance and Power in Organizations*, London: Routledge.

Knights, D. and Willmott, H. (1989) 'Power and Subjectivity at Work: From Degradation to Subjugation in Social Relations', *Sociology*, 23, 4: 535–58.

Korczynski, M. (2002) *Human Resource Management in Service Work*, London: Palgrave.

Korczynski, M., Shire, K., Frenkel, S. and Tam, M. (2000) 'Service Work in Consumer Capitalism: Customers, Control and Contradictions', *Work, Employment and Society*, 14, 4: 669–87.

Kotter, J. (1996) *Leading Change*. Harvard: Harvard Business School Press.

Kotter, J. and Cohen, D. (2002) *Heart of Change*. Harvard: Harvard Business School Press.

Lawler, J. (1991) *Behind the Screens: Nursing, Somology, and the Problem of the Body*. Melbourne: Churchill Livingstone.

Lawrence, P. R. and Lorsch, J. W. (1967) *Organisation and Environment*. Cambridge: Harvard University Press.

Lee-Treweek, G. (1997) 'Women, Resistance and Care: An Ethnographic Study of Nursing Auxiliary Work', *Work, Employment and Society*, 11, 1: 47–63.

Leidner, R. (1996) 'Rethinking Questions of Control: Lessons from McDonalds', in Macdonald, C. and Sirianni, C. (eds), (1996) *Working in the Service Society*, Philadelphia: Temple University Press

Linstead, S. (1985) 'Jokers Wild: The Importance of Humour and the Maintenance of Organisational Culture', *Sociological Review*, 33, 4: 741–67.

Lipsky, M. (1980) *Street-Level Bureaucracy: Dilemmas of the Individual in Public Services*. New York: Russell Sage Foundation.

Lively, K. (2000) 'Reciprocal Emotion Management', *Work and Occupations*, 27, 1: 32–63.

Lively, K. (2002) 'Client Contact and Emotional Labour', *Work and Occupations*, 29, 3: 198–225.

Lorentzon, M. (1990) 'Professional Status and Managerial Tasks: Feminine Service Ideology in British Nursing and Social Work', in Abbott, P. and Wallace, C. (eds), *The Sociology of the Caring Professions*, Basingstoke: The Falmer Press.

Lutz, C. (1988) *Unnatural Emotion*. Chicago: University of Chicago Press.

Lyon, M. (1998) 'The Limitations of Cultural Constructionism in the Study of Emotion' in Bendelow, G. and Williams, S. (eds), *Emotions in Social Life: Critical Themes and Contemporary Issues*, London: Routledge.

MacDonald, C. and Sirianni, C. (eds) (1996) *Working in the Service Society*. Philadelphia: Temple University Press.

Mann, S. (1999) *Hiding What we Feel, Faking What we Don't*. Boston: Element.

Martin, J., Knopoff, K. and Beckman, C. (1998) 'An Alternative to Bureaucratic Impersonality and Emotional Labor: Bounded Emotionality at The Body Shop'. *Administrative Science Quarterly*, June 1998: 429–69.

Maslow, A. H. (1954) *Motivation and Human Personality*. New York: Harper and Row.

Mayer, J. (1999) 'Emotional Intelligence: Popular or Scientific Psychology', *APA Monitor Online*, 30, 8.

Mayer, J. and Salovey, P. (1993) 'The Intelligence of Emotional Intelligence', *Intelligence*, 17: 433–42.

Mayo, E. (1946) *Human Problems of an Industrial Civilisation*. New York: Macmillan.

McGregor, D. (1960) *The Human Side of Enterprise*. New York: Harper and Row.

McKinlay, A. and Starkey, K. (1998) *Foucault, Management and Organization Theory*. London: Sage.

McNay, L. (1999) *Gender and Agency*. Cambridge: Polity Press.

McQueen, A. (1997) 'Gynaecological Nursing', *Journal of Advanced Nursing*, 25: 767–74.

Meerabeau, L. and Page, S. (1998) 'Getting the Job Done: Emotion Management and Cardiopulmonary Resuscitation in Nursing' in Bendelow, G. and Williams, S. (eds), *Emotions in Social Life: Critical Themes and Contemporary Issues*, London: Routledge. 295–312.

Meštrović, S. G. (1997) *Postemotional Society*. London: Sage.

Meyer, J. and Rowan, B. (1977) 'Institutionalized Organizations: Formal Structure as Myth and Ceremony', *American Journal of Sociology*, 83: 340–63.

Mills, A. J. and Murgatroyd, S. J. (1991*) Organizational Rules: a Framework for Understanding Organizational Action*. Milton Keynes: Open University Press.

Mintzberg, H. (1983) *Structure in Fives: Designing Effective Organisations*. New Jersey: Prentice-Hall.

Morris, J. A. and Feldman, D. C. (1996) 'The Dimensions, Antecedents and Consequences of Emotional Labor', *Academy of Management Review*, 21, 4: 986–1000.

Morris, J. A. and Feldman, D. C. (1997) 'Managing Emotions in the Workplace', *Journal of Managerial Issues*, 9, 3: 257–74.

Mouzelis, N. (1975) *Organisation and Bureaucracy*. London: Routledge and Kegan Paul.

Mulkay, M. (1988) *On Humour: Its Nature and its Place in Modern Society*. Cambridge: Polity Press.

Mumby, D. K. and Putman, L. L. (1992) 'The Politics of Emotion: A Feminist Reading of Bounded Rationality', *Academy of Management Review*, 17, 3: 465–86.

Murphy, R. (1995) 'Sociology as if Nature did not Matter: An Ecological Critique', *British Journal of Sociology*, 46: 689–707.

Neuman, J. and Baron, R. (1998) 'Workplace Violence and Aggression', *Journal of Management*, 24, 3: 391–419.

New, C. (1998) 'Realism, Deconstruction and the Feminist Standpoint', *Journal for the Theory of Social Behaviour*, 28, 3: 349–72.

Newton, T. with Handy, J. and Fineman, S. (1995) *'Managing' Stress: Emotion and Power at Work*. London: Sage.

Nichols, T. and Armstrong, P. (1976) *Workers Divided*. London: Collins.

Nichols, T. and Beynon, H. (1977) *Living With Capitalism*. London: Routledge and Kegan Paul.

Nickson, D., Warhurst, C., Cullen, A. M. and Watt, A. (2003) 'Bringing in the Excluded? Aesthetic Labour, Skills and Training in the New Economy', *Journal of Education and Work*, 16, 3.

O'Brien, M. (1994) 'The Managed Heart Revisited: Health and Social Control', *Sociological Review*, 42, 3: 393–413.

O'Doherty, D. and Willmott, H. (2001) 'Debating Labour Process Theory: The Issue of Subjectivity and the Relevance of Poststructuralism', *Sociology*, 35, 2: 457–76.

Parasuraman, A., Berry, L. and Zeithaml, V. (1991) 'Understanding Customer Expectations of Service', *Sloan Management Review*, 32, 3: 39–48.

Parkin, W. (1993) 'The Public and the Private: Gender, Sexuality and Emotion', in Fineman, S. (ed.), *Emotion in Organizations*, London: Sage. 167–89.

Parkinson, B. (1991) 'Emotional Stylists: Strategies of Expressive Management among Trainee Hairdressers', *Cognition and Emotion*, 5: 419–34.

Parson, T. (1956) 'Suggestions for a Sociological Approach to the Theory of Organizations', *Administrative Science Quarterly*, 1, 63–85.

Paules, G. (1996) 'Resisting the Symbolism of Service', in MacDonald, C. and Sirianni, C. (eds), *Working in the Service Society*, Philadelphia: Temple University Press.

Pearce, F. (1989) *The Radical Durkheim*. London: Unwin Hyman.

Peccei, R. and Rosenthal, P. (1997) 'The Antecedents of Employee Commitment to Customer Service from a UK Service Context', *International Journal of Human Resource Management*, 8, 1: 66–86.

Pedlar, M., Burgoyne, J. and Boydell, T. (1997) *The Learning Company: A Strategy for Sustainable Development* (2nd edn) London: McGraw-Hill.

Peters, T. (1987) *Thriving on Chaos*. London: Macmillan.

Peters, T. (1994) *The Tom Peters Seminar: Crazy Times Call for Crazy Organizations*. London: Macmillan.

Peters, T. (1995) *The Pursuit of Wow*. London: Macmillan.

Peters, T. (2003) *Re-imagine: Business Excellence in a Disruptive Age*. London: Dorling Kindersley.

Peters, T. and Austin, N. (1985) *A Passion for Excellence*. London: Guild Publishing.

Peters, T. and Waterman, R. (1982) *In Search of Excellence*. New York: Harper Row.

Phillips, S. (1996) 'Labouring the Emotions: Expanding the Remit of Nursing Work?', *Journal Of Advanced Nursing*, 24: 139–43.

Pilnick, A. and Hindmarsh, J. (1999) 'When you Wake up it will be Over', *Symbolic Interaction*, 22: 345–60.

Pitt, L., Foreman, S. and Bromfield, D. (1995) 'Organizational Commitment and Service Delivery: Evidence from an Industrial Setting in the UK', *The International Journal of Human Resource Management*, 6, 1: 389.

Pollert, A. (1981) *Girls, Wives, Factory Lives*. London: The Macmillan Press.

Pugh, D. S. and Hickson, D. I. (1976) *The Aston Programme I – Organizational Structure in its Context*. Farnborough: Saxon House.

Putman, L. and Mumby, D. (1993) 'Organizations, Emotion and the Myth of Rationality', in Fineman, S. (ed.), *Emotion in Organizations*, London: Sage. 36–57.

Rafaeli, A. and Sutton, R. I. (1987) 'Expression of Emotion as Part of the Work Role', *Academy of Management Review*, 12: 23–37.

Rafaeli, A. and Sutton, R. L. (1990) 'Busy Stores and Demanding Customers: How do they Affect the Display of Positive Emotion', *Academy of Management Journal*, 33, 3: 623–37.

Reed, M. (1992) *The Sociology of Organizations: Themes, Perspectives and Prospects*. Hemel Hempstead: Harvester Wheatsheaf.

Ritzer, G. (1971) 'Professionalism and the Individual' in Freidson, E. (ed.), *The Professions and Their Prospects*, Beverley Hills: Sage. pp. 59–74.

Ritzer, G. (1996) *The Mcdonaldization of Society* (Revised Edition). California: Pine Forge Press.

Ritzer, G. (1999) *Enchanting a Disenchanted World*. California: Pine Forge Press.

Rochberg-Halton, E. (1982) 'Situation, Structure, and the Context of Meaning', The Sociological Quarterly 23: 455–76, in Plummer, K. (ed.) (1991) *Symbolic Interactionism Volume II: Contemporary Issues*, Essex: Edward Elgar Ltd.

Roethlisberger, F. G. and Dickson, W. J. (1939) *Management and the Worker*. Cambridge: Harvard University Press.

Rose, N. (1990) *Governing the Soul: The Shaping of the Private Self*. London: Routledge.

Rose, N. (1999) *Governing the Soul: The Shaping of the Private Self*, London: Free Association Books.

Rosenthal, P., Peccei, R. and Hill, S. (2001) 'Academic Discourses of the Customer' in, Sturdy, A. Grugulis, I. and Willmott, H. (eds), *Customer Service*, London: Palgrave.

Roy, D. F. (1973) 'Banana Time: Job Satisfaction and Informal Interaction', in Salaman, G. and Thompson, K. (eds), *People and Organisations*. London: Longman.

Sabini, J. and Silver, M. (1998) 'The Not Altogether Social Construction of Emotion', *Journal for the Theory of Social Behaviour*, 28, 3: 223–35.

Salaman, G. (1974) *Community and Occupation*. London: Cambridge University Press.

Salaman, G. (1983) 'Roles and Rules', in Salaman, G. and Thompson, K. (eds), *Control and Ideology in Organisations*, Cambridge, Mass.: MIT Press.

Salvage, J. (1985) *The Politics of Nursing*. London: Heinemann Nursing.

Sandelands, L. (1988) 'The Concept of Work Feeling', *Journal for the Theory of Social Behaviour*, 18: 437–57.

Scheff, T. (1990) *Microsociology: Discourse, Emotion and Social Structure*. Chicago and London: The University of Chicago Press.

Schneider, B. and Bowen, D. (1995) *Winning the Service Game*. Boston, MA: Harvard Business School Press.

Schuler, R. and Jackson, S. (1999) *Strategic Human Resource Management: A Reader*. London: Blackwell.

Schutz, A. (1967) *The Phenomenology of the Social World*. Evanston: North Western University Press.

Schwabe, M. (1993) 'Goffman Against Postmodernism: Emotion and the Reality of the Self', *Symbolic Interaction*, 16, 4: 333–50.

Scott, R. A., Aiken, L. H., Mechanic, D. and Moravcsik, J. (1995) 'Organizational Aspects of Caring', *The Millbank Quarterly*, 73, 1: 77–95.

Scott, W. R. (1987) 'The Adolescence of Institutional Theory', *Administrative Science Quarterly*, 32: 493–511.

Selznick, P. (1957) *Leadership in Administration*. Evanston: Row Peterson.

Selznick, P. (1996) 'Institutionalism "Old" and "New"', *Administrative Science Quarterly*, 41: 270–7.

Senge, P. (1990) *The Fifth Discipline*, New York: Doubleday.

Senge, P. (1996) 'The Leader's New Work: Building learning organisations', in *How Organisations Learn*, Starkey, K. (ed.), London: Thomson Business Press.

Senge, P. (1999) *The Dance of Change*. New York: Nicholas Brealey Publishing.

Sewell, G. and Wilkinson, B. (1992) 'Empowerment or Emasculation? Shopfloor Surveillance in a Total Quality Organization', in Blyton, P. and Turnbull, P. (eds), *Reassessing HRM*, London: Sage.

Sharma, U. and Black, P. (2001) 'Look Good, Feel Better: Beauty Therapy as Emotional Labour', *Sociology*, 35, 4: 913–31.

Shields, S. (2002) *Speaking from the Heart*. Cambridge: Cambridge University Press.

Shotter, J. (1990) 'Rom Harré: Realism and the Turn to Social Constructionism' in Bhaskar, R. (ed.), *Harré and His Critics*, Oxford: Basil Blackwell.

Silverman, D. (1970) *The Theory of Organisations*. London: Heinemann.

Smith, P. (1988) 'The Emotional Labour of Nursing', *Nursing Times*, 84: 44.

Smith, P. (1991) 'The Nursing Process: Raising the Profile of Emotional Care in Nursing Training', *Journal of Advanced Nursing*, 16: 74–81.

Smith, P. (1992) *The Emotional Labour of Nursing*. London: Macmillan.

Snow, D. (2001) 'Extending and Broadening Blumer's Conceptualization of Symbolic Interactionism', *Symbolic Interactionism*, 24, 3: 367–77.

Solomon, R. C. (2002) 'Back to Basics: On the Very Idea of "Basic Emotions" ', *Journal for the Theory of Social Behaviour*, 32, 2: 115–46.

Sosteric, M. (1996) 'Subjectivity and the Labour Process: A Case Study in the Restaurant Industry', *Work, Employment and Society*, 10, 2: 297–318.

Sotirin, P. and Gottfried, H. (1999) 'The Ambivalent Dynamics of Secretarial Bitching: Control, Resistance, and the Construction of Identity', *Organization*, 6, 1: 57–80.

Spencer, D. (2000) 'Braverman and the Contribution of Labour Process Analysis to the Critique of Capitalist Production – Twenty-Five Years On', *Work, Employment and Society*, 14, 2: 223–43.

Staden, H. (1998) 'Alertness to the Needs of Others: A Study of the Emotional Labour of Caring', *Journal of Advanced Nursing*, 27: 147–56.

Strauss, A. (1970) *Mirrors and Masks: The Search for Identity*. California: Sociology Press.

Strauss, A. (1975) *Professions, Work and Careers*. London: Transaction Publishers.

Strauss, A., Fagerhaugh, S., Suczek, B. and Wiener, C. (1982) 'Sentimental Work in the Technologized Hospital', *Sociology of Health and Illness*, 4, 3: 255–78.

Sturdy, A. (1998) 'Customer Care in a Consumer Society: Smiling and Sometimes Meaning It?' *Organization*, 5, 1: 27–53.

Sturdy, A. (2000) 'Training in Service- Importing and Imparting Customer Service Culture as an Interactive Process', *International Journal of Human Resource Management*, 11, 6: 1082–103.

Sturdy, A. and Fineman, S. (2001) 'Struggles for the Control of Affect', in, Sturdy, A. Grugulis, I. and Willmott, H. (eds), *Customer Service: Empowerment and Entrapment*, Basingstoke: Palgrave. pp. 140–56.

Sutton, R. I. (1991) 'Maintaining Norms about Expressed Emotions: The Case of Bill Collectors', *Administrative Science Quarterly*, 36: 245–68.

Tancred, P. (1995) 'Women's Work: A Challenge to the Sociology of Work', *Gender, Work and Organisation*, 2, 1: 11–20.

Taylor, F. (1911) *Scientific Management*. New York: Harper and Brothers.

Taylor, S. (1996) 'Something Old, Something New: Investigating Emotion in Organizations', Paper presented to *The Future Of the Sociology of Work, Employment and Organisations*, Grey College, University of Durham, 9th September 1996.

Taylor, S. (1998) 'Emotional Labour and the New Workplace' in Thompson, P. and Warhurst, C. (eds), *Workplaces of the Future*, Basingstoke: Macmillan.

Taylor, P. and Bain, P. (1999) 'An Assembly Line in the Head: The Call Centre Labour Process', *Industrial Relations Journal*, 30, 2: 101–17.

Thompson, P. (1989) *The Nature of Work*. London: Macmillan.

Thompson, P. (1990) 'Crawling from the Wreckage: The Labour Process and the Politics of Production', in Knights, D. and Willmott, H. (eds), *Labour Process Theory*, London: Macmillan.

Thompson, P. (1993) 'Postmodernism: Fatal Distraction', in Hassard, J. and Parker, M. (eds), *Postmodernism and Organizations*, London: Sage.

Thompson, P. (2003) 'Disconnected Capitalism', *Work, Employment and Society*, 17, 2: 359–78.

Thompson, P. and Ackroyd, S. (1995) 'All Quiet on the Workplace Front? A Critique of Recent Trends in British Industrial Sociology', *Sociology*, 29, 4: 615–33.

Thompson, P. and Bannon, E. (1985) *Working the System*. London: Pluto Press.

Thompson, P. and Findlay, P. (1996) 'The Mystery of the Missing Subject', Paper presented to the *14th International Labour Process Conference*, Aston University, March 1996.

Thompson, P. and McHugh, D. (1990) *Work Organisations*. Basingstoke: Macmillan Press.

Thompson, P. and O'Connell Davidson (1996) 'The Continuity of Discontinuity', *Personnel Review*, 24, 4: 17–33.

Thompson, P. and Smith, C. (2001) 'Follow the Redbrick Road: Reflections on Pathways in and out of the Labour Process Debate', *International Studies of Management and Organization*, 30, 4: 40–67.

Thompson, P., Warhurst, C. and Callaghan, G. (2000) 'Human Capital or Capitalising on Humanity? Knowledge, Skills and Competencies in Interactive Service Work', in Pritchard, Hull and Willmott, H. (eds), *Critical Investigations of Work and Learning*, London: Macmillan.

Titmus, R. (1970) *The Gift Relationship*. George Allen and Unwin Ltd: London.

Tolbert, P. S. and Zucker, L. G. (1996) 'The Institutionalization of Institutional Theory', in Clegg, S., Hardy, C. and Nord, W. (eds), *Handbook of Organization Studies*, London: Sage.

Tolich, M. (1993) 'Alienating and Liberating Emotion at Work', *Journal of Contemporary Ethnography*, 22, 3: 361–81.

Townley, B. (1994) *Reframing Human Resource Management*. London: Sage.

Tyler, M. and Taylor, S. (1997) '"Come Fly With Us" Emotional Labour and the Commodification of Sexual Difference in the Airline Industry', Paper Presented to the 15th *Annual International Labour Process Conference*, University of Edinburgh, 25–27 March 1997.

Tyler, M. and Taylor, S. (1998) 'The Exchange of Aesthetics: Women's Work and "The Gift"', *Gender, Work and Organization*, 5, 3: 165–71.

Tyler, M. and Taylor, S. (2001) 'Juggling Justice and Care: Gendered Customer Service in the Contemporary Airline Industry', in Sturdy, A., Grugulis, I. and Willmott, H. (eds), *Customer Service: Empowerment and Entrapment*, London: Palgrave.

Van de Vliet, A. (1994) 'Order from Chaos', *Management Today*, November 1994.

Van Maanen, J. and Kunda, G. (1989) 'Real Feelings: Emotional Expression and Organizational Culture', *Research in Organizational Behaviour*, 11: 43–103.

Van Maanen, J. (1991) 'The Smile Factory: Work at Disneyland', in Frost, P., Moore, L., Luis, M., Lundberg, C. and Martin, J. (eds), *Reframing Organizational Culture*, California: Sage.

Wajcman, J. (1998) *Managing Like a Man: Women and Men in Corporate Management*. St Leonards: Allen and Unwin.

Weatherly, K. and Tansik, D. (1992) 'Tactics Used by Customer-Contact Workers: Effects of Role Stress, Boundary Spanning and Control', *International Journal of Service Industry Management*, 4, 3: 4–17.

Weber, M. (1947) *The Theory of Social and Economic Action*. Translated by A. M. Henderson and Talcott Parsons, Talcott Parsons (ed.), New York: The Free Press.

Wellington, C. A. and Bryson, J. (2001) 'At Face Value? Image Consultancy, Emotional Labour and Professional Work', *Sociology*, 35, 4: 933–46.

Wentworth, W. M. and Ryan, J. (1994) Introduction. *Social Perspectives on Emotion* (Vol. 12). Greenwich, Connecticut: JAI Press Inc.

West, C. and Zimmerman, D. (1987) 'Doing Gender', *Gender and Society*, 1: 125–51.

Westwood, S. (1984) *All Day Every Day*. London: Pluto Press.

Wharton, A. (1996) 'Service with a Smile: Understanding the Consequences of Emotional Labour', in MacDonald, C. and Sirianni, C. (eds), *Working in the Service Society*, Philadelphia: Temple University Press.

Whyte, W. (1948) *Human Relations in the Restaurant Industry*. New York: McGraw-Hill.

Wickens, D. (1993) 'Lean Production: The System, its Critics and the Future', *Human Resource Management Journal*, 3.

Williams, S. J. (2001) *Emotion and Social Theory*. London: Sage.

Williams, S. J. and Bendelow, G. A. (1996a) 'Emotions and "Sociological Imperialism": A Rejoinder to Craib', *Sociology*, 30, 1: 145–53.

Williams, S. J. and Bendelow, G. A. (1996b) 'The "Emotional" Body', *Body and Society*, 2: 125–39.

Willmott, H. (1993) 'Strength is Ignorance, Slavery is Freedom: Managing Culture in Modern Organisations', *Journal of Management Studies*, 30, 4: 515–52.

Willmott, R. (1997) 'Structure, Culture and Agency: Rejecting the Current Orthodoxy of Organisation Theory', *Journal for the Theory of Social Behaviour*, 27, 1: 93–123.

Witz, A., Warhurst, C. and Nickson, D. (2003) 'The Labour of Aesthetics and the Aesthetics of Organization', *Organization*, 10, 1: 33–54.

Woodruffe, C. (2001) 'Promotional Intelligence', *People Management*, 11, January: 26–9.

Woodward, J. (1965) *Industrial Organization: Theory and Practice*. London: Oxford University Press.

Wouters, C. (1989a) 'The Sociology of Emotions and Flight Attendants: Hochschild's Managed Heart', *Theory, Culture and Society*, 6: 95–123.

Wouters, C. (1989b) 'Response to Hochschild's Reply', *Theory, Culture and Society*, 6: 447–50.

Wray-Bliss, E. (2001) 'Representing Customer Service: Telephones and Texts' in Sturdy, A. Grugulis, I. and Willmott, H. (eds), *Customer Service*, London: Palgrave.

Zimmerman, D. (1971) 'The Practicalities of Rule Use', in Douglas, J. (ed.), *Understanding Everyday Life*, London: Routledge and Kegan Paul.

Author Index

Subject Index

customer satisfaction   60, 63, 91, 103, 113,
    120, 126
  attempt to maintain   159
  commercial feeling rules producing   128
  creating   155
  profitable product of   113
customer service   20, 119, 157–9
  as abuse   120–2
  conceptualised as a form of social
      encounter   161
  current (mis)representations of   115–18
  disturbed and disturbing act of   95
  front-line 94, 161
  investment of feeling into   95
  predetermined standards of   94
'cycle of unease'   95, 161, 162
cynical distance   108
cynicism   61, 82, 95, 97, 102, 120, 137

'damp corners'   138, 139, 147
day-to-day contact   2, 115, 121, 123, 124
debt collectors   51, 102, 103
decision-making   28, 41
deep acting   48, 51, 63, 79–80, 82, 83, 90,
    117, 140
deference   4, 97, 119, 127, 142, 147, 156,
    161, 162
  resistance and defiance against   138
defiance   119, 138, 144
Delta Airline   120, 141–2
demands   6, 59, 78, 117, 138, 146
  conflicting   99
  constrictions imposed by   115
  emotional   123
  escape from   129
  invasive   138, 150
  material   141
  organisational   100, 101
  resistance to   135
demeanour   4, 97, 122, 142, 147,
    156, 161, 162
  desirable   113, 119, 156
  organisationally prescribed   94
depersonalisation   73, 118
desires   20, 116
de-skilling   29, 30, 32, 34
despair   33
determinism   72
deviance   18, 84
  pathological   136
dignity   95, 158
  denied   119, 138
  restoration of   160–3
dirty work   127, 146

disaffection   115, 138
discipline   15
discontent   136, 144
discord   8, 111
'discourse of enterprise'   154
discretion   126
discriminatory remarks   97
Disney   48, 114
disquiet   121
dissatisfaction   6, 21, 119
dissent   144
dissonance   53, 141
distaste   142
diversity   96
  cultural   71
division of labour   17, 29, 30, 57, 109
  definitional   143
  emotional   54, 58
  medical   124
  specialised   16
'docile bodies'   38, 136
doctors   52, 95, 122, 123, 124–5, 130
  profiteering   96
domination   29, 136, 144, 148
dress code   96

'economy of gratitude'   97
efficiency   13, 15, 16, 17, 18, 114, 126, 128
  financial   127
  humour and   101
EI (emotional intelligence)   35, 36, 45–6
emotional detachment   120
'emotional ecology'   145
'emotional numbness'   129
'emotional proletariat'   113–14, 128,
    129, 155
'emotional zones'   134
empathy   34, 95, 98, 102, 117, 140, 141, 145
empowerment   34
enterprise culture   6, 154, 159
EQ (emotional quotient)   35
equilibrium   17, 22, 23, 24, 35, 41, 136
esprit de corps   18
ethnographic studies   142
Europe   53
executive role/functions   17, 18
expectations   75, 109, 110, 119
  colleagues   122
  interaction conflict with   129
  official   107
  raised   6, 94, 159
  unmet   159
exploitation   93, 136
'expressive order'   7

'exquisite drama' 120
extroverts 155

face-saving activity 77, 78, 98–9, 140, 144, 156
face-to-face contact 32, 51, 88, 98, 112, 113, 114
face-work 78, 87, 120
   'sincere' and 'cynical' 82
'factor X' 14
factors of production 18
fast-food workers 95, 141
feedback 80, 117
feeling rules 48, 55, 74, 75, 96, 127
   alien 96
   blurred 102
   cynical embracement of 137
   externally imposed 94, 108
   forcefully applied 97
   implicit 50, 77, 80, 122, 145
   instrumentally motivated/inspired 95, 128
   managerially designed 90
   motivations and 98
   negotiating between 3
   new 8, 84, 86, 88, 92
   prescribed 137, 138
   prevailing, sole concentration on 93
   rigidly prescribed 95
   see also commercial feeling rules;
        organisational feeling rules; professional
        feeling rules; social feeling rules
feelings 3, 38, 83
   ability to monitor 35
   capitalism and 2
   captured 49
   induced 52
   mixed 153–64
   organisations have 1, 45–7, 63
   'real', death of 4
   social regulation of 45
   suppressed 52
   'transmutation' of 39, 49, 61, 90, 103
feminine qualities 156
feminists 31, 45, 59, 148
flat ontology 72
'folk symbols' 124
Fordism 16, 97
fragmentation 77, 78
freedom 75
friendship 145, 147
front-line service workers 94, 95, 101,
     113–15, 118, 119, 149, 155
   benefits of granting autonomy to 158
   customer care programmes 117
   empowered 116, 118, 119, 149, 155
   little autonomy 141

recalcitrant 119
routinised 159
self-actualising 116
subjugated 120
view of provision of customer service 161
frustrations 3, 123, 160
   common 145
fulfilment 13
fun 142
functionalism 72, 90, 91

game-playing activity 31, 97, 145
gender 53, 75, 125, 156
   feminist analysis of 45
   power relations 148
   social construction of 32
gestures 139, 147, 149
gift exchange 32, 48, 51, 57, 63, 84, 97,
     98, 135, 145
   spaces for 139–42
global markets 47
goal-oriented activity 18, 98, 107
good work 146
grief 72
group dynamics 20
'Gung Ho' principle 23

habitus 75–6
hairdressers 111, 120
handbooks and guides 114
'happy' workers 91
harassment 2, 62, 139
   sexual 97, 147, 148
hatred 1, 64
'have-a-nice-day' culture 114
Hawthorne Plant 19, 34
health and safety 141
help 32
heroes and villains 125
heterosexual masculinity 148
hierarchy 17, 41, 114
   formal 15, 30
   informal 148
   of needs 20, 34
   power relationships 93
   skills 155
homogenous groups 123, 124
HRM (Human Resource Management)
    1, 20, 136
   'soft' 37, 137
'Human Relations' school 19, 20
human resources 34–7, 114
humanity 5, 140, 149
humiliation 123, 147

status passages   109–10
  see also social status
street-level bureaucrats   125, 126, 129, 130
stress   119–20, 150
structuralism   69, 70
sub-cultures   97, 145
subjectivity   101
  captured   37–40, 43
subordination   17, 18, 138, 147
supermarket chains   114
surface acting   48, 79–80, 81, 82, 83, 90, 111,
  120, 137
surplus value   154
surveillance   8, 64, 114, 117
survival   17, 20, 22, 63, 126
  labour market   94
symbolic interactionism   25, 26, 28, 69, 70, 153
symbols   109
sympathy   6, 102
synthesizers   103
systems approach, *see* open-systems approach

tainted work   146
Taylorism   20, 30, 137
teachers   129, 159
teamwork   146, 157
teasing   144, 149
telephone queries   94, 121
  see also TSAs
'tender loving care'   56
Theory X/Theory Y   34
time and energy   26
time and motion   18
TQM (Total Quality Management)   38, 55
training   98, 112
  explicit   114
  intensive periods of   113
  professional   122
'transmutation'   39, 49, 61, 64, 90, 103, 110
TSAs (tele-sales agents)   55, 63, 95, 97, 101,
  102, 128
  certain pre-requisites expected of   111

unconventional practices   136
'underlife'   8, 139

understanding   26, 163
  shared   109
uneasiness   121
unequal exchange   3, 5–7, 62
unique mission   122
United States   30
'universal human nature'   133
'unmanaged condition'   62
unmanaged organization   90
unpredictability   36, 161
unsocial hours   146
urges   20

values   14, 19, 125
  commercial   129
  company   111, 112
  core   34, 35
  corporate   90
  cultural   78, 115
  internalised   96
  managerial   127
  organisational   101, 111
violations   145, 147–9
violence   14, 63, 139, 148
  customer, directed at service-providers
    149
  physical   147
vision   35
'vocabulary of motive'   110
voice-to-voice contact   51, 113
'vulgar tendency'   5
vulnerability   127, 143

waitresses   119–20, 141, 150
ways of being   137, 147
weakness   17, 119, 144
well-being   48, 58, 91, 114
women   13, 31, 54, 75
  adept emotion workers   125
  emotional distance   125
  middle-class   76
'women's work'   156
wow factors   35, 91

X-factors   35, 45, 91